Maqtal Mutahhar

(Majalis and Martyrdom of the Purified Ahlul Bayt)

By:

Ayatullah Murtadha Mutahhari

Translated by:
Syed Maqsood Athar

Checked and Edited:
Syed Athar Husain S.H. Rizvi

This book is printed with the permission of Islamic Seminary Pakistan

Title	: Maqtal Mutahhar
Research	: Ja'far Salihan
English Translation	: Syed Maqsood Athar
Checked & Edited	: Syed Athar Husain S.H. Rizvi
Printed	: Lantern Publications (Australia)
ISBN	:978-1-922583-67-3

Islam

"Have you fully realized what Islam is?

It is indeed a religion founded on truth. It is such a fountainhead of learning that several streams of wisdom and knowledge flow from it. It is such a lamp that several lamps will be lighted from it. It is a lofty beacon of light illuminating the path of Allah. It is such a set of principles and beliefs that will satisfy every seeker of truth and reality. Know you all that Allah has made Islam the most sublime path for the attainment of His supreme pleasure and the highest standard of His worship and obedience. He has favoured it with noble precepts, exalted principles, undoubtable arguments, unchallengeable supremacy and undeniable wisdom. It is up to you to maintain the eminence and dignity granted to it by the Lord, to follow it sincerely, to do justice to its articles of faith and belief, to obey implicitly its tenets and orders and to give it the proper place in your lives."

Imam Ali

About Us

The Islamic Seminary Pakistan was founded by Hazrat Ayatullah Sayyid Abul Qasim Musawi Khoei and today under the leadership of Hazrat Ayatullah al-Uzma Sayyid Ali Husaini Sistani, this international organisation is endeavoring to supply authentic Islamic literature to the public. This organization aims to satisfy the spiritual needs of the present age, make people aware of authoritative Islamic knowledge and to guard this great heritage of knowledge that the Ahlul Bayt of the Prophet has entrusted to us as a divine trust.

So far, this organization has published many books in Urdu, English, and other languages that, due to their fine appearance, style, and subject matter, have obtained a special place among printed books. If Allah wills, these publications will continue to show the right path to humanity.

In addition to this, the organization is also engaged in imparting religious knowledge and training to students in more than 500 Madressas and Makatibs.

Propagating the message of Islam requires the cooperation of all. The Seminary invites you to join in this task so that Islamic teachings may be popularized worldwide.

We pray to God, that for the sake of Muhammad and Aale Muhammad to send blessings and mercy on all.

Shaykh Yusuf Nafsi
Representative of Ayatullah al-Uzma Sistani (d.a.)

Table of Contents

Foreword

بِسْمِ اللّهِ الرَّحْمَنِ الرَّحِيمِ

Peace be on you, O Ahlul Bayt of the Prophet.

One day I was sitting alone and taking the account of my self and going through the register of my deeds. As much I thought upon it as much loss I found in the account of my deeds and it seemed difficult to traverse the paths of the hereafter. I told myself 'the caravan has departed while you were asleep. Now there is an unending desert before you. Where would you go? Whom will you ask for directions to reach your destination? And how will you survive? How can you cross empty-handed, the terrifying stages that lie ahead?'

I was engrossed in these thoughts when a ray of hope appeared. From the depths of my distressed heart a voice said: "O you that is confused in doubts, if you want to reach the banks of your aspiration, why don't you board the Ark of Salvation? Have you forgotten that those who board it shall be saved and those you leave it, would drown?[1] Why don't you take the support of ones who are the ultimate piety and true refuge? They are the leading lights of the caravan of monotheism. They have scaled the heights of absolute guardianship. They are the doors of God, they shall lead you to God. In the sacred court of these intercessors of the world and the hereafter, express natural love in such a way that all the obstacles on the straight path are eliminated and the way becomes clear for you, because if the chaste leaders of the caravan of

---

[1] Extract from *Salawat* related on the authority of Imam Zainul Abideen (a.s.), which is recited everyday in the month of Shaban.

guidance lead your way, you will reach the destination without fail; but if you continue without them you will never find your way.

It had been my heartfelt desire since the past few months that I should undertake some writing work as is the habit of the scholars of religion and the wayfarers so that I can present the fruits of my labour as a gift to those divine personalities. Perhaps this humble gift would be accepted and this sinful one rewarded with a glance of mercy so that the luster of his heart and eyes is regained and his besmeared heart may obtain purity and his worthless being is changed into something worthwhile.

Thus I remembered that great scholar who has written authoritatively on different subjects and whose writings are sources of religious knowledge. I mean the great religious intellectual, Ustad Shaheed Murtada Mutahhari. As far as I know, none of his books deals with Ahlul Bayt's sufferings. So I thought, what could be better than to collect material on this topic from the various writings of this thinker?

With this purpose in mind I began to go through the books of Ustad Shaheed and compiled the present work. After that I conducted research and added references to give the final shape.

The following points are worth noting:

1. In this book, we have collected the sufferings of Ahlul Bayt 🕮 from 61 Majalis (mourning speeches) of Ustad Shaheed, which can fulfil the need of Dhakireen (Majlis speakers) to some extent.

2. In compiling and researching the material, we have tried our best to retain Ustad Shaheed's original style.

3. Most of the material was in audio format, so there was a possibility of missing words and phrases. Hence, we have compared them with the original sources, and if the matter is mentioned differently, we have pointed it out in the footnotes.

4. In the present age, given the cultural assault of the enemies of Islam, it is very important to make the young generation aware of the thoughts of this great scholar. Therefore, it would be better if our Dhakireen recited the accounts of Karbala tragedy on the authority of Ustad Shaheed so that the incomparable service rendered by him is duly acknowledged. We hope that through this, the intellectual level of our youth shall be increased, and our lectures will gain academic authority.

5. All the merits of this book are a result of the intellectual and practical struggle of the Ustad, his sincerity, internal purity and integrity, whereas if there are any shortcomings, they are due to this humble servant.

At the end of this foreword, we present the reply of Ustad Shaheed to a question posed to him during the days of mourning for Imam Husain ۱ and in it he has explained the need and importance of narrating the sufferings of Ahlul Bayt; and also clarified the philosophy behind it.

Philosophy and Necessity of Narrating the Sufferings of Ahlul Bayt ۱

The Ustad says: "Yesterday, a young man asked me a question, so I shall mention a point here with reference to that same query. In fact, I have never insisted that the sufferings of Ahlul Bayt 🕮 should be recited at the end of every Majlis. If the talk is at a point from where I can move forward in another direction, I don't narrate the sufferings, but in most of the speeches, especially during the mourning season, I make it a point to mention some account of sorrow, however brief it may be.

This young man had asked me if there was any necessity and benefit of narrating the sufferings. If our aim is to revive the School of Husain 🕮, is it necessary to recount the tragedy of Karbala? I told him: Yes, it is something that the Holy Imams 🕮 have commanded us and there is a philosophy behind this. If there is no warmth of true emotions in a school of thought and it is merely a collection of dry ideas and principles, it will not affect the souls of the people and it will not endure forever. However, if a school has the power to warm up the hearts and pull the people towards itself, this same attraction keeps that school alive. The philosophy of a school plays a basic role in propagating that school and it bestows speech to it; that it makes it talk.

Doubtlessly, the school of Husain is a school whose philosophy fires the emotions and that is why it survives to this day. We have to understand this philosophy and appreciate it. If we present this life-creating school as merely a school of thought, the flame of this school which imparts a tongue to human emotions, will be gradually extinguished and this school will become outdated and useless. That is why we must continue to recount the sufferings of Karbala."

The deep insight and comprehensive understanding of this learned scholar is apparent from the above statements. Indeed, the narration of the sufferings of Imam Ali 🕮, Imam Husain 🕮, Imam Hasan 🕮, or Lady Zahra (s.a.)

touches human emotions, and it bestows speech to these emotions. People obtain warmth from the flame of these emotions, and these emotions rekindle in them a perception of responsibility and understanding to protect, which we must always endeavour.

3 Shawwal 1420 A.H.

Ja'far Salihan

Majlis 1

Imam Ali ﷺ awaits the Night of Attack

O mourners of His Eminence, Amirul Mu'minīn ﷺ!

Today is the 13th of the holy month of Ramadan. We are approaching the nights of wakefulness and worship, and the day of the martyrdom of the Commander of the Faithful. It is narrated that the Commander of the Faithful was delivering a sermon on the 13th of the holy month of Ramadan, which was Friday. His sons, Imam Hasan ﷺ and Imam Husain ﷺ were seated among the audience.

In the course of the sermon, he suddenly asked Imam Hasan ﷺ: "Son, Hasan! How many days of this month have passed till now?"

He replied: "Thirteen days have passed, father."

It seems that Imam wanted to convey an important message because he already knew how many days had passed.

After that he asked Imam Husain ﷺ: "Son! How many days are left in this month?"

Imam Husain ﷺ said: "Seventeen days are left, father."

Hearing this, Imam Ali ﷺ held his beard and said: "Very less time is left for this beard to be dyed by the blood of this head."[1]

The Commander of the Faithful did not declare the exact time and conditions of his martyrdom but used to point out a particular state that made the people in general and his family in particular restless and troubled.[2]

There is no power and might except by Allah the High and the Mighty.

---

[1] *Muntahal Amaal,* Vol. 1, Pg. 330 and *Manaqib Murtazviyah,* Pg. 390

[2] *Ashnai ba Quran,* Murtadha Mutahhari, Vol. 6, Pg. 146-147

Majlis 2

Martyrdom in the View of Imam Ali ﷺ

The last Ramadan of the life of Imam Ali ﷺ had restlessness in it as was apparent from the behavior of the Imam. This month was different from all the months of Ramadan of previous years. It was clearly felt by the family members of Imam ﷺ. Nonetheless I would like to mention the differentiating feature, which is also narrated in *Nahjul Balagha*. Imam Ali ﷺ said: When Allah, the Glorified sent down the verse:

Alif Laam Meem. What! Do people imagine that they will be let off on (their) saying: "We believe!" and they will not be tried?[1]

I came to know that the disturbance would not befall us as long as the Prophet (peace and blessing of Allah be upon him and his progeny) is among us. So I said, "O Prophet of Allah, what is this mischief about which Allah, the Sublime, has informed you?"[2] And he replied, "O Ali, my Ummah will soon undergo trials after me."

When Ali ﷺ heard that after the passing away of the Prophet, they would have to undergo tribulations, he remembered something from the past, and he asked:

---

[1] Surah Ankaboot 29:1-2
[2] The Faiz al-Islam Edition of *Nahjul Balagha* does not contain the word 'taa'la'.

"O Messenger of Allah 🕮, on the day of Uhud did you not tell me that those Muslims who were supposed to be martyred have obtained the status of martyrdom?"

On that day, seventy Muslims were martyred, among whom the chief of the martyrs, His Eminence Hamza, was the most important.

While martyrdom evaded me, which was very annoying to me,[1] and I asked you: Why have I been denied this honor?"

His Eminence, had said: "Cheer up, as martyrdom is in your pursuit. So what if you were not martyred? Martyrdom has already been written in your destiny. Saying this His Eminence asked me:

"It will indeed come to pass, but tell me how will your patience be at the time of your martyrdom?" Imam Ali 🕮 said: O Messenger of Allah 🕮 it is not an occasion for patience, but rather an occasion for joy and gratefulness."[2]

Last Days of Ali's Life

The family and companions of Imam Ali 🕮 were restless and worried because of the news the Holy Prophet 🕮 had given and because of those signs, which were made apparent by Imam Ali 🕮 because he was talking of strange things. During this Ramadan month he used to conclude

---

[1] Imam Ali (a.s.) was in his prime youth in the battle of Uhad. He was only twenty-five years old at that time. He was newly married to Lady Sayyada and Imam Hasan (a.s.) was born to them. Normally, a young couple wishes for a long life but the greatest wish of Ali (a.s.) was martyrdom. (Ustad Mutahhari)

[2] *Nahjul Balagha*, Faizul Islam, Sermon 155, Pg. 1481 and *Nahjul Balagha,* Subhi Salih, Sermon 156.

his fast at one of his children's house.[1] Every night he used to be the guest of one of them. He ate at Imam Hasan's 🕮 house one night and then Imam Husain's 🕮 house on the next and then Lady Zainab's house and so on. But he ate very little.[2]

The Imam's children used to become sad on this condition of Imam. They used to cry out of sadness. Once, one of them asked: "O father! Why do you eat so less?" The Imam replied: "I want to meet the Almighty Allah with an empty stomach."[3] (His children used to understand that His Eminence, Ali was waiting). Sometimes he used to look at the sky and say: "My beloved one, the Holy Prophet 🕮 has informed me and what he had told me is absolutely true. He cannot be wrong. The time is near."[4]

On 13th Rajab, he stated something, which increased the trouble. It was Friday and the Imam was delivering a sermon.

During the sermon he asked Imam Husain 🕮: "Son, how many days are left in this month?"

He replied: "Seventeen days are left, father."

Imam Ali 🕮 said: "Yes, very soon my beard will be dyed with my blood. The time for this beard to be dyed with blood is near."[5]

---

[1] Perhaps, it was his practice in the previous months of Ramadan also. (Ustad Mutahhari)
[2] *Muntahal Amaal,* Vol. 1, Pg. 329
[3] *Biharul Anwār,* Vol. 42, Pg. 224
[4] *Biharul Anwār,* Vol. 42, Pg. 277
[5] *Muntahal Amaal,* Vol. 1, Pg. 330; *Manaqib Murtazviyah,* Pg. 490

Imam Ali's ﷺ Dream on the Eve of Attack

O mourners! The children spent sometime with His Eminence, Ali ﷺ on the eve of the 19th. After everyone had departed, Imam Ali ﷺ came to the prayer-mat.[1] Imam Ali ﷺ was on his prayer-mat and it was not yet dawn. Imam Hasan ﷺ arrived and sat down near him. Either it was because of restlessness or it was his usual habit.

The Commander of the Faithful gave special respect to Imams Hasan and Husain ﷺ because they were children of Lady Zahra. He used to consider honoring them as honoring the Holy Prophet ﷺ and Lady Zahra. He told Imam Hasan ﷺ: "I was sitting when I dozed for some moments. I saw the Prophet of Allah appear before me, and I said, 'Your Ummah has made me cry tears of blood.'"[2] Really, it is strange that people opposed His Eminence, Ali ﷺ and did not walk on the path shown by him. People had troubled him no end. The companions of Ayesha broke the allegiance and Muawiyah constantly conspired against him. It was very tough for His Eminence, Ali ﷺ to bear all this. Muawiyah was a cunning brute. He knew what hurts His Eminence, Ali ﷺ the most. Thus, he used to do the same. What did the Khawarij and so-called religious groups, who used to accuse Imam Ali ﷺ and call him an infidel, do in the end?

It is a fact that a person wonders after looking at the grief-stricken life of Imam Ali ﷺ. Even a mountain does

---

[1] It is recommended that a place should be reserved in one's house for worship. Imam Ali's prayer-mat was reserved during his stay in Darul Imarah as a caliph and he used to worship on it. Normally, he did not sleep during the nights and used to start his worship on this mat after completing all his chores. (Ustad Mutahhari)

[2] *Nahjul Balagha*, Faizul Islam, Sermon 69, Pg. 156; *Nahjul Balagha,* Subhi Salih, Sermon 70

not have the power to bear so many calamities as he did. To whom can Ali ☩ tell about his sufferings? When he saw the Holy Prophet ﷺ in his dream, Imam Ali ☩ opened his heart to him and said: "O Messenger of Allah! Your Ummah has troubled me a lot. Tell me, what I should do about it?" Then he told Imam Hasan ☩: "Father's dearest! Your grandfather ordered me, 'O Ali! Curse this Ummah' And in the dream I said, 'O Lord! Take me from this world at the soonest and appoint over them in my place someone who is worse than me.'" You can estimate the trouble and restlessness from this statement.

The Ducks Protest

When the Imam started to set out for the mosque, the ducks began to quack loudly. Imam said: "Now only these ducks are quacking but the time is near when the earth and the skies will tremble and people will start mourning."[1]

Hearing this, the children came forward and said: "O father! We won't allow you to go to the mosque. Please send us or someone else in your place." Imam Ali ☩ said: "All right, send my nephew, Joada bin Hubaira." Then he immediately said: "No, I will go to the mosque myself." The children asked the Imam to permit them to accompany him but he refused saying: "I don't want anyone to accompany me."[2]

How pleasant was this night for him! Only God knows what his feelings were. He said: I myself tried a lot to know the secret but I could know only the outline; that

---

[1] *Kashful Ghumma,* Vol. 2, Pg. 62; *Manaqib Ibne Shahr Aashob,* Vol. 3, Pg. 310
[2] *Biharul Anwār,* Vol. 42, Pg. 226; *Muntahal Amaal,* Vol. 1 Pg. 335

a great tragedy was expected to happen. It is apparent from his words in *Nahjul Balagha*:

"I tried a lot to reach the hidden secret but God denied, because He wanted to keep it secret."[1]

Imam Ali's Last Call for Prayer (*Azaan*)

Imam used to call out the Azaan of the Morning Prayer. Dawn was approaching when the Imam went to the place of Azaan and recited it.[2] After that he bid farewell to whiteness of dawn and said: "O whiteness of dawn! Have you ever witnessed a day when Ali ﷺ was sleeping when you appeared in the sky since the time Ali has opened his eyes?" It means that it has not happen prior to this but now the eyes of Ali were going to be closed forever. After returning from the place of Azaan, the Imam recited the following couplets:

"Make way for the believer warrior fighting in the way of Allah[3]

He is a believer who follows the divine commandments

And steps into the battlefield of martyrdom willingly

One who does not worship anyone except God and enjoins people to offer Prayer regularly."

---

[1] *Nahjul Balagha*, Faizul Islam, Sermon 149, Pg. 445; *Nahjul Balagha*, Subhi Salih, Sermon 149
[2] *Biharul Anwār,* Vol. 42, Pg. 279
[3] *Manaqib Ibne Shahr Aashob,* Vol. 3, Pg. 310; *Biharul Anwār*, Vol. 42, Pg. 238

Here, the Imam is introducing himself as a believer and a warrior.

His family members were not permitted to move from their places. Imam Ali ؑ had already said that after his cries, people will start mourning. Lady Zainab, Lady Umme Kulthum and other family members were awake and restless. Their hearts were beating fast with anxiety because they didn't know what catastrophe would occur before the darkness of this night disappears. Suddenly a voice caught the attention of everyone:

"O mourners! O mourners of Ali!" This sound was coming from every nook and corner at this unfortunate hour:

"By Allah, the pillars of guidance have been demolished. By Allah, signs of piety have been erased. The strong rope of truth is broken. The cousin of Mustafa is martyred. The successor of the chosen prophet of Allah is martyred. Ali al-Murtada is martyred. The worst person from the formers and the latters has martyred him."[1]

In the name of Allah and by Allah and on the religion of the Messenger of Allah ﷺ

Majlis 3

Imam Ali ﷺ prepares to meet the Lord

Imam Ali ﷺ had chosen a special program in the last Ramadan of his life. He used to go to the house of one of his sons or daughters for Iftar (concluding the fast). He did not eat more than three morsels in Iftar.[1] On the insistence of his children to eat more, he used to say: "I don't want to meet Allah with a full stomach."[2]

He frequently said: "According to the portents the Holy Prophet ﷺ has indicated to me, soon my beard will be smeared with the blood of my head."[3]

He visited the house of his younger daughter, Umme Kulthum, on the eve of the nineteenth. The signs of awaiting were more apparent in him as compared to the previous nights. When everybody retired for the night, the Imam went to his prayer-mat and began to pray.[4]

O Lord! Take me away soon

Imam Hasan ﷺ came to him just before dawn. Imam Ali ﷺ told his beloved son: "I haven't slept the whole night and have woken up the people of house because today is Friday eve and this night is equal to Shab-e-Badr (or Shab-

---

[1] *Muntahal Amaal,* Vol. 1, Pg. 329
[2] *Biharul Anwār,* Vol. 42, Pg. 224
[3] *Biharul Anwār,* Vol. 42, Pg. 227
[4] *Biharul Anwār,* Vol. 42, Pg. 226

e-Qadr).[1] I was sitting when I dozed for some moments. I saw your grandfather in my dream. The Holy Prophet ﷺ told me, 'Curse this Ummah' I said, 'O Lord! Take me away from these people soon and gather me among those who are better than them. Give power on them to one who is worse than me as they are deserving of it.'"[2]

The Muezzin arrived and informed that it was the time for Prayer. Imam Ali ﷺ set out for the mosque.[3] There were a few pet ducks for children in the Imam's house. The ducks began to quack as if they were crying. When a family member tried to silence them, the Imam said: "Do not stop them because they are mourning."[4]

"I have triumphed, by the Lord of Kaaba!"

Abdur Rahman Ibne Muljim and his evil companions were awaiting the arrival of Imam Ali ﷺ impatiently. Their plan was not known to anyone except Quttam and Ashath bin Qais, who had a wicked mentality and was conniving with Muawiyah as he disliked the equitable behavior of Imam Ali ﷺ.

It was likely that a small incident would have spilled the beans of this conspiracy of assassination but a coincidence prevented it. Ashath came running to Ibne Muljim and said: "Very little time is left before daylight. If

---

[1] The Battle of Badr was fought on 17th or 19th Ramadan 2 A.H. ref. *History of the Messenger of Islam*, Pg. 253
[2] *Biharul Anwār*, Vol. 42, Pg. 226
[3] *Muntahal Amaal*, Vol. 1, Pg. 335
[4] *Kashful Ghumma*, Vol. 2, Pg. 62; *Manaqib Ibne Shahr Aashob*, Vol. 3, Pg. 310

it is light you will be disgraced. So finish this job as early as possible."[1]

Hujr bin Adi, who was a close companion of Imam Ali ﷺ overheard the conversation and sensed that they had a dangerous plan. Hujr had returned a little while ago after completing an official chore and his horse was outside the mosque. It seems that he wanted to report this to the Commander of the Faithful.

When Hujr heard the words of Ashath, he rushed to Imam Ali ﷺ to caution him of the danger. However, he reached the house of Imam Ali ﷺ only to find that the latter has gone to the mosque from another route.[2]

Even though the sons and companions of Imam Ali ﷺ insisted that he should be accompanied by a guard, Imam Ali ﷺ always turned down their offer. Imam ﷺ used to stay unguarded. They put forward the same offer to the Imam on that night also but he did not accept it.[3]

Upon entering the mosque, Imam Ali ﷺ called out: "O people! The Prayer! The Prayer!" He had walked a few steps towards the prayer-mat after reciting the Azaan when two swords flashed in the darkness and the people were shocked to hear the shouts of: *"Al-Hukmu Lillaah Ya Aliyyu laa lak."*[4] The first blow was given by Shabeeb, the accursed one, but the sword hit the wall and it was unsuccessful. The second blow was given by Ibne Muljim, which hit the holy head of Imam Ali ﷺ. Hujr returned as soon as he could only to find the people wailing and mourning in the Kufa mosque. People were crying: "The

---

[1] *Irshad,* Shaykh Mufid, Pg. 17

[2] *Irshad,* Shaykh Mufid, Pg. 17; *Tatmah al-Muntaha*, Pg. 39

[3] *Muntahal Amaal,* Vol. 1, Pg. 336

[4] *Biharul Anwār,* Vol. 42, Pg. 239

Commander of the Faithful is killed! The Commander of the Faithful is killed."[1]

"Thanks to Allah, my old wish is finally fulfilled"

The first words of Imam Ali ﷺ after being attacked were: "I have succeeded, by the Lord of the Kaaba."[2] In the words of the poet, Ali was saying:

"Thanks to Allah, my old wish is finally fulfilled"

Then he shouted, "Don't let this man escape."[3]

Abdur Rahman, Shabeeb and Wardan[4] tried to run away. Wardan had not come forward in this attack and was not recognized.[5] As soon as Shabeeb tried to run away, a companion of His Eminence, Ali ﷺ caught him and snatched the sword from his hands. He threw Shabeeb on the ground and mounted his chest with the intention of killing him. However, when he saw people coming towards them, he feared that they might mistake him to be the real killer. Hence he climbed down from his chest. Shabeeb ran away and hid himself in a house. When Shabeeb's cousin came to know that he was involved in the martyrdom of Imam Ali ﷺ, he went to his house and killed him with his sword.[6]

---

[1] *Biharul Anwār,* Vol. 42, Pg. 230

[2] *Biharul Anwār,* Vol. 42, Pg. 239

[3] *Biharul Anwār,* Vol. 42, Pg. 230

[4] His full name was Wardan bin Mujalid; *Irshad,* Shaykh Mufid, Pg. 16

[5] *Irshad,* Shaykh Mufid, Pg. 17; *Biharul Anwār,* Vol. 42, Pg. 231

[6] *Biharul Anwār,* Vol. 42, Pg. 230

Abdur Rahman Ibne Muljim was caught by the people and brought to the mosque with his hands tied behind him. The people were so enraged that they would have lynched him.[1]

Imam Ali ﷺ ordered the people to bring Abdur Rahman to him. When he was brought to the Imam, he asked: "Have I not done good to you?" He said, "Yes, why not?" Imam asked: "Then why did you do this?"[2] He said: "Whatever was bound to happen has happened. I had immersed this sword in poison for forty days and had prayed to Allah to kill the worst person with it." Imam said: "Your prayers are answered. Very soon you will be killed with this sword."[3]

Then Imam Ali ﷺ told his relatives who were gathered there: "O sons of Abdul Muttalib! Beware! Do not make my martyrdom an excuse for accusing someone of a conspiracy and do not start bloodshed."

Then he told Imam Hasan ﷺ: "O son! If I survive, I will take revenge from this person. If I die, you can take the revenge by hitting him not more than once because he hit me only once. Avoid doing any damage to his corpse[4] because the Holy Prophet ﷺ has ordered us not to mutilate

---

[1] *Biharul Anwār,* Vol. 42, Pg. 231, 284

[2] *Biharul Anwār,* Vol. 42, Pg. 287

[3] *Biharul Anwār,* Vol. 42. Pg. 239

[4] The hatred of Bani Umayyah with the Holy Prophet (s.a.w.s.) was so grave that Yazid's grandmother Hinda was not content even after getting His Eminence, Hamza martyred and she chewed his heart as revenge and wore his nose and ears after cutting them off from his body. The followers of Yazid were not content even after slaying Imam Husain (a.s.) and they rode their horses on his body. Yazid's heart was not content until he shook the soul of the Holy Prophet by hitting the lips and teeth of Imam Husain (a.s.) with a cane. (Rizwani)

the corpse even if it is of a mad dog.[1] Take care of this prisoner and feed him well."[2]

Upon Imam Hasan's orders the famous and experienced physician, Athir bin Amr was called. After examining the wound of the Commander of the Faithful he said: "The sword was smeared with poison and its effects have reached the brain. No treatment would be effective."[3]

Imam Ali's Will on the bed of Martyrdom

Imam remained alive for 48 hours after being hit by the sword. However he did not waste this time also. There was no moment in which the Imam did not dispense an advice. He willed as follows:

In the name of Allah, the most Beneficent, the most Merciful

These are things regarding which Ali Ibne Abi Talib 🕮 is making a will to you.

Ali testifies that god is One and testifies that Muhammad is the servant and messenger of God. God has sent him to make His religion dominate over other religions. Indeed, my Prayer, my worship, my life and my death is for this God, Who has no partner. I have been commanded this only and I submit to God. To you, O my son Hasan, to my other children, to my relatives and to all who come to know about this will of mine, regarding the following matters:

---

[1] *Biharul Anwār,* Vol. 42, Pg. 288
[2] *Biharul Anwār,* Vol. 42, Pg. 206, 248
[3] Ibid. Pg. 234

(1) Under no circumstances must you ignore the fear of Allah and try to remain on the religion of God till the moment of your death.

(2) All of you hold the rope of Allah together. All of you remain united on the foundations of faith and recognition of God and avoid disunity and disintegration. The Messenger of Allah ﷺ has said, "To remove mutual enmity, ill-feeling and hatred is better than recommended prayers and fasting. And that which destroys faith is disunity and disintegration."

(3) Take care of your blood and close relatives. Maintain good relations with them because the accounting of one who does good to relatives becomes easy in the presence of God.

(4) For the sake of Allah, take care of the orphans. Do not leave them hungry and uncared.

(5) For the sake of Allah, keep a tab on the well being of the neighbors. The Messenger of Allah ﷺ stressed so much regarding the neighbors that we though he would include them among ones heirs.

(6) Fear Allah in respect of the Holy Quran, lest others should excel and surpass you in following its tenets and in acting according to its orders.

(7) Fear Allah so far as prayers are concerned, because prayers are pillars of your faith.

(8) Fear Allah in the matter of His Holy House (Kaaba). Let it not be deserted because if it is deserted, you (the Muslims) will be lost.

(9) Do not forget Allah, struggle in His cause with your tongue, with your wealth and with your lives.

(10) For the sake of Allah pay Zakat regularly. Payment of Zakat cools divine anger.

(11) For the sake of Allah, refrain from oppressing the descendants of the Prophet.

(12) For the sake of Allah, accord respect to the companions of the Prophet. The Messenger of Allah ﷺ has recommended them.

(13) For the sake of Allah, take care of the poor and the deprived and allow them to share your life.

(14) For the sake of Allah, have a good behavior with the slaves because the last recommendation of the Messenger of Allah ﷺ was regarding them only.

(15) Do that which pleases God and do not care for people's criticism in this regard.

(16) Deal with love and goodness with the people as the Holy Quran has commanded.

(17) Exhort people to do good and restrain them from evil, otherwise the vicious and the wicked will dominate you and if you willingly allow such persons to be your rulers, your prayers will not be heard by Allah.

(18) Develop mutual liking, friendship and love and help one another. Take care that you do not spurn and treat one another badly and unsympathetically.

(19) Cooperate with each other on good works and perform them in a communal way. And do not help each other in sinful acts and acts that cause hatred and enmity.

(20) Fear the chastisement of God, because the hold of God is very strong. May Allah keep you all in His refuge and may He give good sense to the Ummah of the Messenger that they continue to hold you and the Messenger of Allah ﷺ in respect. I entrust you all to Allah. Peace be on you all, as is wont.

After this bequest no one heard any other statement from Amirul Mu'minīn ؏ except the two testimonies of Islamic faith, till he finally surrendered his soul to the Creator.[12]

---

[1] This will of the Imam shows how important unity is according to Islam. Holy Prophet (s.a.w.s.) said: 'Allah's protects the congregation.' Islam wants to see unity in people in addition to the presence of faith everywhere because progress and success results from unity only. Breaking unity and separating oneself is against Islam. Certainly, Islam possesses such a wealth that it can play a role of awakening the people of the entire world and gathering them at one place because this is the religion of the Lord of human beings. Professor of Arabic literature in the University of Cairo, Dr. Hamid Hanafi Dawood says, "The secrets of Islam are hidden in the fundamentals of Islam and the secrets of fundamentals is hidden in Islam." A society is successful only if it is united. Being united means that people work for common benefit and different classes of society have strong basis of communication among them and the entire society benefits from them. Thus, a person who gathers Muslims at one place is worth praising and a person who destroys their unity is worth condemnation. (Rizwani)

[2] *Irshad,* Shaykh Mufid, Pg. 15-18; *Kamil Ibne Athir,* Vol. 3, Pg. 387-392, *Muruj al-Zahab,* Vol. 2, Pg. 423-426; *Biharul Anwār,* Vol. 42, Pg. 248; *Sharh Nahjul Balagha,* Ibne Abil Hadīd, Vol. 6, Pg. 120; *Nahjul Balagha,* Faizul Islam, Sermon 47, Pg. 967; *Muntahal Amaal,* Vol. 1, Pg. 332-341; *Dastan Raastan,* Vol. 2, Pg. 268-274

There is no power and might except by Allah the High and the Mighty.

Majlis 4

"I was waiting for this Day."

O mourners!

When Ibne Muljim, the accursed one hit Imam Ali bin Abi Talib ؏ on his head with the sword, a slash was made in the skull till his eyebrows. Imam ؏ said: By Allah! Sudden death and sudden attack are not something that I dislike. My case is like that of a lover who has reached his beloved.[1] In the words of a poet:

"Do you know the happiness of meeting a lost friend? The happiness is like that of a thirsty person in a desert when a cloud starts raining on him."

The Commander of the Faithful gave an example, which was well-known among the Arabs. The Arabs living in deserts were nomads. They used to settle down wherever they found water and vegetation. When the resources got over, they shifted from that place. In summer, they traveled during nights in search of a place where water was available. The Commander of the Faithful told his companions: My state is like that of a person who has reached his beloved. My state of happiness

---

[1] *Biharul Anwār,* Vol. 42, Pg. 254; *Nahjul Balagha,* Faizul Islam, Sermon 23, Pg. 865; *Sharh Nahjul Balagha,* Ibne Abil Hadīd, Vol. 15, Pg. 143; the words of the master of faithful, in which he cursed Ibne Muljim after he was attacked and before his martyrdom are presented excerpts.

is like that of a person that searches for water during nights in lonely forests and becomes overjoyed on finding it. It is quoted very well as below:

"I was given freedom from grief yesterday morning and in the darkness tonight I was given the elixir of life."[1]

In the name of Allah and by Allah and on the religion of the Messenger of Allah.

---

[1] *Hamasa Husaini,* Vol. 1 (the Urdu version of this book is published by Dar al-Thaqafiyatul Islamiya, Karachi)

Majlis 5

Last moments of Imam Ali ﷺ

O mourners!

The last 25 hours of Imam Ali's ﷺ life are most astounding although his entire life is full of important lessons, from birth to declaration of Islam, from declaration to Islam to migration, from migration to the demise of the Holy Prophet ﷺ, which was the third period of the Imam's life and it was entirely different. The fourth period of Imam Ali's ﷺ life was from the demise of the Holy Prophet ﷺ to his appointment as caliph. After that, came the period of his rule for four and a half years, which was one of the important periods of the Imam's life.

Nonetheless, another period of Imam Ali's ﷺ life of two days and nights is very strange. It is the period from the time when Imam ﷺ was attacked until his passing away, which proved that the Imam was a perfect man. Even though his end was near, what duties did he shirk? When the Imam was struck on his holy head, two statements spoken by him were heard. First was, "I swear by the Lord of Kaaba, I have succeeded. I got martyrdom and it is the proof of my success." The second statement was, "Do not let that man escape."

The Doctor of Kufa examines Ali ﷺ

Imam Ali ﷺ was brought to his house from the mosque after being attacked. He was made to lie on a bed. An Arab named Athir bin Amr[1] who had studied medicine in Jundi Shahpur was practicing in Kufa. He was brought to treat the Commander of the Faithful. He began diagnosing the Imam's condition.[2] He understood that the poison had already entered the veins of Imam ﷺ and said that no treatment would be effective. (Normally such patients are not informed that no treatment would be useful for them. Only the relatives of the patient are informed about it). However, the doctor knew that it was not appropriate to hide the fact from a personality like Imam Ali ﷺ and inform only his relatives about his deteriorating condition. So he told him:

"O Commander of the Faithful! If you want to make a will, do it now."[3]

Umme Kulthum speaks to Ibne Muljim

When Lady Umme Kulthum came to know about this accursed one from first to last, she told him hatefully: "What wrong did my father do to you? Why did you attack him?" Then she said, "God willing, my father will be

---

[1] Among the renowned physicians of Kufa, no one was more experienced than Athir bin Amr. He was one of the nine youths who were arrested by Khalid bin Walid during the caliphate of Abu Bakr. He had taken shelter in Kufa. *Biharul Anwār,* Vol. 42, Pg. 234

[2] It is narrated that this physician heated the windpipe of a ram and filled the wound with it.

[3] O master of faithful! Please complete your vow because the impact of the attack of the enemy of God has reached your brain. *Biharul Anwār,* Vol. 42, Pg. 234; *Muntahal Amaal,* Vol. 1, Pg. 343

well soon and you will have to suffer deprivation and failure." At this, the accursed one told her:

"Do not hope that your father will get well, because I bought this sword for one thousand dirhams (or dinars) and spent one thousand dirhams (or dinars) more to smear it with poison. I have smeared it with such a poison that this sword is enough to kill the entire population of Kufa."[1]

Imam Ali's ﷺ recommendation for the killer

The humanistic miracle of Imam Ali ﷺ, which astounds others, appeared when he ordered that proper care should be taken of his prisoner. Then he said: "O children of Abdul Muttalib! Do not go about saying: "so and so person is involved in the martyrdom of the Commander of the Faithful" and "so and so person is also a part of conspiracy". It should not be that you start accusing one or more. I don't want you to fall into these things because only this man is my killer."[2]

A cup of milk for Ibne Muljim

He told Imam Hasan ﷺ: "O son! You have the right decide the fate of this man after me. You may set him free or punish him. If you want to punish him, hit him only once, because he has hit your father only once. If he does not die in one blow, set him free. Then he asked once

---

[1] *Biharul Anwār,* Vol. 42, Pg. 231

[2] *Nahjul Balagha,* Subhi Salih, Sermon 47; *Nahjul Balagha,* Faizul Islam, Sermon 47, Pg. 969 – the word 'yaqtulna' is included in *Nahjul Balagha* of Faizul Islam.

again: "Did you provide food to your prisoner? Did you provide him water? Did you take proper care of him?"[1]

When a cup of milk was brought for the Imam to drink, he took a few sips and gave the remaining to Ibne Muljim so that he does not remain hungry.[2]

Commenting on his treatment towards an enemy, Maulana Rumi says:

"No one can equal Ali in daring and courage. And no one could reach the level of his lofty manners and forbearance."

What can be better than Martyrdom during Worship?

Imam was on his death-bed. His health was deteriorating with the passage of time. The poison had spread to his entire body. His companions were aggrieved. All of them had surrounded him and were crying. However, the Imam was calm and was smiling patiently. Expressing his joy at the turn of these events he said: "By Allah, whatever has happened to me is certainly not disliked by me because it was my old wish to get martyred in the way of Allah. What can be better for me than getting martyred while in worship...?"

Imam Ali ﷺ gives an example that Arabs were well-aware of. The nomads used to stay at a place depending on the weather. They stayed at a place as long as food and water was available for them and their animals. When the resources exhausted they set out in search of another place

---

[1] *Biharul Anwār,* Vol. 42, Pg. 289
[2] *Mathnawi Manawi,* (Nicholson Edition) Vol. 1, Pg. 229

where they could find food and water. Since it was extremely hot during the days of summer they traveled during the night (Arabs called such persons who used to travel during night in search of water as "Qaarib"). Imam Ali ☪ said:

"O people! Think upon it. A person who is in search of water during the darkness of night and he finds it suddenly, how happy he would be? My happiness is also like a lover who has met his beloved or like a person who is in search of water at night and finds it suddenly."[1]

"I was freed from grief yesterday morning and given the elixir of life in the darkness of tonight. How blessed was that dawn and how blessed was that night, that Night of Power in which I was given a new permit of salvation."

These couplets of Hafiz also imply that which the Imam said: "I swear by the Lord of Kaaba, I have succeeded."[2] The most astonishing words of Imam Ali ☪ were those spoken in his last 45 hours. He was struck on 19th Ramadan a few minutes after dawn and his soul departed at midnight of 21st Ramadan.

Imam Ali's ☪ last advice

During his last moments, when the spectacle of death was before him and people surrounded his bed, the effects of poison had spread in his entire body. Sometimes he writhed in pain and sometimes lost consciousness. Whenever he used to regain consciousness, pearls of advices full of wisdom came out from him. The twenty-

---

[1] *Diwan-e-Hafiz*, Pg. 114
[2] *Biharul Anwār*, Vol. 42, Pg. 239

point bequest of the Imam, which we mentioned in the previous Majlis, is full of the enthusiasm of faith. He first addressed Imams Hasan and Husain ※ and then his other relatives:

"My (son) Hasan, My (son) Hasan! After that the Imam addressed all his sons and all the generations that were to some till the Judgment Day and told them about the comprehensiveness of Islam:

Fear Allah regarding the orphans.

Fear Allah regarding the Quran.

Fear Allah regarding your neighbors.

Fear Allah regarding the house of your Lord.

Fear Allah regarding the Ritual Prayer.

Fear Allah regarding Zakat tax.

He stressed upon each point in turn.[1]

The Imam continued to emphasize the points that were before him. Those persons whose eyes were on the illuminated face of Imam Ali ※, saw that in a moment the Imam's condition changed. Beads of cold perspiration began to glitter upon his wide forehead and he took away his attention from the people who had surrounded him. All of them waited for the lips of the Imam to move again, so that they may hear a word from him. People waited for the

---

[1] *Nahjul Balagha*, Faizul Islam, Sermon 47, Pg. 967; *Biharul Anwār*, Vol. 42, Pg. 249

magnificent personality of history and the beloved of the Prophet to utter the last sentence of his life:

I testify that there is no god except Allah and I testify that Muhammad is His servant and Messenger.

Majlis 6

Value of Dower – Ali's Blood!

Abdur Rahman Ibne Muljim was among those so-called nine 'famous pure and pious persons' who had gone to Mecca to take a well-known oath. They believed that only Ali, Muawiyah and Amr bin Aas were responsible for all the troubles in the world of Islam.[1]

Ibne Muljim was entrusted with the job of assassinating Ali ﷺ in Kufa. They fixed the 19th eve of Ramadan for this purpose. Ibne Abil Hadid says that the fools had chosen the 19th eve because according to their mistaken notion, if they committed this act of 'worship' in the Night of Power (Shab-e-Qadr) they shall get more reward.[2]

Ibne Muljim arrived in Kufa and wandered here and there waiting for the fixed night. During this time, he fell for the virgin, Quttam[3] (binte Akhzar) also of Khariji sect. He was so mad in her love that he even forgot his mission. When he proposed to her, she said: "I am ready to marry you but I would demand a huge and tough dower from you." Ibne Muljim wanted to marry her at any cost and he agreed to fulfill all her demands.

---

[1] *Sharh Nahjul Balagha,* Ibne Abil Hadīd, Vol. 6, Pg. 112,113
[2] *Sharh Nahjul Balagha,* Ibne Abil Hadīd, Vol. 6, Pg. 112,113
[3] Quttam was very clever. She demanded Ali's blood in her Dower because many of her relatives were killed in the battle of Nahrawan (Rizwani).

Quttam stated four demands for the marriage:

1. Three thousand dirhams in cash

2. A slave boy

3. A slave girl

4. Murder of Ali bin Abi Talib ﷺ

Ibne Muljim accepted the first three conditions happily but was worried at the third and he said: "Ali's murder would become a barrier in the way of our happy married life." Quttam said: "If you want me you will have to kill Ali. After that, if you survive you will get me and if not, it would be the end."[1] Ibne Muljim was stunned to hear these conditions of Quttam and a poet has composed the following verses on this:

(It was) three thousand (dirhams), a slave and a young servant, and the striking of Ali with a sharp piercing sword.

(There has been) no dowry more precious – and no violence except that it was less than the violence of Ibne Muljim.[2]

How true is the statement of this poet!

---

[1] *Irshad,* Shaykh Mufid, Pg. 16; *Sharh Nahjul Balagha,* Ibne Abil Hadīd, Vol. 6, Pg. 115

[2] *Biharul Anwār,* Vol. 42, Pg. 266; *Irshad,* Shaykh Mufid, Pg. 18 also has following verse before the above verses:
"I have never seen a dowry, given by a generous man, like the dowry of Quttam (whether the man was) rich or needy."

Do not kill the Khawarij after me

Keeping the above fact in mind, let us review the will of Imam Ali 🌿. When Imam Ali 🌿 was on his death-bed, he had both the mischievous groups in his mind that he had crushed before. One of them was that of the hypocrites, called *Qasiteen* in terminology. Muawiyah was the leader of this group. Another was *Mariqeen* or Khawarij who were wearing the veil of purity. There were mutual differences in this group. Hence the Imam advises his companions about how to fight these two groups:

"Do not kill these people after me. It is true that they have killed me but you do not kill them after me. If you go about increasing bloodshed, you will be included among the helpers of Muawiyah. You would not be included among the people working in the way of truth. The danger to Muawiyah is something else." Imam Ali 🌿 said: Do not fight the Kharijites after me, because one who seeks right but does not find it, is not like one who seeks wrong and finds it."[1] Sayyid ar-Radi says: Amirul Mu'minīn means Muawiyah and his men.

Imam Ali 🌿 neither had any malice towards anyone nor did he harbor enmity for any. He always spoke the truth. Consider the example of Ibne Muljim. When he was arrested and brought to the Imam, he asked in a painful voice because of his injury: "Why did you do this? Was I a bad Imam for you?" (I don't know whether Imam Ali 🌿 spoke these words once or twice but everybody has narrated the same statements). This oppressor was moved by the Imam's spirituality and he said: "Can you save an

---

[1] *Nahjul Balagha*, Faizul Islam, Sermon 60, Pg. 141; *Nahjul Balagha,* Subhi Salih, Sermon 61 has 'laa tuqaatiloo' substituted in place of 'laa taqtuloo'

unfortunate man from the fire?[1] I was wretched to have committed such an act."[2] It is also mentioned in books that when Imam Ali 🕮 was speaking to him, the killer addressed the Imam in the most vicious manner and asked:

"O Ali! When I bought this sword, I prayed to Allah that the worst person among the creatures of Allah should be killed with this sword."

Imam Ali 🕮 said: "Fortunately, your prayers are answered because soon you will be killed with this sword."[3]

Attending the Funeral at Night

Imam Ali 🕮 was martyred in a city like Kufa where all people except the Khawarij of Nahrawan wanted to attend his funeral and mourn for him. People had no information of Imam Ali's 🕮 martyrdom till the midnight of the twenty-first of Ramadan because he passed away after midnight.

Imam Ali's sons, viz. Imams Hasan and Husain 🕮, Muhammad bin Hanafiyyah and Abul Fazl al-Abbas and some of his close companions who numbered six or seven performed his funeral bath, shrouded him and buried him secretly at the place as willed by Imam Ali 🕮. He was taken to the place where he is buried today in the darkness of the night and no one was informed about this. According to traditions, it is the place where some of the

---

[1] Surah Zumar 39:19
[2] *Muntahal Amaal,* Vol. 1, Pg. 340; *Biharul Anwār,* Vol. 42, Pg. 287
[3] *Biharul Anwār,* Vol. 42, Pg. 239-244

great prophets are buried. The place of Imam's grave was kept confidential and no one was informed about it.[1]

Next day, the people came to know that Ali ﷺ was buried the previous night. When they asked about the place of his burial, they were told that it was not necessary for them to know it. It is also mentioned in some books that Imam Hasan ﷺ prepared a bier and sent it to Medina so that the people may believe that Ali's ﷺ bier has been sent to Medina for burial.[2]

Why was it done in this way? It was because of these Khawarij only. If they had known where Imam Ali ﷺ was buried they would have taken out his holy body from the grave and defiled it.

As long as Khawarij lived in this world and were in power, no one except the descendants of Imam Ali ﷺ and holy Imams knew the place of his burial. After a hundred years, Khawarij lost power and they were eliminated and there was no possibility of insult to Imam Ali's ﷺ grave. Then Imam Ja'far Sadiq ﷺ informed the people about the location of Imam Ali's ﷺ grave for the first time.

The supplication recited by us in Ziarat Ashura has a famous companion of the Imam, Safwan Jamal as one of the narrators. Safwan narrates: I was with Imam Ja'far

---

[1] *Biharul Anwār,* Vol. 42, Pg. 239
Holy Prophet had said about Fatima Zahra: "Fatima is a piece of my heart" (*Sahih Bukhari,* Vol. 5, Tr. 209). Also the Holy Prophet had said about Ali Murtadha, "O Ali! Are you not pleased with the fact that you are to me as Haroon was to Musa, except that there is no prophet after me?" (*Sahih Bukhari,* Vol. 6, Tr. 408). Doesn't the Ummah wonder why their burial took place in the darkness of night instead of doing it in presence of the entire community? (Rizwani)
[2] *Muntahal Amaal,* Vol. 1, Pg. 353

Sadiq in Kufa and the Imam took us to the holy grave of Imam Ali ﷺ. Imam ﷺ pointed out the holy grave of Imam Ali ﷺ and probably he arranged for a shelter for the holy grave. After that the secret of Imam Ali's ﷺ grave became known.[1] The atrocities on Imam Ali ﷺ were not limited till his martyrdom. The place of his burial was kept secret for more than a hundred years after his martyrdom.

Victimization of Ali ﷺ

Peace be on you, O Abul Hasan! Peace be on you, O Commander of the Faithful!

How oppressed he and his children were! I don't know whether my master, the Commander of the Faithful was more oppressed or his dear son, Imam Husain ﷺ. Just as the holy body of Imam Ali ﷺ was not safe from the mischief of the enemies, the holy body of his son and the son of Lady Zahra was also unsafe from the mischief of his enemies. Probably, that was the reason he said: "None of the days are like the unfortunate days of my oppressed Husain." Why did Imam Hasan ﷺ hide the body of his holy father? Because he didn't want anyone to harm it; but alas, the situation was entirely different in Karbala. Imam Sajjad ﷺ was so helpless that he could not hide the body of

---

[1] *Irshad,* Shaykh Mufid, Pg. 12; *Muntahal Amaal,* Vol. 2, Pg. 271 and *Safinatul Bihar,* Vol. 2, Pg. 37

(Safwan was a camel-driver and he used to rent his camels. He had taken Imam Ja'far Sadiq (a.s.) from Medina to Kufa once in the past. He got a chance of performing the Ziarat of the holy grave of Imam Ali along with Imam Ja'far Sadiq (a.s.). He had complete knowledge of Imam Ali's grave and it is mentioned at Pg. 37 of *Kamiluz Ziaraat* that Safwan used to regularly go for the Ziarat of the holy grave of Imam Ali for sixty years. He used to offer Prayer near the Imam's grave.

Imam Husain ﷺ after his martyrdom. What was the result? I don't want to mention it. A person has said:[1]

What is the use of an old dress when one is trampled by the hooves?

Nobody remained to cover it with clothes.

---

[1] *Seeri dar Seerat-e-Aimma-e-Athaar,* Pg. 49-54

Majlis 7

Imam Ali ﷺ was buried secretly

O mourners of the Commander of the Faithful!

Why have we gathered here today? Today we have gathered to mourn that perfect personality who was buried secretly at night. This was done because the perfect personality i.e. Ali bin Abi Talib ﷺ had as many enemies as he had relatives and friends. I have discussed this in detail in my book, *Jaziba wa Dafia-e-Ali* ﷺ that some people in this world have tremendous power in them. There are also some people who have boundless resistance power in them. The followers of those who have extraordinary power of attraction are so committed that they feel pride in sacrificing their lives for their leader. Also, the enemies of such persons are bitterest. Especially those who stay near him or his internal enemies. The enemies of Imam Ali ﷺ were of the same type. They veiled their faces with purity and stood up against Imam Ali ﷺ. Khawarij were those who had faith, but were illiterate and extremely adamant. Imam Ali ﷺ had himself confessed that these people had faith but were illiterate and foolish. Imam Ali ﷺ compared Khawarij with the hypocrites by saying: "Do not fight Khawarij after me because there is a difference between them and the followers of Muawiyah. These Khawarij seek truth but they are foolish. They have fallen prey to misunderstanding while the hypocrites know the truth but they want to go against it."

Why was Imam Ali ﷺ buried secretly in the darkness of night in spite of having so many followers?[1] It was because of the fear of Khawarij only because they used to say that Ali ﷺ is not a Muslim. Hence, there was a risk that these people might have dug up his grave in the darkness of night and exhumed his pure remains.

Towards the end of Imam Ja'far Sadiq's time i.e. approximately for a hundred years,[2] why did no one except the holy Imams and some special companions knew the grave of Imam Ali ﷺ?

On the morning of the 21st Ramadan, Imam Hasan ﷺ prepared a bier and gave it to a group of people to take it to Medina so that the people think that Imam Ali ﷺ is buried in Medina.[3]

The children of Imam Ali ﷺ and his close Shias knew the location of his grave because they had buried him on the 21st eve of Ramadan. They used to go to the place for Ziarat, which was near Kufa. When the Khawarij lost power during the time of Imam Ja'far Sadiq, the risk of any damage to the grave of Imam Ali ﷺ was eliminated. Eventually, Imam Ja'far Sadiq ﷺ ordered Safwan who is a narrator in the chain of narrators of Dua Alqamah to prepare a shade over the grave of Imam Ali ﷺ so that people could recognize it. After that, people came to know about the grave of Imam Ali ﷺ and it became a place of visitation for all.

---

[1] *Biharul Anwār,* Vol. 42, Pg. 222
[2] Imam Ali was martyred in 40 A.H. while Imam Ja'far Sadiq's martyrdom took place in 148 A.H.
[3] *Muntahal Amaal,* Vol. 1, Pg. 353

Sasa'ah's Elegy at Imam Ali's 🕮 grave

Only a handful of people had attended Imam Ali's 🕮 funeral. Only his sons and a few close companions were present. One of his companions, Sasa'ah bin Sauhan[1] who was a sincere friend was also present. He was an excellent speaker and orator.[2] He had delivered a number of speeches during the time of Imam Ali 🕮.

All those gathered at the funeral of Imam Ali 🕮 were filled with sadness, grief and anger. Sasa'ah's heart was

---

[1] Muhaddith Shaykh Abbas Qummi has written in the section of Amaal of Masjid Sahla that Masjid Zaid is one of the holiest mosques of Kufa. It is related to Zaid bin Sauhan. He was a senior companion of Imam Ali. He is included among devoted persons. He was martyred on the side of Imam Ali (a.s.) in the battle of Jamal. There is a mosque called Masjid Sasa'ah near this mosque, which is related to his brother, Sasa'ah bin Sauhan. He was also a senior companion of the master of the faithful. He is included among those believers who had great recognition of Imam Ali (a.s.). He was such an eloquent orator that Imam Ali (a.s.) had given him the title of 'Khatib-e-shahshah' and had praised his oratory skills and eloquence. On the twenty-first night, when his coffin was taken to holy Najaf from Kufa, Sasa'ah was along with them. When Imam Ali (a.s.) was buried, Sasa'ah took a handful of mud from the Imam's grave and kept it on his head and said, "O master of faithful! May my parents be sacrificed for you. O Abul Hasan! May Allah's blessings be upon you. Certainly, the place of your birth is pure. Your patience is strong and jihad is great. You got whatever you desired. Your trade was very profitable and returned to truth." He spoke many such statements and cried a lot and made others cry. In fact, Majlis-e-Aza was conducted at the grave of Imam Ali (a.s.) in the darkness of this night. Sasa'ah was the speaker and listeners included Imam Hasan, Imam Husain, Muhammad bin Hanafiyyah, His Eminence, Abbas and other sons and great companions of Imam Ali (a.s.). After this Majlis, he turned towards Imam Hasan, Imam Husain and other sons of Imam Ali (a.s.) and expressed his condolence. After that, everybody returned to Kufa.

[2] Jahiz has narrated from him in *al-Bayan wa al-Tibiyyin*.

full of remorse. He picked up a handful of sand from Imam Ali's ﷺ grave and put it on his head. He controlled his emotions and said: "Peace be upon you, O Commander of the Faithful! You led a successful life and passed away in a successful manner."[1] You were born in the holy Kaaba and drank the potion of martyrdom in the house of Allah.

This concept is expressed beautifully by a poet in the following lines:

"You were born in Kaaba and got martyred in a mosque. I am proud of your beautiful start and beautiful end."

O my master! You were so great and people were so base. By Allah, if people had followed the path shown by you, mercy would have rained on their heads and bounties would have flowed under their feet.[2] They would have obtained material and abstract bounties. Alas, people did not care about you. They hurt your feelings in many ways instead of following your lofty principles. At last, they split your holy head into two and bathed you in mud and blood.[3]

وَسَيَعْلَمُ الَّذِينَ ظَلَمُوا أَيَّ مُنقَلَبٍ يَنقَلِبُونَ

And they who act unjustly shall know to what final place of turning they shall turn back.[4]

---

[1] *Biharul Anwār,* Vol. 42, Pg. 295; *Muntahal Amaal,* Vol. 1, Pg. 352
[2] *Biharul Anwār,* Vol. 42, Pg. 296
[3] *Insan-e-Kamil,* Pg. 144-146
[4] Surah Shuara 26:227

Majlis 8

Sasa'ah, the Great Companion of Ali ﷺ

O mourners of the master!

Sasa'ah bin Sauhan Abdi was a great companion of the Commander of the Faithful. The Imam was very fond of him. He was a well-known orator whose speeches were effective. Jahiz has praised his powerful oratory and way of reasoning in his book, *Al-Bayan wa al-Tibbiyyin* in the following words: "Sasa'ah was such a nice orator that at times, Imam Ali ﷺ used to invite him to speak in public and he used to speak in the Imam's presence."[1]

Sasa'ah had spoken briefly about the Imam on the first day of his caliphate. He spoke about him for the second time when Imam Ali ﷺ was struck by Ibne Muljim's sword. After that, he talked in detail about the Imam after his burial.

The First Day of Ali's Caliphate

On the first day of Imam Ali's ﷺ caliphate, Sasa'ah turned towards the Imam and said: "O Commander of the Faithful! You have decorated caliphate and caliphate has not decorated you. The respect of caliphate has increased after you became the caliph and caliphate has not

---

[1] Jahiz, *al-Bayan wat Tibiyyin*, Vol. 1, Pg. 266

increased your respect. The Caliphate needs you and you do not need caliphate."[1]

After Imam Ali ﷺ was wounded

Sasa'ah talked about him for the second time after the Commander of the Faithful was injured. The blow had severe impact on him like other special companions of Imam Ali ﷺ. In fact, Sasa'ah had come to visit Imam ﷺ however he did not get a chance to meet him. Eventually, he conveyed two verses through the person who was allowed to enter the room where the Imam was kept. Sasa'ah expressed his sorrow by conveying his salutation to Imam and by reciting the following two verses: "May Allah's mercy be with you in your life and death, O Commander of the Faithful! You consider God the greatest and you have divine recognition of the Unique Being."[2]

When Imam Ali ﷺ received the message, he replied to Sasa'ah saying: "May Allah's mercy be upon you too, O Sasa'ah! You are our best friend and helper. You did not expect much, gave least trouble and spent less. You were also hard working; you served much and gave many sacrifices."[3]

After Ali's burial

The third poem recited by Sasa'ah was after the burial of Imam Ali ﷺ. Sasa'ah was one of the special companions of the Imam present at the time of his burial. After Imam's burial, Sasa'ah kept one of his hands on his chest and took a handful of mud from the grave and kept it on his head.

---

[1] *Al-Sawarim al-Muhriqa,* Pg. 6; *Usudul Ghaba,* Vol. 4, Pg. 32
[2] *Biharul Anwār,* Vol. 42, Pg. 234; *Safinatul Bihar,* Vol. 2, Pg. 31
[3] *Biharul Anwār,* Vol. 42, Pg. 234; *Safinatul Bihar,* Vol. 2, Pg. 30

Then he said: "May my parents be sacrificed for you, O Commander of the Faithful! O Abul Hasan! May you find pleasing all the honors and successes you gained through this martyrdom and the rank you obtained near Allah."

Then he said: "Surely, the place of your birth is pure, your patience is strong and your Jihad is great. You made a profitable trade and reached your Lord. I pray to Allah that He grants us the good sense to follow your footsteps. You reached a place none can reach. You have gained that honor, which could not be gained by anyone." He again said: "O Abul Hasan! I am happy for you. Allah has made your rank more honorable. May Allah not keep us away from the great reward, which we seek through you. May Allah not let us get misguided after you. By Allah, your holy life was the key to goodness and a lock for mischief.[1] If people had obeyed you and sought your recognition, heaven would have rained mercy and earth would have thrown up its treasures. Alas, they did not care about you. This temporal world misled them."[2] Saying this, Sasa'ah began crying excessively and all the people gathered there were full of remorse. They began to weep aloud in extreme grief.[3]

---

[1] *Biharul Anwār,* Vol. 42, Pg. 295
[2] *Biharul Anwār,* Vol. 42, Pg. 295
[3] *Sukhan,* Jame Talimaat-e-Islami, Pakistan

Majlis 9

Ali ﷺ and Justice are synonymous

Imam Ali's ﷺ name became a synonym for 'justice' after him. He became an ideal of human justice amongst the common people and the nobility. Umar bin Abdul Aziz said: "Ali neglected the predecessors and made the successors fall in a difficult situation. When people compared the characteristics of the caliphs with immaculate and just character of Imam Ali ﷺ, they could not help criticizing the caliphs.

Darmiyya praises Ali ﷺ in Muawiyah's presence

Muawiyah had come to Mecca for Hajj and found about Darmiyya Hujuniya who was famous for supporting Imam Ali ﷺ and opposing Muawiyah. Muawiyah was informed that she is alive and he summoned her. He asked her: "Do you know why I called you? I want to know the reason why you love Ali and hate me." Darmiyya replied: "It is better that you don't ask me this question?" Muawiyah said: "You will have to reply this question in any case."

Darmiyya said: "Because Ali was the standard bearer of justice and equity. You fought him without justification. I love Ali because he took care of the poor. I hate you because you shed unlawful blood. You created a rift among

Muslims, gave unjust verdicts and fell a prey to your selfish desires."

Muawiyah was ashamed to hear this and be became furious. He could not control his anger and abused Darmiyya. Then he controlled his anger and as usual told her politely, "Never mind, have you seen Ali yourself?"

Darmiyya: "Yes."

Muawiyah: "How did you find him?"

Darmiyya: "By Allah, I saw him in a state such that he was not intoxicated by kingdom like you are."

Muawiyah asked: "Did you hear Ali's voice?"

Darmiyya said: "Yes, I have heard him. His voice polishes the hearts and removes turbidity from them as olive oil removes rust."

Muawiyah asked: "Do you want anything?"

Darmiyya said: "Would you give me what I ask?"

Muawiyah replied: "Yes, why not?"

Darmiyya said: "I want a hundred red-haired camels."

Muawiyah said: "If I give you these camels, would you equate me with Ali?"

Darmiyya said: "Never."

Muawiyah ordered the wish of Darmiyya to be fulfilled. A hundred camels were given to Darmiyya.

Muawiyah said: "By Allah, if Ali had been alive, he would not have given you even a single camel."

Darmiyya said: "You are talking about one camel? I swear by Allah, Ali would not have given me even a single camel hair because it is communal property of Muslims."[1]

Adi recites a poem in Ali's praise

Adi bin Hatim Tai was one of the great and pious companions of the Master of the Pious. He loved Imam Ali ﷺ from the depths of his heart. He accepted Islam during the last days of the Holy Prophet ﷺ. Accepting Islam brought him lots of good luck. He came very close to Imam Ali ﷺ during the days of his caliphate. His three sons – Tareef, Tarfa and Taarif were alongside Imam Ali ﷺ in the battle of Siffeen and got martyred in the battle. Adi happened to meet Muawiyah face to face one day after the martyrdom of Imam Ali ﷺ. Muawiyah tried to reopen the wounds of Adi by making him recollect the memories of his martyred sons and make Adi say what he wanted.

Muawiyah asked: "Where are Tareef, Tarfa and Taarif?"

Adi replied courageously: "They were martyred in front of Ali bin Abi Talib ﷺ in the battle of Siffeen."

Adi emphasized the phrase "in front of Ali" in order to express his pleasure.

---

[1] *Al Iqdul Farid*, Vol. 2, Pg. 113. This statement "We should follow the footsteps of His Eminence, Ali" seems amusing when spoken by those who loan lacs and crores of rupees collected as taxes from people to whomever they wish and then waive their loans. (Rizwani)

Muawiyah said: "Ali has not done justice with you. He sent your sons to the front so that they may be killed but he did not send his sons so that they might live."

Adi said: "No, the fact is that I have not done justice to Ali 🕮 because he got martyred and I am still alive."[1]

When Muawiyah saw that his purpose was not getting fulfilled, his tactics changed and he said, "Narrate the attributes of Ali."

Adi said: "Please excuse me."

Muawiyah said: "No, I won't leave you like this."

When Muawiyah insisted much, Adi began reciting a poem in praise of Imam Ali 🕮 as follows:

"By Allah, Ali 🕮 was foresighted and very brave. He used to talk justly and decide responsibly. The fountains of knowledge and wisdom flowed around him. He hated the glamour of this world. He was attracted towards the darkness of night and solitude. He used to cry out of fear of Allah and pondered on every matter. He used to account for his deeds when he was alone and used to repent for his past. When he was around us, he looked like us. He used to give whatever we asked. When we visited him, he made us sit near him and he never sat away from us. Even though he was so close to us, we awed him so much that we did not dare to speak in front of him. We did not dare to look into his eyes because of his greatness. When he smiled, his teeth shone like pearls. He respected generosity and piety. He loved the helpless. Strong people

---

[1] *Safinatul Bihar,* Vol. 2, Pg. 170

never feared that he would do injustice and weak never lost hope in his justice.

I swear by Allah, one night I saw Ali ؑ standing in the niche of the mosque. There was silence everywhere. His beard was wet with his tears. He was trembling and shivering like a troubled person. His words still strike my mind. He was saying: 'O world! Why are you after me? Go away and deceive someone else. Your magic will have no effect on Ali ؑ. I have divorced you thrice and there is no possibility of reconciliation now. You are tasteless and unpredictable. Alas, provisions for journey are meager and journey is long and there is no companion.'"[1]

Adi told this much and tears began flowing from Muawiyah's eyes. He wiped his tears with his sleeves and said: "May Allah bless Ali ؑ. Surely, he was just as you have described."[2]

Now tell me, how do you feel without him?

Adi said: "I feel like a mother whose son was slaughtered in her lap."

Muawiyah asked: "Wouldn't you be able to ever forget Ali?"

Adi said: "No, but the ointment of time might make me forget the pain."

Shaykh Mufeed writes in *Al-Irshad* that the period of the Imamate of Commander of the Faithful was for thirty years after the Holy Prophet ؐ. Out of which, he held the

---

[1] *Safinatul Bihar,* Vol. 2, Pg. 170
[2] *Safinatul Bihar,* Vol. 2, Pg. 170

reins of government for five years and six months. During this short tenure also he fought the hypocrites. He was martyred on the 21st of holy Ramadan, Friday at sunrise. He was martyred due to the effect of the sword strike of Ibne Muljim Muradi.[1]

The famous will of the Commander of the Faithful is mentioned in *Kafi* in detail. This will is addressed to his sons as well as to all the human beings till the Judgment Day. It is written at the end of the will that Imam Ali ؏ said: "May Allah protect you Ahlul Bayt. I entrust you all to Allah."

It is mentioned in *Kafi* that Imam Ali ؏ continued to repeat the statement "There is no god except Allah" till his holy soul departed for the heavenly abode.[2]

Blessings of Allah upon him and his progeny.[3]

---

[1] *Kafi*, Vol. 7, Pg. 52; *Mirat al-Uqool fi Sharh Kafi*, Vol. 23, Pg. 88
[2] *Kafi*, Vol. 7, Pg. 52; *Mirat al-Uqool fi Sharh Kafi*, Vol. 23, Pg. 88
[3] *Beest Guftar*, Pg. 67-71

Majlis 10

O mourners of Fatima Zahra!

An aspect of the matter of Fadak with reference to Lady Zahra is extremely strange and complex. It should be kept in mind in general that Imam Ali ﷺ and Lady Zahra was such a couple who did not have greed of accumulating wealth. Imam Ali ﷺ had said: "What interest can I have in Fadak and other property while the real house of human beings is their grave in future." Therefore, Imam Ali ﷺ did not have any interest in Fadak.[1]

What will one who has already shunned the world do with Fadak? What can the sky do for one who has jumped to one side?

A person who is free from the deception and fraud of the material world and its wealth, which is considered as achievement of life by people; when he is so wealthy, what has he got to do with Fadak?

Lady Fatima's meaningful smile

The tradition I narrate here is an accepted fact in the history of Islam and narrated by Ahlul Sunnat narrators. When the Holy Prophet ﷺ was in his last moments, his beloved daughter Lady Zahra was weeping much on his condition. The Holy Prophet ﷺ whispered something in

---

[1] *Nahjul Balagha*, Faizul Islam, Sermon 45, Pg. 958

her ears and she began to weep louder. Then the Holy Prophet ﷺ whispered something in her ears and she smiled. It was really strange! Later on she was asked what the Prophet had whispered into her ears. She said:

"At first, my father informed me that he was departing from this world. I wept louder due to the grief of separation. However, when he told me: O daughter! You will be the first to meet me after I go away, I smiled happily."[1]

Lady Zahra's Courage

We also know that Lady Zahra used to remain ill and was mostly bed-ridden after the passing away of the Holy Prophet ﷺ. She definitely knew that the lamp of her life would go off soon. In spite of this, her claim over custody of Fadak appears strange. The answer to this question arising in our minds is that the property of Fadak had no value for Lady Zahra but it was her legal right. When one's right is usurped, it is necessary to claim it back. Therefore, Lady Zahra considered it important and went to the Prophet's mosque in order to defend her right. She was surrounded by women of Bani Hashim and other devoted women as she went to the mosque.[2] She delivered a sermon in front of the ruler of the time, which shook him. She demanded her right. She criticized the claim of the opposing party and did not fear a bit. Why didn't Lady Zahra fear the ruler of time? Was this act against the teachings of Islam? Was this act improper for a woman? Is it wrong for a woman to come to the mosque like this and talk about worldly wealth in front of thousands of people?

---

[1] *Tarikh Kamil,* Vol. 3, Pg. 323; *Irshad,* Shaykh Mufid, Pg. 100; *Biharul Anwār,* Vol. 22, Pg. 470

[2] *Biharul Anwār,* Vol. 9, Pg. 216; Ibne Abil Hadīd, *Sharh Nahjul Balagha,* Vol. 16, Pg. 211

Is it wrong to defend one's right? No, absolutely not. It was not wrong to defend her right.

Lady Zahra had no attachment with worldly wealth and considered it valueless, which resulted in personal wealth and lust of an individual. She also knew that she would depart from this temporary abode soon. When a person knows that he is going to leave this world soon, naturally, his worldly desires come to an end. Considering this fact, Lady Zahra's stand was to defend the right in all situations so that the society does not get into the habit of crushing the rights of others. That is why she stepped forward bravely and defended her right well.

She went to the house of the caliph of her time and obtained the sanction letter to restore Fadak from him. However, this sanction letter was soon taken away from her forcibly. After that, she went to the mosque accompanied by the Commander of the Faithful. An unmentionable incident occurred in the mosque and she was forced to challenge the usurpers.

Lady Zainab's Courage

You find the same conditions if you look at the character of Lady Zainab. If good character demands that a woman should be timid then Lady Zainab should also have become timid like other women. According to a famous phrase, she should not have come out of her 'feminine cover'.

What forced Lady Zainab to come to the gate of Kufa and deliver a sermon? Can anybody be forced to give a sermon? Then what forced Lady Zainab to express her courage and address Ibne Ziyad with such names in his court, which put her life and the life of her family members to risk? Yazid's court was even more magnificent and its greatness more noticeable because Ibne Ziyad was a governor while Yazid was a caliph. Secondly, Ibne Ziyad was in Kufa whereas Yazid was in Syria, which was in the neighborhood of Constantinople. The regime had decorated the palaces thoroughly on pretext of keeping up the apparent glory of Islam. It is mentioned in books of history that 'the green palace' was so huge that after entering from a gate, one had to pass through a number of courtyards, doors and groups of servants in order to reach the next gate. Its decorated court had royal thrones, dining tables and beautiful chairs for the rich. It was a magnificent court but the lion-hearted daughter of Ali ﷺ did not care about those things and said: "O Yazid! You are too lowly and base in my view that I should talk to you."[1]

Can a cowardly woman disgrace Yazid in front of all royal courtiers? The greatest risk to Lady Zainab was losing her life at the hands of that unjust king but she did not fear for her life at all. There was no risk to her honor. In fact, her honor increased because of her bravery.

Therefore this difference is related to a special condition which a woman has. Then the important thing is that this difference is related to character and not to morals or personality.

There is no difference between a man and a woman as regards ethical personality. We all know that even if a man faces such a situation where he is responsible for protecting the trust of society it is no occasion of forgiving and displaying bravery and neither is there scope to show helplessness and weakness. He has to remain trustworthy

---

[1] *Luhūf,* Sayyid bin Tawoos, Pg. 181

and act cautiously. He must show courage so that the usurper is not allowed to usurp.[1]

And there is no power and strength except by Allah the High and the Mighty

---

[1] *Talim wa Tarbiyat dar Islam,* Pg. 178-181

Majlis 11

Lady Zahra grieves for her father

O mourners of Fatima Zahra!

These days are related to the demise of Lady Zahra and are associated with her holy being. Hence I would say a few words about her sufferings and conclude the speech. It is narrated that after her father passed away, Lady Zahra was never seen without a strip of cloth tied around her forehead. She was becoming thinner as the days passed. She used to weep all the time for the remorseful demise of her father.[1]

The phrase 'pillars were destroyed' has a strange implication. Pillars mean support; like the pillars of a building, on which the structure stands. In human anatomy, legs and backbone joints are pillars of human body, using which one stands. Sometimes, from the bodily aspect a pillar is damaged. For instance, legs of a human being are amputated or the joints of his backbone become impaired. In that case, the person cannot stand. Similarly, human soul falls prey to destruction in such a way that it seems that the pillars supporting the human soul are shattered. The state of Lady Zahra after her father's demise was said to be like this.

O mourners!

---

[1] *Biharul Anwār,* Vol. 43, Pg. 181; *Baitul Ahzan,* Pg. 238

Lady Zahra and the Holy Prophet ﷺ loved each other very much. That is why you must have heard that Lady Zahra used to embrace her sons, Imam Hasan and Husain ؑ very much and cry:

"My dearest ones! O light of my eyes! Where has your affectionate and kind father gone who loved you most of all? He used to go about carrying you on his shoulders and placing you in his lap passed his hand on your heads lovingly.[1]

In the name of Allah and by Allah and on the religion of the Messenger of Allah.

---

[1] *Biharul Anwār,* Vol. 43, Pg. 181; *Baitul Ahzan,* Pg. 238; *Seeri dar Seerah-e-Nabawi,* Pg. 59-60

Majlis 12

Days of Fatima

These days are associated with Lady Fatima (s.a.). Try to think why there is so much reward of narrating the pure life-histories and virtues of Ahlul Bayt of the Holy Prophet ﷺ?[1] It is so much rewarding because they were created in a human form, which is the highest example for humanity. They were role models. They are made as 'perfect example' by God, the creator of human beings.

The Holy Prophet ﷺ said: "I am taught morals from God and Ali ؑ has been taught morals by me."[2] Ali ؑ is an ideal man who is perfect. He is the best person as regards speech, movement and character. Lady Zahra was also an ideal for human beings.

Lady Zahra's Will

Now Lady Zahra felt that she was going to depart. According to a narration, she wrote a will in solitude and kept it under her pillow. It is worth noting how an ideal wife's behavior with her husband should be. When Imam Ali ؑ came near the bed of Lady Zahra, she expressed her desire to make a will. Imam Ali ؑ sat near her and took her head in his lap. Lady Sayyada said: "O Abal Hasan! I

---

[1] The wordings after this statement are absent from the cassette.
[2] *Biharul Anwār,* Vol. 16, Pg. 231; *Mizanul Hikma,* Vol. 1, Pg. 78

want to make a few wills." Imam Ali ﷺ said: "I would listen and obey. You can say what you want."

Lady Zahra humbly started with an introduction, hearing which Imam Ali ﷺ was moved. She said: "O Ali! Whatever duration I lived in your house I lived like your slave-girl. I spent time in your house most trustfully. I was in such a state in your house..." Hearing these words, Imam Ali's ﷺ eyes were filled with tears. He pressed her head against his chest as if trying to convey: "I never want you to apologize like this" because Lady Zahra's statements implied that she was apologizing for any discrepancy in her services. Whereas Imam Ali's ﷺ act only meant: "O Zahra! I don't want you to speak like this because I am pained by it."[1]

Fatima's Etiquette with Ali ﷺ

I leave this matter here and present another scenario to you. As you know Lady Zahra was furious at the people who inflicted atrocities on her. When they came to know that her malady has become serious, they sent a message to her seeking permission to visit her. Actually, they wanted to apologize and ask her to forget what they had done in the past on the pretext of visiting her during her illness. Lady Zahra did not permit them to visit her and said: "I am not pleased with those people who hurt me and usurped the right of my husband. I don't want them to enter my house and step on the floor of my house."

Eventually, they came to Imam Ali ﷺ and said: "O Abal Hasan! We have requested the daughter of the Prophet to permit us to visit her during her illness but she did not allow us. So, we have come to you to seek your

---

[1] *Biharul Anwār*, Vol. 43, Pg. 191; *Baitul Ahzan*, Pg. 253

permission." Now note the respect that Imam Ali 🕮 accorded to Lady Zahra. He did not come to her and told her flatly: "Would you give me whatever I ask for?" or "So and so situation demands..." The Imam said: "Zahra (or daughter of Prophet)! The two have sought my mediation." That is, the decision is yours, whether you permit them or not. However, note what Lady Sayyada replied. She said: "O Ali! This is your house. I am your wife and would not object to your decision."[1]

Imam Ali's 🕮 restlessness on being separated from Lady Zahra

This couple had souls tied together in the same way as the saying goes: "Birds of feather flock together". There was a wonderful unity between the two. Therefore, did Imam Ali 🕮 not have the right to wish for his death after the passing away of Lady Zahra who was so great that neither she had a replacement nor a successor?

Imam Ali 🕮 himself says:

"We were spending the days of our youth happily like a couple of pigeons. However, time separated us from each

---

[1] *Biharul Anwār,* Vol. 28, Pg. 303

Imam Ali told Lady Fatima that so and so persons were standing at the door and wanted to salute her and asked if they were permitted inside. Lady Fatima replied, "This is your house and I am your wife. It is up to you to do whatever you wish."

The tradition of *Biharul Anwār,* Vol. 43, Pg. 246 and *Baitul Ahzan,* Pg. 246 is as follows:

"This is your house and women must obey their husbands. I would not object to any of your decisions. You may permit whoever you want."

another. Surely, time separates the friends from one another."[1]

What should a person do who is shattered by the loss of a helper who is unique? When he used to visit the holy grave of Lady Zahra, he used to salute her and then narrate his feelings to her. He used to speak to her about a thing and then give the reply himself.

Imam Ali ﷺ used to tell himself:

"Why do I stand at the grave of my beloved saluting her when I don't get a reply to the salutation from the beloved's grave? What kind of beloved you are! You do not reply to my salutations. Did you forget our friendship after passing away from this world? Did you forget Ali?"[2]

Then he used to himself say:

"My beloved said: O Ali! How do I reply you? Don't you know that your Zahra is sleeping under the cover of dust?"[3]

---

[1] *Diwan Imam Ali,* Pg. 86
[2] *Diwan Imam Ali,* Pg. 89
[3] *Ashnai ba Quran,* Vol. 7, Pg. 56-58

Majlis 13

Ali embraced Batool

O devotees of Ali and Batool!

The series of our Majalis is ending today. Tonight is a special night. Therefore it is necessary to relate the calamities of Lady Fatima Zahra on the occasion of the days of Fatima.

It was unbearable for Imam Ali ﷺ to get separated from Lady Zahra. The condition was Lady Zahra had become very weak. She was lying on her bed and Imam Ali ﷺ was sitting beside her. Lady Zahra started the discussion expressing humility, which moved Imam Ali ﷺ. His eyes became filled with tears. Lady Zahra's words can be summarized as follows:

O Ali! Our companionship in this world is coming to an end. I am departing from this world. I tried to be obedient in your house as much as possible and did not oppose you in any matter...and other such words. These words moved Ali so much that he immediately embraced her. Lady Zahra's head was pressed against Imam Ali's ﷺ chest and he said with his eyes filled with tears:

"O daughter of Prophet (s.a.)! You are far better than these words; then why do you express so much helplessness?"[1]

The boundless love between Ali and Zahra cannot be explained. Therefore we can understand how difficult it would have been for Ali to bear the loneliness after the demise of Lady Zahra. Regarding this, I would like to narrate only the statement of Imam Ali ﷺ that he spoke on her holy grave. This statement is also mentioned in *Nahjul Balagha*.

Why was Lady Fatima buried in the darkness of the night?

Lady Zahra had willed: "O Ali! Bury me in the darkness of night after giving the funeral bath and shroud. I don't want those who hurt me to attend my funeral." History is always prone to be distorted. Some people commit a crime and try to prove their innocence so that they can distort history. Mamoon Rashid did same. He martyred Imam Ali Reḍa ﷺ, but during the Imam's funeral he picked up a handful of earth and poured it on his head. Then he wept crocodile tears and recited an elegy.[2] In this way, history became distorted and many people could not believe that Mamoon the Abbaside had martyred Imam Reḍa ﷺ. This is called distortion of history.

Lady Zahra wanted to save history from distortion. So she said: "Please bury me in the darkness of night" so that the question should remain in history forever as to why

---

[1] *Biharul Anwār,* Vol. 43, Pg. 191; *Baitul Ahzan,* Pg. 253
[2] *Muntahal Amaal,* Vol. 2, Pg. 491
(Such examples are found in large numbers in modern day politics) – Rizwani

the only daughter of the Prophet (s.a.) was buried in a dark night? Why is her grave unknown? This was the policy of Lady Zahra, because of which even after more than a thousand years there exists an unanswered question in history:

"Why was the beloved daughter of the Prophet (s.a.) buried in the dark night? Why is her grave unknown?"[1]

History is asking: Why was the daughter of the Prophet (s.a.) buried on a dark night? Isn't attending a funeral a recommended act? Then why did only a handful of people attend the funeral prayer of the only daughter of the Prophet (s.a.)? Why the location of the grave of Lady Zahra was kept secret? Why were people unaware of the place she was buried?

"O Ali, after burial, stay with me for a while."

After Imam Ali ؏ had buried Lady Zahra according to her will, suddenly he heard her voice from her grave: "O Ali! Please sit near my grave for some time and do not go away because I need you the most in these moments of fear of the grave."

Imam Ali ؏ had acted exactly as Lady Zahra had willed. Just think what the Imam must be going through at that time. I cannot describe his state in words how he must have lowered Lady Zahra in grave with his own hands and the way he put soil over the grave. I only know that it is written in history: "When he spread the soil of the grave with his hands, his grief swelled up."[2] Imam Ali ؏ began

---

[1] *Baitul Ahzan,* Pg. 266
[2] *Muntahal Amaal,* Vol. 1, Pg. 273; *Baitul Ahzan,* Pg. 264

dusting his clothes after making her grave. Till then, he was busy with work and when someone is busy with work, he concentrates fully on the work. Hence the grief is limited to some extent. However, now the time had come when Imam Ali ؏ was supposed to sit near the grave of Lady Zahra after burying her as per her will and he felt he needed someone whom he could narrate his feelings to.

Ali expresses his feelings

As you know, Imam Ali ؏ used to feel lonely some times. When he was unable to express his feelings to anyone, he used to lean inside a well and narrate his feelings. However, today his heart was completely shattered due to the separation of Lady Zahra. The Imam found no one better than the beloved Prophet of Allah to expressing his feelings to. Eventually, Ali turned towards the grave of the Holy Prophet ﷺ with a heavy heart and said:

"Salutations to you, O Messenger of Allah from me and from your beloved daughter who is sleeping on the dust before you and is going to meet you very soon. O Messenger of Allah! Your beloved daughter has reduced the level of my patience.[1]

O Messenger of Allah! If you want to know the condition of Ali; listen. Ali's patience has decreased." That is why Ali ؏ said:

---

[1] *Nahjul Balagha*, Faizul Islam, Sermon 193, Pg. 642; *Sharh Nahjul Balagha,* Ibne Abil Hadīd, Vol. 10, Pg. 265

"Soon your daughter will let you know how the Ummah united in order to inflict atrocities on her."[1][2]

وَسَيَعْلَمُ الَّذِينَ ظَلَمُوا أَيَّ مُنقَلَبٍ يَنقَلِبُونَ

And they who act unjustly shall know to what final place of turning they shall turn back.[3]

---

[1] *Nahjul Balagha*, Faizul Islam, Sermon 193; *Sharh Nahjul Balagha*, Ibne Abil Hadīd, Vol. 1, Pg. 265
[2] *Falsafa Akhlaq,* Pg. 248, 250
[3] Surah Shuara 26:227

Majlis 14

Simple lifestyle of the Holy Prophet ﷺ

One of the basic principles of the Prophet's life was simplicity. It is narrated that he followed this principle till the last moments of his life.[1]

It is mentioned in a tradition that one day Umar bin Khattab entered the Prophet's house to see that the Prophet had turned his face away from his wives and was saying: "You are free to take divorce or in order to lead a simple life or you make patience your motto." It was so because some wives of the Prophet had told him: "We cannot lead such a simple life. We also want ornaments and jewels like others; so please give us something from the war booty."

His Eminence was telling them: "I lead a very simple life. Thus, if you want I am ready to divorce you and also prepared to pay you some monies as ordered by the holy Quran. It is all right if you want to live a simple life, otherwise I am ready to divorce you."[2] Upon this, all the wives of the Prophet replied in unison: "O Messenger of

---

[1] *Irshadul Quloob,* Ch. 32, Pg. 155

[2] *O Prophet! Say to your wives: If you desire this world's life and its adornment, then come, I will give you a provision and allow you to depart a goodly departing; and if you desire Allah and His Apostle and the latter abode, then surely Allah has prepared for the doers of good among you a mighty reward.* (Surah Ahzab 33:28-29)

Allah! We are ready to lead a simple life." This incident has been narrated in great detail.[1] Books of Ahlul Sunnat also contain this tradition.

It is narrated that when Umar came to know about the problems of the wives of Prophet, he went to speak to the Prophet. He says that when he reached there, an Ethiopian was sitting outside with orders not to allow anyone to meet the Prophet. Umar told the sentry to inform the Prophet about his arrival. He went inside and then came back and said: "The Holy Prophet ﷺ did not give any reply." After that, Umar tried to seek permission twice again but he did not get it. When he went there for the third time, he was permitted to enter. He saw the Holy Prophet ﷺ resting on a mat of date-palm. When the Holy Prophet ﷺ moved, marks of mat appeared on his holy body. He was moved on seeing this and said: O Messenger of Allah! Why is it that worldly kings are surrounded by wealth and the Messenger of Allah is in such a state?"

The Holy Prophet ﷺ was annoyed at these words of Umar. He got up from his place and said:

"What are you saying? What rubbish is this? On the basis of what you have seen you are wondering why I don't have wealth? In your view it is a sort of deprivation for me and a bounty for them. By Allah, even if all these luxuries come to Muslims, even then they would not be worth boasting on."[2]

O mourners! You have seen how simple the lifestyle of the Holy Prophet ﷺ was! When he passed away from this world, what did he leave behind? Later, when Imam Ali ﷺ departed from this world, what did he leave behind?

---

[1] *Al-Mizan fi Tafseer al-Quran,* Vol. 16, Pg. 314
[2] *Sirat-e-Halabiya,* Vol. 3, Pg. 316

Simplicity of Lady Fatima

As we know the Holy Prophet ﷺ was survived by only one daughter. Generally, every father out of his fatherly love and according to our customs, tries to leave behind something for his daughter before passing away. For example, he might buy a house for her where she can live peacefully. However, history says that one day the Holy Prophet ﷺ visited his daughter's house. He saw her wearing a silver bangle and the house had a colorful curtain. In spite of the boundless love of his daughter, he went away without speaking to her. Lady Zahra understood that her father did not like even this much wealth for her. Why? Because it was the period of the folks of the *Suffa* (a platform in the Prophet's mosque where homeless folks took shelter).[1]

Lady Zahra was always present in the rows of generous people. She used to give off whatever worldly wealth she had to others. As soon as she saw that her father has gone, she took off her bangle and that colorful curtain and sent them to the Holy Prophet ﷺ along with a message: "O Messenger of Allah! This is gifted to you by your daughter and you may use them as you wish." When the Holy Prophet ﷺ heard this, his face lit up with happiness and he said: "O daughter! May your father be sacrificed for you."[2]

Wedding Night Dress

It was the wedding night of Lady Zahra. Only a single dress was purchased for her wedding night. Apart from this, she did not have any other new dress.

---

[1] That is it was a period of extreme poverty.
[2] *Biharul Anwār,* Vol. 43 Pg. 83

On her wedding night, a beggar came to her house and called out, "I am without clothes. Can anybody give me clothes?" Nobody paid heed to his call. However, when the bride sitting on her bed, Lady Zahra saw that nobody was paying heed to the beggar, she got up and going to an isolated place, changed her wedding dress putting on her old clothes. Then she gave away the wedding dress to that beggar. When guests arrived and inquired about her new dress, Lady Zahra replied that she has given it in the way of Allah.[1] Think about the greatness and importance of this act in the view of Lady Zahra? What was a new dress for her? What was apparent glitter and adoration for her?

Then why did Fatima go to claim Fadak?

If Lady Zahra went to claim Fadak in the court of caliphate it was so be in Islam it is obligatory to defend one's right. Otherwise, what worth Fadak had for her? However, if she had not demanded her right to Fadak it would have been injustice to herself. She could have sacrificed a thousand Fadaks in the way of Allah but she went to seek her right for not doing injustice to herself. That is, Lady Zahra considered Fadak important because it was her right and not because it was a material thing and a property. The only importance of Fadak as a property was that she could help the poor through its income.

Last moments of Lady Fatima

Yes, the state of Lady Zahra on her wedding night was same as I narrated just now. However, at the time of her death, she particularly wore a pure dress so that she takes her last breath in these clothes only. Asma binte Umais says: "One day (there are two traditions regarding the

---

[1] *Nuzhatul Majalis,* Vol. 3, Pg. 235

demise of Lady Zahra. According to one tradition, Lady Zahra passed away 75 days after the Prophet's demise and according to another tradition, she passed away after 90 days) I saw that the condition of Lady Zahra was quite better because she got up from her place and then sat down again. Then she got up again and went to perform the ritual bath (*Ghusl*) and then said: 'Asma! Bring such and such dress of mine.'"[1]

Asma says that she became happy seeing all this but the statement spoken by Lady Zahra later on turned all her happiness into grief. Lady Zahra said: "Asma! I am lying down facing Qibla. Don't talk to me for some time. After some time has passed, you should call out to me. If I don't reply; know that that my final moments have arrived."

Upon this, all the expectations of Asma were destroyed. Not much time passed when Asma started wailing and came out in search of Ali. She reached the mosque and called out for Imam Ali ﷺ and Imams Hasan and Husain ﷺ also arrived.[2]

---

[1] Lady Asma binte Umais was not a servant. She was the sister-in-law of Lady Zahra i.e. wife of His Eminence, Ja'far Tayyar. After his martyrdom, she was married to Abu Bakr and Muhammad bin Abi Bakr, an honest person was born to them. After Abu Bakr, Imam Ali had married her. Thus, Muhammad bin Abi Bakr was also called the son of Imam Ali (a.s.). He was brought up by Imam Ali (a.s.). Hence he loved Imam Ali (a.s.) very much and had nothing to do with his father. The purpose of narrating this is to make it clear that Asma binte Umais was a woman of high status. When she was married to Abu Bakr, she had faith in the caliphate of Imam Ali only. She was among the supporters of Ali (a.s.) and loved the family of the Imam very much and had faith in them. She did not like the family of Abu Bakr at all. (Ustad Mutahhari)

[2] *Muntahal Amaal,* Vol. 2, Pg. 270; *Biharul Anwār,* Vol. 43, Pg. 186

Majlis 15

A Glimpse of Imam Hasan's Character

Since today is the day of Imam Hasan's martyrdom, I would say something about his character. It is narrated that twice[1] during his lifetime, Imam Hasan 🕊 divided his entire wealth into two parts. He kept one with himself and distributed the other among poor and spent it in other charitable ways.[2]

Imam Hasan 🕊 went from Medina to Mecca for Hajj a number of times on foot. Even if he had a mount, he did not use it. He used to consider it a penance and a worship act for himself to go on foot. The rank of the Imam is so great that there is no need to mention these virtues. However, there is no doubt that the reward of performing Hajj with all facilities is not as great as performing Hajj on foot even for a common man.

Atrocities on Imam Hasan 🕊

Imam Hasan Mujtaba 🕊 used to worship a lot but his enemies accused him excessively be they Bani Umayyah and Bani Abbas who were worse. During the tyrannical rule of Bani Abbas, Sayyids of Imam Hasan 🕊 launched a

---

[1] It is mentioned in History that Imam Hasan Mujtaba (a.s.) performed Hajj twenty times on foot.
He gave away all his wealth in charity twice and gave away half of his wealth in charity thrice. *Biharul Anwār,* Vol. 43, Pg. 339 and 349
[2] *Biharul Anwār,* Vol. 43, Pg. 331, 358

number of movements against Bani Abbas. Eventually, the Bani Abbas rulers and other ministers started a propaganda in order to crush the Sayyids of Imam Hasan's family by falsely accusing their holy ancestor (Imam Hasan). They alleged that he had married a number of times and was extravagant. Similarly, he was falsely accused by Bani Abbas of being responsible for other such mischief. However, Imam Hasan 🕮 was the greatest worshipper of his time.

Whenever Imam Hasan Mujtaba 🕮 prayed, tears flowed from his eyes. When he recited the holy Quran and came across a verse describing divine chastisement, he used to fall down unconscious.[1] Indeed, he was a true copy of the character of his father, Imam Ali 🕮 al-Murtada.

O mourners of Imam Hasan 🕮!

Whatever you have heard about the Commander of the Faithful, the same is true for Imam Hasan 🕮 as well, without any exaggeration.

Muawiyah's Atrocities and Crimes

The tale of atrocities inflicted on Imam Hasan 🕮 during his lifetime and the propaganda against him after his martyrdom is a lengthy and a remorseful one.

Imam Hasan 🕮 remained in this world for about ten years after the passing away of his honorable father. The Commander of the Faithful was martyred in the year 40 A.H. and Imam Hasan 🕮 was martyred in 49 A.H. These nine or ten years were the darkest days of the inauspicious rule of Muawiyah. Imam Hasan 🕮 was greatly oppressed

---

[1] *Muntahal Amaal,* Vol. 1, Pg. 422; *Biharul Anwār,* Vol. 43, Pg. 331

during this time. Muawiyah did not waste even a single minute without spreading false propaganda to demean Imam Hasan ﷺ.

During the initial period of the caliphate of Bani Umayyah, the true colors of Muawiyah and Bani Umayyah were not fully apparent to the public. However, the veil was taken off the face of Bani Umayyah during the last days of Muawiyah and start of Yazid's rule and their real color became known to all. In the beginning, people thought that Muawiyah was a 'sensible person'.

Muawiyah wanted his son to succeed him in caliphate. Therefore he started removing all the barriers one by one in his own lifetime. This matter was not limited to Imam Hasan ﷺ. According to Muawiyah, there were some other people also who could have contested for caliphate. They could have been elected as caliph. Hence he continued to remove them from the way. Saad bin Abi Waqqas, the father of Umar bin Saad was poisoned and killed by Muawiyah because Saad was one of those six persons whom Umar had selected for the Shura committee. Therefore, it was natural to have been famous among people that Saad is eligible for caliphate.[1]

Similarly, Abdur Rahman, son of Khalid bin Walid was also killed by Muawiyah through poisoning because his father was a famous chief and could have proclaimed his leadership. Muawiyah had also removed some people of Bani Umayyah from his way whom he feared as being desirous of caliphate.

---

[1] *Mojam Rijalul Hadith,* Vol. 8, Pg. 53; *Tanqihul Maqal,* Vol. 2, Pg. 12

Order to Curse Ali ﷺ in Imam Hasan's presence

These people were eliminated so that they cannot become candidates for caliphate. However, his intentions were different in the case of Imam Hasan ﷺ. He wanted that the love and faith of Imam Hasan ﷺ should be removed from the hearts of people. Even though he knew that people have faith on Ahlul Bayt, he wanted to torture Imam Hasan ﷺ mentally while he was alive. Therefore, he wrote to the governor of Medina and asked him to curse his father, Imam Ali ﷺ in his presence, every Friday in the Prophet's mosque.[1]

We recite the verse in Friday prayer that when it is the time of Friday prayer, it is obligatory for all to join it. (Thus, Muawiyah and his followers used to force people to attend the Prayer by quoting the compulsory order of this verse). Anyone who opposed the Friday prayer on the pretext that those people were not worthy of leading Friday prayer, was accused of being an infidel. Whenever the group of extremists found such a person, they used to kill him. Hence, Imam Hasan ﷺ was forced to attend the Prayer in such a state. I have already discussed the obligation of the Imam of the congregation standing on the pulpit near the grave of the Holy Prophet ﷺ in the sermon of Friday prayer in my lecture on 'sermon and pulpit'.[2] This obligation was changed with curses on Imam Ali ﷺ.[3] At last Muawiyah decided to eliminate the son of the Holy Prophet ﷺ, Imam Hasan ﷺ and because of this decision, he poisoned the Imam. Imam was not

---

[1] *Sharh Nahjul Balagha,* Ibne Abil Hadīd, Vol. 4, Pg. 56
[2] Both speeches are present in Ustad Mutahhari's *Sukhan* published by Jame Taalimaat-e-Islami
[3] *Muntahal Amaal,* Vol. 1, Pg. 450; *Al-Ghadeer,* Vol. 10, Pg. 257

administered poison only once but it was done twice or thrice.[1]

وَسَيَعْلَمُ الَّذِينَ ظَلَمُوا أَيَّ مُنقَلَبٍ يَنقَلِبُونَ

And they who act unjustly shall know to what final place of turning they shall turn back.[2]

---

[1] After this, the some part of the lecture was not recorded; *Ashnai ba Quran,* Vol. 7, Pg. 118, 120

[2] Surah Shuara 26:227

Majlis 16

Dream of Martyr Mutahhari at the advent of Muharram

O mourners of the oppressed one of Karbala!

These days, all of us are preparing to welcome Muharram. Husainiyyahs are being decorated to commemorate the sorrow of the apple of Fatima's eyes. It is a strange coincidence, in 1962, when Aqa Burujardi expired, I saw him in my dream (Aqa Burujardi expired in the month of Shawwal) but the state of that dream was such that even I could not interpret it.

"Do not leave the pulpit."

In those days, Haji Ahmad Qummi was famous for giving strange interpretations of dreams. At times, even Ayatullah Burujardi went to him for interpretation of his dreams. Thus, I asked him the interpretation of my dream on phone. It is true that even I couldn't understand what was so special in that dream, which led me to seek interpretation from the respected Qummi on phone. (In those days, I had stopped preaching from the pulpit. He told me not to leave the pulpit at all. I don't know from where he extracted this interpretation. He told me not to leave the service of Imam Husain 鑑. I did as I was told and tried to put into practice as advised in the interpretation.

Service of the Chief of the Martyrs

As usual, I slept for some time after the Morning Prayer yesterday. I dreamt a huge gathering of Majlis, which was attended by scholars who were all waiting for the arrival of Aqa Burujardi. After sometime, he arrived. The entire gathering of people got up to welcome him as it used to happen during his lifetime. As I tried to get up suddenly my cloak got entangled in my hand and foot. I moved myself aside, adjusted my clothes and got up. At that very moment, Aqa reached the place where I was sitting. I immediately vacated that place as if I knew that he wanted to occupy it. Then I saw that he went and sat on the chair and it appeared as if he did not want to lecture and instead he would be reciting a Majlis. As soon as he sat on the pulpit, he said:

"We Majlis reciters (*Dhakireen*)!" I was extremely astonished in my dream after hearing this term. I thought: Why did Aqa Burujardi call himself a Majlis reciter? (Although I know that he used to sometimes recite Majlis in the city of Burujard during Ramadan when he was a main jurist. However, he was a chief jurist and not a speaker).

Then I saw a white shawl on his head and I was even more surprised because scenes usually change in dream. I saw him sitting on pulpit in another city but with respect as a jurist. Then I saw him in a garden full of greenery. Suddenly I saw him sitting near flowing water as if he wanted to perform ablution. I remembered in my dream that I had been his student in the past. Hence, I moved forward to kiss his hands. When I reached the place, I saw half his face immersed in the clean and pure water and half outside. He had closed his eyes like a Gnostic in meditation. Suddenly, he started wailing with the heart beats. He shouted the name of the chief of martyrs and said: O Husain! O Husain bin Ali! O son of Zahra. He used to shout his name and then wail. He used to narrate the calamities of Imam himself and then cry. And what a type of wailing! This wailing was not such that its effects would have become explicit from his tears. Instead he was wailing without caring about the world around him. He was immersed in the grief of Imam Husain ؏ so much that he was unaware of the world. After that, I awoke from sleep. I remembered that I had seen a dream two or three days before the month of Muharram a few years back. This time also, I saw a dream before the advent of Muharram.[1]

There is no power and might except by Allah the High and the Mighty.

---

[1] After this, some part of the lecture was not recorded; *Ashnai ba Quran,* Vol. 6, Pg. 259-261

Majlis 17

The tragedy of Ashura has so much emotion of sadness and a state of faithfulness that if we have even an iota of faith in our hearts our eyes would be flooded with tears on hearing the name of the oppressed Husain. "Certainly, the love of Imam Husain ﷺ is hidden in the hearts of believers."[1] (Perhaps that is why Imam Husain ﷺ said: "I am a martyr who shall be mourned."[2]

Imam Sadiq mourns for Husain ﷺ

During the days of my study in the holy city of Mashad, I had memorized a remorseful five-line poem of a companion of Imam Ja'far Sadiq from Shaykh Abbas Qummi's *Nafthat al-Masdur*.

Muhaddith Qummi writes that Abu Harūn Makfuf who was almost blind and hence given the title of 'Makfuf' was an extempore poet and he recited elegies of Imam Husain ﷺ. He used to say: "One day, I came to Imam Ja'far Sadiq. He asked me to recite the latest elegy I had composed about his great grandfather. I said: As you wish. Imam Ja'far Sadiq asked the ladies of his house to gather behind a curtain so that they may also listen to the elegy. Eventually, all women gathered behind the curtain."

---

[1] *Khasais al-Husainia,* Pg. 48
[2] *Mausuat-e-Kalimat al-Imam al-Husain,* Pg. 649; *Biharul Anwār,* Vol. 44, Pg. 279

Makfuf started reciting the elegy. You may also try to understand the meaning of those verses and take lesson from them.

Even though it comprised of only five verses, everyone in the house of Imam Ja'far Sadiq ﷺ was wailing aloud. The Imam was himself crying in such a way that pearls of tears were falling from his eyes and his shoulders were shaking. The sounds of weeping and wailing became so loud in his holy house that finally the Imam said that it was enough.

I could not find an elegy equivalent to this one. Abu Harūn Makfuf had said:

O current of the morning breeze!

When you pass by Karbala, convey the message and salutation of us, the lovers, and tell the sanctified bones of his pure body that they would be continuously watered by the tears of the mourners of Husain. They would continue to shed tears in order to quench your thirst. One day, you were denied water and Master Husain was martyred thirsty. However, now his Shias will always sacrifice tears on him.

O morning breeze!

When you pass by the grave of Husain, do not say only this much. Do wait there for sometime and cry much upon his sufferings. Your weeping should not be like an ordinary person. Cry like a mother whose only son has died. Yes, cry like a distressed mother separated from her only son for Imam Husain ﷺ

who was pure and his mother and father were also pure.[1]

In the name of Allah and by Allah and on the religion of the Messenger of Allah ﷺ

---

[1] *Nafthatul Masdur,* Pg. 254; *Aghani,* Vol. 7, 260; *Muntahal Amaal,* Vol. 1, Pg. 541; *Seeri dar Seerah-e-Nabawi,* Pg. 172-175

Majlis 18

Speech of Imam Husain ﷺ after he prepares to set out for Karbala

Imam Husain ﷺ was a like his holy father in all aspects. In oratory also it was the same though he did not get as much opportunity as Imam Ali ﷺ during his apparent caliphate. The little opportunity he got was on his way from Mecca to Karbala. Then the jewels of his oratory became manifest during the last eight days in Karbala. Most sermons of Imam Husain ﷺ present today were delivered during this period. The style of Imam Husain ﷺ resembled his father's and a sea of essence and wisdom is seen surging in them.

Imam Ali ﷺ had said that the tongue is the medium of the expression of the soul. If gems of wisdom do not emerge from the tongue, what is the use of it? And if wisdom is present in the soul, the tongue cannot stop its emergence. Imam ﷺ said: "We Ahlul Bayt are masters of oratory. We are sovereigns of the country of oratory. The roots of elocution are buried in our existence and its branches provide shade only to us."[1]

The first sermon of Imam Husain ﷺ while departing for Karbala from Mecca is full of magnificence and eloquence. It comprises of guidance, bravery, high-mindedness and faith in the unseen. After announcing his

---

[1] *Nahjul Balagha*, Faizul Islam, Sermon 224, Pg. 72; *Nahjul Balagha,* Subhi Salih, Sermon 233

decision of traveling to Karbala Imam ﷺ informed the people that whoever supported his ideas could join him. Imam ﷺ said:

"Death has left a mark on the progeny of Adam like a mark is left on the neck a young woman because of her necklace. Death in the way of rightfulness is a matter of pride. I am eager to meet my ancestors as Yaqoob was eager to meet Yusuf." Further on, the Imam ﷺ said:

"Whoever wants to meet Allah after getting martyred in our way should prepare to accompany us. God willing, we will depart from here tomorrow morning."[1]

The Imam says: "O people! Whoever among you desires to sacrifice a small thing in the right way should think what to sacrifice. Come, let me show you that to end the fear hidden inside you, you must buy an arrow so that you can depart to meet your Lord. God willing, I will also depart tomorrow morning with the same intention. If Allah wills."

---

[1] *Luhūf,* Pg. 60; *Biharul Anwār,* Vol. 44, Pg. 366; *Mausuat-e-Kalimat al-Imam al-Husain,* Pg. 328

Majlis 19

Martyrdom of Muslim bin Aqeel

The pilgrims had entered Mecca on the 8th of Zilhajj with full enthusiasm and eagerness. On the very day the pilgrims were supposed to depart for Mina and Arafat, Imam Husain ؏ was leaving Mecca. At that time, he delivered a famous sermon, which is narrated by Sayyid bin Tawoos. Then the Imam passed each stage of the journey till he reached near the Iraq border. What were the conditions in Kufa? What was going on there? Only God knows better.

On the way Imam Husain ؏ saw a person who was coming from Kufa and was heading in the direction of the Imam. (In Arabia there were no one-way roads, so that people going to and fro may pass each other close by. It was a desert and a person coming from the opposite direction used to cross the person going that way at a long distance). Eventually, the Imam waited for a while. He wanted to signal to the person coming from the opposite direction to stop so that he can speak to him. It is narrated that the person also knew Imam Husain ؏ and had bad news with him. He thought that if he met Imam Husain ؏ the latter would surely ask him about Kufa and he will have to relate the bad news to him. The person did not want to give the bad news to the Imam, so he changed his route and went in another direction.

On the other hand two persons from Bani Asad tribe who were present in Mecca for Hajj; intended to assist the

Imam. Hence, they completed the Hajj rituals and set out at great speed in order to catch up with the Imam. When they were a station behind the Imam, they met the person coming from Kufa. They exchanged greetings with him and as was the custom of Arabs, asked to which tribe he belonged. He replied that he was from Bani Asad. They were surprised and said that they too were from Bani Asad. They enquired about his father and grandfather and the person replied their questions till all of them recognized each other. After that, both of them asked that person about the news of Kufa. He replied that there was very sad news about Kufa. He said, "Imam Husain ﷺ was going to Karbala from Mecca and he saw me and stopped. I knew that the Imam would enquire me about Kufa and I did not want to give him this unfortunate news. Therefore I changed my route." Then he told them everything in detail.

These two men sped on and caught up with the Imam at the next station but did not talk to him about anything. They waited for the Imam to halt at the next stop. After passing by the man from Kufa, the Imam's caravan had traveled for a day and a night before reaching that station. Imam ﷺ was in his tent along with some of his companions. These two men came to the Imam and said respectfully:

"O Aba Abdillah! We have news for you. Do you want us to tell you before everybody or in private?"

The Imam replied: "I don't hide anything from my companions. Say whatever you want in front of everybody." Hearing this, they said:

"O son of Allah's Messenger! We met the person for whom you had halted yesterday and he did not meet you.

He is a reliable person. We know him. He is from our tribe only. When we enquired about Kufa, he said that when he left Kufa, Muslim bin Aqeel and Hani bin Urwah were martyred. Their bodies were tied with ropes and dragged through the streets of Kufa."

When Imam Husain 🕮 got the grievous news of Muslim bin Aqeel's martyrdom, tears began to flow from his eyes but he recited the following verse immediately:

"Of the believers are men who are true to the covenant which they made with Allah: so of them is he who accomplished his vow, and of them is he who yet waits, and they have not changed in the least." (Surah Ahzab 33:23)

On this occasion Imam Husain 🕮 did not say that Muslim bin Aqeel and Hani bin Urwah are martyred and Kufa is captured by enemies. We have lost the battle and therefore it is better that we return from here. Instead Imam said something, which pointed to a different aim. The above mentioned verse is apparently related to the battle of Ahzab, in which some believers had kept the promise they made to Allah and laid their lives in the right path while others were waiting for their turn to sacrifice their lives. Imam Husain 🕮 recited this verse and said, "Muslim has fulfilled his obligation and now its our turn".[1]

---

[1] Whatever is narrated about Imam Husain (a.s.) in history is the meaning of verse 23 of Surah Ahzab and not the actual verse. It is recorded that even when Imam Husain (a.s.) was informed about the martyrdom of Muslim he repeated *'innaa lillaahi...'* a few times. Some narrators have recorded that the Imam said: "May Allah grant salvation to Muslim who went towards divine neighborhood, Paradise and Rizwan. He fulfilled his duty while we are yet to do so."
Biharul Anwār, Vol. 44 Pg. 374; *Mausuat-e-Kalimat al-Imam al-Husain,* Pg. 349

Now we must fulfill our obligation. At this, every companion expressed his opinion, which displayed their inner emotions. Some people who met Imam ﷺ on the way did not have the level of recognition as desired by Imam Husain ﷺ. Thus the Imam was upset and he separated them from himself. When they realized that they would not get everything on a platter after reaching Kufa, they left the Imam, as happens in most battles. Only his Ahlul Bayt and special companions were left with him and they were very few (When those who had left the Imam woke up from their sleep of ignorance, one by one, they left Umar Ibne Saad's army and joined Imam Husain).

At the time Imam Husain ﷺ received the news of Muslim's martyrdom, his companions did not even number twenty. You can estimate what Imam Husain ﷺ and his loyal companions would have felt at the news of the martyrdom of Muslim bin Aqeel and Hani bin Urwah. The author of *Lisanul Ghaib* says that some historians have written that since Imam Husain ﷺ did not hide anything from his companions, hence, after receiving the news of Muslim's martyrdom, it became necessary for him to visit the harem and inform ladies also of this news in spite of the presence of his cousin sister and other relatives in addition to his younger siblings. God knows how the oppressed Imam must have conveyed this terrible news to them!

It is also narrated that Imam Husain recited verse 23 of Surah Ahzab on getting the news of the martyrdom of Qais bin Musahhar Saidawi; *Mausuat-e-Kalimat al-Imam al-Husain*, Pg. 363

Informing Muslim's daughter about the news of Muslim's martyrdom

The holy Imam ﷺ entered the tent and taking a seat called for Muslim's little daughter. When she came, Imam seated her in his lap and passed his hand over her head lovingly. This little girl of the family of prophethood was very sensible. When she saw this extraordinary behavior of the Imam, she asked fearfully, "O Aba Abdillah! O son of Allah's Messenger! Is my father dead? That you are comforting me so much...?"[1]

Imam ﷺ was extremely moved on hearing this and he said: "Daughter! I am also like your father. After your father, I will give love to you like a father." As the Imam said this, there was mayhem in the camp of Ahlul Bayt.

Aqeel's sons promise loyalty

Imam Husain ﷺ addressed the sons of Aqeel and said:

"O sons of Aqeel! You have given the sacrifice of a Muslim. This sacrifice is enough for the entire family of Aqeel. If you want you can go back."

All of them replied in unison: "O son of Allah's Messenger! We did not present Muslim for martyrdom. We accompanied you till now and now that we also have to avenge for Muslim, how can we leave you now?

---

[1] After this some words are missing from the cassette.

Absolutely not, we will accompany you so that we too meet the same fate as Muslim did."[1]

---

[1] *Irshad,* Shaykh Mufid, Pg. 222; *Muntahal Amaal,* Vol. 1, Pg. 603; *Biharul Anwār,* Vol. 44, Pg. 373; *Mausuat-e-Kalimat al-Imam al-Husain,* Pg. 344

Majlis 20

Title of the Chief of the Martyrs

O mourners of the Chief of the Martyrs!

His Eminence, Hamza was called the chief of martyrs before the event of Karbala. However, this title was conferred to Imam Husain ﷺ afterwards. It was as if the martyrdom of Imam Husain ﷺ eclipsed the martyrdom of His Eminence, Hamza. The loyal companions of Imam Husain ﷺ were also somewhat like this because they acquired precedence over all the martyrs of the past. Imam Husain ﷺ himself said: "Certainly, I have not seen companions more loyal and better than mine." Also, "I do not know people better than my Ahlul Bayt."[1]

Imam Husain ﷺ was free from the side of his friends as well as from his enemies.

The Imam himself said: "Look (O my loyal companions)! They do not have anything against anyone except me. I willingly permit you to go if you like."

After that he said: "Go away, taking advantage of the darkness of night." Saying this, the holy Imam bowed his head so that when the companions look up, they do not have to feel ashamed looking into the eyes of the Imam. The condition of the companions of Imam Husain ﷺ was

---

[1] *Mausuat-e-Kalimat al-Imam al-Husain,* Pg. 395

not like that of the companions of Tariq who had burnt their rations (leaving behind only a day's supply) and their ships; nor their condition was like that of a person forced to stand at the doorstep by a friend. Imam Husain ﷺ bowed his head so that his eyes do not have any forceful effect on his companions.[1]

Status of Husain's Companions

Just as the companions of Imam Husain ﷺ were better than the companions of the Prophet who fought in the battle of Badr and companions of Imam Ali ﷺ who fought for him in the battle of Siffeen, in the same way the army of Umar Saad was more stone-hearted and worse than the army of Abu Sufyan at Badr and the army of Muawiyah at Siffeen because the army of Umar bin Saad was not fighting for their 'faith' like the people of Badr; nor did they have any controversial issue like the people of Siffeen had of revenging Uthman's murder. They were committing this crime in spite of repeated opposition from their conscience. Their state was like the saying goes "their hearts supported him but their swords were against him".[2] How strange it is that Umar Saad's army was weeping as well as slaying the Prophet's grandson. It was shedding tears and at the same time snatching earrings from the ears of the innocent children of Husain. It was

---

[1] Apparently, the words of Ibne Abil Hadīd: "They preferred death." are appropriate for those companions. According to Imam Ali, "The riders will come down from their mounts at this place and this place would become a battlefield of devotees." Neither the martyrs of the past nor future are better than these.; *Biharul Anwār,* Vol. 41, Pg. 295

[2] *Mausuat-e-Kalimat al-Imam al-Husain,* Pg. 370

beheading Husain ﷺ with the dagger of oppression and was trembling at the same time.[1]

In the name of Allah and by Allah and on the religion of the Messenger of Allah ﷺ

---

[1] *Hamasa-e-Husaini,* Vol. 3, Pg. 56-57

Majlis 21

Better to be tested

In the Ziarat of Imam Husain ﷺ we recite, "O Aba Abdillah! We wish we had been with you in Karbala to confront falsehood and sacrifice our lives like the loyal companions of the Imam had achieved a great success through martyrdom."[1] This sentence has become a mere recital and we don't pay any attention to its meaning. Think for a while. Is our claim true? Are we such people who can truly make such a claim? (No, absolutely not) Most of us are such that we only read the words of the Ziarat without taking them seriously.

Most Loyal Companions

Imam Husain ﷺ extolled his companions on Ashura eve saying: "I have not seen companions better and more loyal than mine."

A senior Shia scholar was once of the view that perhaps Imam Husain ﷺ did not issue this statement. According to him, the companions of Imam Husain ﷺ did not perform any extraordinary feat. Then why would the Imam say so? However, his enemies had really displayed

---

[1] The statement *"Yaa laitanee kuntu ma'akum fa-afooza fauzan a'z'eemaa"* is present in one of the Ziarats of Imam Husain.
The special Ziarat of the day of Arafah has a statement: *"Yaa laitanee kuntu ma'akum fa-afooza ma'akum fil h'inaani maa'sh shuhadaa-I was' s'aalih'eena wa h'asuna oolaa-ika rafeeqaa".*

the worst cruelty. Imam Husain ﷺ was a flower of the garden of prophethood. He was the Imam of his time and the most beloved of Ali and Batool (Fatima). Therefore, any Muslim who would see the Imam surrounded by such calamities would have surely come forward to assist him. Thus, according to that scholar, those people were worst creatures who did not help the Imam but those who helped him did not perform any extraordinary feat.

That great scholar says: Perhaps God wanted me to come out of ignorance. Therefore, I saw the battlefield of Karbala in my dream and I was present there. I was telling the Imam, "O son of the Messenger! I have come to help you." The Imam said, "Wait". I waited till it was the time for Prayer.

(I have read in the books of Karbala Tragedy that Saeed bin Abdullah Hanafi and other companions became a human-shield in front of the Imam so that he could pray. They were people having true enthusiasm. When the parts of their bodies were getting cut and falling to the ground), they were thinking:

The life I sacrificed was given by him only.

The fact is that, we have not the debt we owed.

The scholar says that the Imam told him in his dream:

"I want to offer Prayer. You stand in front of us. When the enemies shoot arrows, stop them and do not let them reach us." The scholar said: "By all means". He stood in front of the Imam while the Imam started to pray. He says: "I saw a fierce arrow coming towards the Imam. When the arrow came closer, I bent down involuntarily and the arrow hit the holy Imam. I said: I seek the forgiveness of

Allah and to Him I repent. That was too bad. I will not let that happen again. Now I will stop every arrow at my chest. Suddenly, another arrow came and I again bent down to save my life. This arrow also injured the holy Imam. Then a third and a fourth arrow came and hit Imam only because every time I was trying to save my life. Then suddenly my eyes fell on the Imam, and I saw that he was smiling and saying: "I have not seen companions better and more loyal than mine."[1]

Sitting at home and reciting "I wish I had been..." does not make one reach that rank. It requires the courage of putting it to practice.[2] When the time comes, it would be known who can put his words to practice. The companions of Imam Husain ﷺ did not merely make a promise, but they acted upon their words. They used to say:

To die below your feet,

Is our only heartfelt desire.

Courageous Nature

My discussion has automatically reached the Zuhr Prayer of Imam Husain ﷺ and the time of our Zuhr Prayer is also near. As you know most companions of the Imam were martyred before the Zuhr Prayer itself. Thus, only a

---

[1] Imam Husain said on the eve of Ashura: "I don't know any companions better and more loyal than mine and any family more virtuous and better than my Ahle Bayt." *Mausuat-e-Kalimat al-Imam al-Husain,* Pg. 395

[2] As Imam Husain entered Karbala he said, "People are slaves of this world and religion is at the tip of their tongues. They work for religion as long as their life has comforts. When time comes for test, very few religious people are left." *Tohafful Uqool,* Pg. 245

few companions and family members were alive till the Zuhr of Ashura.

The first stage of martyrdom of the companions of Husain was the shooting of arrows by the rows standing on both the sides. Imam Husain's ﷺ side had only seventy-two persons but they were very brave. They were in high spirits and the fact was that there was no match for their spirit and courage.

Imam Husain ﷺ did not want to give even the slightest imagination of defeat regarding himself. He divided his army into the left wing, right wing and central wing. Zuhair bin Qayn led the right wing, Habib bin Mazahir commanded the left and his younger brother, Abbas, headed the heart of the army. He was given the flag of the army and thus, the title *Alamdar* became a part of his holy name. Companions of the Imam asked for permission to start the battle but the Imam said:

"No, till the enemy does not begin hostilities we will not attack."

Religion and the World

In the beginning, Ibne Saad launched delayed attacks because he wanted to hold onto faith as well as the world. He wanted to get the kingdom of Rayy from Ibne Ziyad as well as avoid smearing his hands with the holy blood of Imam Husain ﷺ. Thus, he continuously wrote to Ibne Ziyad proposing a peace treaty with Imam Husain ﷺ so that the battle does not start. When Ibne Ziyad realized this, he wrote a letter and strictly ordered him to accomplish the task given to him or surrender the command of the army to one who is given this responsibility in addition to him. Ibne Saad did not want the world to slip away from his hands. Therefore, when the choice was between faith and the world, he bade farewell to religion saying: "I would fight in order to fulfill the Governor's command."

Beginning of the battle and its consequences

On Ashura day, in the desert of Karbala, Ibne Saad committed a number of immoral acts because he wanted to prove himself a loyal commander of Ibne Ziyad and disprove the reports made to Ibne Ziyad that Umar bin Saad was dilly dallying as he was a well wisher of Husain. Thus, when the two armies stood opposite each other, Ibne Saad told his shooters to be ready. They all became ready. Then he shot an arrow towards the Imam's army saying:[1]

"O people! Be witness to the Amir, Ibne Ziyad that I was the first to shoot an arrow at the army of Husain."

Whenever I reach this statement of Ibne Saad, I remember a statement of my friend and a friend of you Narmikis also,[2] late Ibrahim Ayati, who was a great scholar and reciter of Majlis and who passed away ten years ago, which I had heard from him and perhaps also read it in his book. He used to say:

"The battle of Karbala started with an arrow and ended with an arrow."

---

[1] Ibne Saad was the son of a companion of Holy Prophet, Saad bin Abi Waqqas and incidentally, he was an expert archer and was very famous in entire Arabia. Thus, Ibne Saad had helped in many battles through his skill. (Ustad Mutahhari)

[2] The people addressed are of Jame Masjid Narmik (Tehran) where Martyr Mutahhari was reciting this Majlis.

The battle started because of the arrow shot by Umar bin Saad; but do you know which arrow ended it? Arrows were shot from the left and the right and both targeted the Imam. Imam ﷺ was fighting continuously and killing the ones damned to hell. But he was exhausted due to injuries and fatigue of the battle. Suddenly, someone hit him on his forehead brutally with a stone; and blood gushed out. Imam ﷺ picked up the tail of his shirt to wipe the blood when one of two poisonous six branched arrows hit the oppressed Imam in his holy chest and the Imam's jihad ended.

Now, the tyrants noticed that Husain was not saying: "Is there anyone..."Instead he was addressing only God and saying:

In the name of Allah and by Allah and on the religion of the Messenger of Allah ﷺ

Anyhow, I was saying that the first arrow was shot by Ibne Saad. After that, arrows started raining on the companions of Imam Husain ﷺ. What valor and courage the companions of Imam Husain ﷺ had! They kneeled down and shot all the arrows present in their quivers one by one immediately and dispatched a large number of the enemies to hell.

Some soldiers of Imam Husain's small army were martyred by the arrows of the enemies. After that, one to one battle started. Whenever a person from Imam Husain's ﷺ side used to go out in the battlefield, some infidels used to confront him. However, the spirit of faith of Imam Husain ﷺ triumphed every time. Even an elderly fighter from Imam Husain's army used to send five to ten enemies to hell.

Martyrdom of Abis bin Abi Shabeeb Shakri

A companion of Imam Husain ﷺ, Abis bin Abi Shabeeb Shakri was such that his soul was full of the 'Husainite enthusiasm'. When he entered the battlefield he recited the war poem (Rajaz)[1] as was the custom, and challenged the enemy for a single combat. However, no one from the enemy's side dared to confront this lion-hearted companion of Imam Husain ﷺ.

When in spite of repeated calls no one dared to come forward to fight Abis, he became angry and returned from the field. He took off his helmet, armor and shoes and went to the battlefield barefoot and called out: "Come out to fight Abis at least now."[2]

But not dared to come forward. At last Umar Saad's army stooped to cowardice and they began to throw stones and pieces of broken swords on Abis and in this way they martyred him.

The courage and sincerity displayed by the loyal companions of Imam Husain ﷺ on the Ashura day cannot be equaled. It was not limited to men. Even the ladies had this state. They left behind those marks in the history of humanity, which will remain till the world exists. If such signs were to be found in the history of Europeans we would have seen how they would have benefited from them.[3]

---

[1] The Rajaz of Abis was "ala rajulun? ala rajulun?" i.e. "is there no man among you that can come to combat with me?"

[2] *Biharul Anwār,* Vol. 45, Pg. 28; *Maqtal-e-Husain,* Muqarram, Pg. 251

[3] It is a serious thing. The basic element of the formation of communities comes from such things only. Poets, thinkers and

political leaders who are builders of communities, make such characters heroes of community and change the entire community.

We know that political and satanic forces have remained in power from the beginning but according to the philosophy of conflicts, consciousness among people goes on becoming solid because of social conflicts. Thus, people would go on understanding revelation and Islam would encompass the world because it is in accordance with human nature. For instance, a human being naturally loves justice and hates injustice. People love freedom and hate slavery. They love freedom of gathering, freedom of thinking, freedom of practicing any religion, political freedom, economic and personal freedom. The teachings of Islam are enlightening the minds of people all over the world without taking the name of the Lord of the universe. That is why enemies of Islam are trying in vain to extinguish this lamp.

The Holy Prophet was the first to protest against racism. He held that blacks, whites and all humans are equal. The level of one's honor is dependent only on his piety and good character. The Holy Prophet had informed the people through Quran the reward of freeing slaves. Thus, he awakened that thinking of human beings, which is still under evolution.

Latin America and Europe stood against slavery more than one and half centuries ago. Martin Luther king fought for equal rights of blacks in the United States of America. Nelson Mandela struggled for independence of South Africa. All these efforts had an unnamed Islamic hand in it because Islam teaches freedom and equity. The teachings of Islam are for every age, race and generation. The Holy Prophet had said, "O people! Women have rights on you in the same way as you have rights on them." Islam advocates the rights of women and their respect. Following the practice of the Holy Prophet would guarantee "blessings" for the entire humanity.

The character of Imam Ali Murtadha is an ideal one in the vast field of history as regards unveiling hypocrites, fighting the autocracy, supporting the oppressed, considering wealth of community as trust and leading the people who support a republican government.

There is one more character in history; that of Imam Husain (a.s.) who dared to defy and refused to pay allegiance to an unjust tyrant. He taught freedom-lovers that it is better to die respectfully instead of living with disgrace. When mouths are shut because of oppression, silence spreads everywhere and people bow down in front of injustice. After the death of Stalin, the new general secretary

117

Self-sacrificing mother of Abdullah bin Umair

Abdullah bin Umair was present along with his mother and wife in Karbala. He was a very brave and strong man. When he intended to go to the battlefield, his wife asked him: "Whom are you entrusting me to? What will happen to me after you?" The couple was newly married. When the mother of Abdullah bin Umair heard their conversation, she said:

"Son! Do not heed what your bride says. Today is the day of your test. If you do not sacrifice yourself today, I would not condone suckling you." Abdullah fought a severe battle and was martyred. After that, his mother wielded a tent-pole and attacked the unscrupulous enemies. Seeing the bravery of this woman, Imam Husain ﷺ said aloud: "May Allah reward you! Go back to the ladies tent and stay there. Jihad is not obligatory on women." Hearing the order of her master, she bowed down obediently and returned to her tent.

On the other hand the enemy beheaded Abdullah and threw his severed head towards his mother saying: "Take this, keep your son with you." The mother lifted the

---

of communist party, Khuruchev was criticizing Stalin in one of the party meetings. One of the members commented, "Why were you silent in front of Stalin?" Khrushchev said, "Whoever has made this remark should stand up." However, no one stood up. Seeing this, Khrushchev laughed and said, "As none of you dares to speak in front of me, I did not dare to speak in front of Stalin." A Christian padre says that if they would have had Imam Husain in place of Prophet Isa they would have ruled this earth. Bernard Shaw has predicted, "Europe (and America) would accept Islam in future." When this happens, these glowing personalities would become the beacon in the way of guidance for Muslims.

severed head of her young son, pressed it against her chest, kissed it and said: Congratulations son, you are very brave. I am pleased with you now and I have condoned your suckling." Then she threw the severed head back in the direction of the enemy and said: "We do not take back whatever we give in the way of Allah."[1]

Praiseworthy child

A time also arrived when Imam Husain ☒ saw that only a few people remained to go to the battlefield and who were seeking permission from him. At that moment, a twelve-year old boy came out from the gathering of the companions with a sword hanging from his waist. He told Imam Husain ☒, "Maula! Please allow me to go to the battlefield."

The father of this child was martyred sometime before in the battle.

The Imam said: "You cannot go. You are too young."

The child said: "Maula! Please allow me to go."

---

[1] The incident narrated by Ustad Mutahhari is of Wahab bin Abdullah bin Habbab Kalbi. A similar tradition is narrated about Abdullah bin Umair Kalbi who lived in Kufa and had come to Karbala with his wife Umme Wahab. Late Allamah Sherani has written in the margin of *Damaus Sujum*, Pg. 147 that this incident is proved true because of its repeated narration by two persons.

Wahab bin Abdullah Kalbi was young and new-married while Abdullah bin Umair Kalbi was a companion of the Holy Prophet and was elderly. (Rizwani)

Luhūf, Pg. 105; *Biharul Anwār*, Vol. 45, Pg. 17; *Muntahal Amaal*, Vol. 1, Pg. 651; *Mausuat-e-Kalimat al-Imam al-Husain*, Pg. 435

Imam ﷺ said: "No, I fear your widowed mother will be distressed."

Hearing this, the child said: "Maula! My mother has ordered me go and sacrifice myself on you. She said that if I do not sacrifice myself on the Imam she would not be pleased with me."

This child who was seeking permission from the Imam was so well-mannered; and he got such honor, which no one else could, because every warrior introduced himself upon reaching the field according to Arabian custom, but this child did not introduce himself and it could not be recorded who that child was.[1]

Writers of Karbala Tragedy could not identify this child. They have written only that:

"And out came a young boy whose father had been killed in the attack."

Didn't that child recite this war poem?

"O people! Listen, my chief is Husain and it is enough for my introduction."

"I am one whose master is Husain; who is the best master; who is the joy of the heart of the Prophet who gave glad tidings and warned."[2]

---

[1] The name of this child is mentioned as Amr bin Junada Ansari in *Maqtal-e-Muqarram*. His father, Junada Ansari was martyred in the first attack

[2] *Biharul Anwār*, Vol. 45, Pg. 27; *Mausuat-e-Kalimat al-Imam al-Husain*, Pg. 457

Majlis 22

Caravan of sacrificing people

Imam Husain ﷺ addressed the gathering of pilgrims and visitors of Kaaba before departing from Mecca and said: "Only those among you who wishes to sacrifice his life for me and meet his Lord should accompany me. God willing, I shall depart tomorrow morning."[1] As if the holy Imam was informing the people that those who loved wealth and power and those who considered their lives important should not accompany him because their caravan was that of the sacrificing people only.

The close relatives of Imam Husain ﷺ were also present among those sacrificing people. If the Imam had left them behind in Medina would anyone have objected to it? Absolutely not. However, consider if Imam Husain ﷺ had not taken his relatives along and got martyred alone, would his martyrdom earned the status it has now got? Would the incident of Karbala got that importance, which it has now? Absolutely not.

Imam Husain ﷺ performed such an extraordinary feat that he explained the meaning of sacrificing everything in the way of Allah. Imam accomplished this task and made it clear that there was nothing left to be sacrificed.

---

[1] *Luhūf,* Pg. 61; *Biharul Anwār,* Vol. 44, Pg. 366; *Mausuat-e-Kalimat al-Imam al-Husain,* Pg. 329

The relatives of Imam Husain ﷺ were not forced to accompany him but they had the same faith and thinking as the Imam had.

"Whoever does not have the spirit of sacrifice should not come."

Basically, Imam Husain ﷺ had decided that in the caravan of self-sacrificing people there should not be anyone who has even a trace of "weakness" in him. That is why the Imam tested his companions two or three times during the journey and sent back a few weak people every time. Before departing from Mecca, Imam ﷺ had announced aloud: "Whoever does not have the spirit of sacrificing his life should not accompany us." In spite of hearing his frightening announcement, some weak-hearted people thought that it was possible that when they reach Kufa, they would benefit from the act of joining the Imam. They thought that they would also get a good governmental post over there. Therefore some weak-hearted people also accompanied the Imam in his journey. In addition to that, a few nomadic Arabs also joined the Imam's caravan.

Companions of Husain are tested

Imam Husain ﷺ told his companions during the journey:

"Whoever among you thinks that he would get some official post on reaching there should cut short his expectations and return home." Hearing this, many people went back.[1]

After that, the Imam tested his companions once again on the Ashura eve. All great historians are of the opinion that there was none among his companions who went back during this night. The Divine hand had already removed cowardly men from the group of Imam Husain ؏. The author of *Nasikhut Tawarikh* has made a mistake by writing that when Imam Husain ؏ allowed his companions to go back if they so wished taking the advantage of the darkness of night, some companions left him and went away. However, this report is incorrect because it is not proved by any other book of history. No historian has made this mistake except for the author of *Nasikhut Tawarikh*. It is an established fact that none of the helpers of Imam Husain ؏ left him on the Ashura day. This proves that no companion of Imam Husain ؏ lacked the highest level of faith and none of them had any weakness of faith.

The greatest achievement of Imam Husain's movement

If on the Ashura Day even a single companion or child had displayed an iota of cowardice and joined the enemy's large and strong army in order to save his life it would have been a defect for Imam Husain ؏ and the Husainite School.

On the contrary, some men of the enemy's army who were safe from all dangers, joined the Imam, leaving all the

---

[1] *Irshad,* Shaykh Mufid, Pg. 223; *Biharul Anwār,* Vol. 44, Pg. 374; *Mausuat-e-Kalimat al-Imam al-Husain,* Pg. 348

luxuries and dared to enter the danger zone while the people surrounded by dangers did not go towards luxury.

If Imam Husain 🕮 had not announced the dangers and had not tested his companions before, half of the companions would have left Imam Husain 🕮 and would have spoken against Imam Husain 🕮. Because whoever runs away does not accept the weakness of his faith but he presents a number of excuses in order to hide his defect and says, "After proper investigation, I supported whomever I found to be on the right path...if I has found the divine will (in favor of my martyrdom) I would have laid down my life. However, it was not the case. We thought that the opposite party was right and joined them." Such persons present a crooked logic. However, such a case was not found in the caravan of Husain and it is a great achievement and a matter of pride for the Husainite School.

Hurr, an example of awakened conscience

In Karbala, the movement of Imam Husain 🕮 pulled a great general of the enemy's army, Hurr bin Yazid Riyahi towards itself. Hurr was not an ordinary man. After Umar bin Saad, he was the most important person of Yazid's army. In the beginning, he was made the commander. He was the first to be given the command of a thousand-strong cavalry and dispatched to block the way of Imam Husain 🕮. In spite of the fact that he was the first to pull the sword against Imam Husain 🕮 on day one, he was full of faith and spirit of performing good deeds. In the end this same spirit made him bow down in front of Imam 🕮 and repent for his initial blunder. In this way, Hurr joined the group of 'the repenters' about whom there is a verse:

"They who turn (to Allah), who serve (Him), who praise (Him), who fast, who bow down, who prostrate themselves, who enjoin what is good and forbid what is evil, and who keep the limits of Allah; and give good news to the believers." (Surah Taubah 9:112)

Hurr repents

He was renowned for his daring and bravery. It is proved by the fact that he was made the commander of a thousand-strong cavalry and dispatched to block Imam Husain's way. But Imam Husain ﷺ transformed the thinking of this man.

Just as the fire that burns in the center of the samovar boils the water and the steam created by it shakes up the whole container, in the same way the candle of truth, which Imam Husain ﷺ had lit in the heart of Hurr, had shaken his entire existence. (Hurr also cared about worldly life like you and me. He also wanted wealth, post and safety but the 'fire of truth' was pressurizing him to join Imam Husain).

The material needs of human beings were inciting Hurr. Hurr was standing at a junction and thinking that if he joined Husain he would be martyred within the next hour and would not be able to see his wife and children. The government will seize his property. His wife will become a widow. Such thoughts were stopping him from moving towards the Imam.

These two opposing powers were pressurizing him. Suddenly someone saw that Hurr was shivering. He came forward and asked: "What am I seeing? Why is a brave man like you shivering?" Perhaps the questioner thought that Hurr was fearing for his life. Hurr replied: "No, I do not fear my death. You don't know what suffering my heart is going through. Currently, I am finding myself standing at the junction of hell and heaven; free to choose one of the paths. I might take Paradise, which is a credit and I can take this world, which is cash but which would lead me to hell."

Hurr remained in this state of inner tug-of-war for a long time. At last, he paid heed to his conscience in the final moments and became Hurr, as per the saying of Imam Husain 彌. Fearing that the enemy would stop him, he moved away slowly. Then he spurred his horse and moved swiftly towards Imam Husain's 彌 camp. He waved a truce so that the companions of Imam Husain 彌 do not take him to be an attacker.

"Can my repentance be accepted?"

It is narrated that Hurr had overturned his shield in order to signal that he was not coming to fight but to take refuge. The first personality to come before Hurr was Imam Husain 彌. He was standing outside the camp of his family members. Hurr came near and said: "Peace be upon you, O Aba Abdillah!" and then said:

"Maula! I am a sinner. I was the first to commit the crime of blocking your way." Then Hurr prayed to the Almighty God:

"O Lord! Forgive my sins. I terrorized the hearts of your friends and intimidated them." (When the Ahlul Bayt of Imam Husain 彌 saw Hurr on their way for the first time, he was accompanied by one thousand armed soldiers who blocked the Imam's way. Therefore, it was natural for them to get intimidated.)

"Maula! I have repented for my sins. The blackness of my face cannot be washed off with anything except my blood. I have come to you to repent after seeking your permission. However, Maula! First tell me whether my repentance can be accepted?"

Now look at the character of Imam Husain ﷺ. The Imam did not care about his personal matter. He knew that even if Hurr repented for his deeds, the current circumstances would not change. However, Imam ﷺ did not care about himself but only and only about Allah. Thus he replied: "Indeed your repentance will be accepted. How can your repentance not be accepted? Has the door of divine mercy ever closed for any repentant? Never!"

Why Hurr didn't enter the Imam's tent?

When Hurr came to know that his repentance was accepted, he praised Allah and said: "Master! Now that my repentance is accepted, I want to sacrifice myself on you. I want to give up my blood in your way."

Imam Husain ﷺ said: "O Hurr! You are my guest. Dismount from your horse. Sit with me for a while so that we may serve you somewhat." (I don't know what Imam Husain ﷺ was going to serve to Hurr). But Hurr continued to seek permission from the Imam so that he does not have to get down from his horse. The Imam insisted a lot but he did not dismount.

Some writers of Karbala tragedy have explained that Hurr wanted to sit with the Imam for sometime but he feared that if he sat with him, one of the children of the Imam may come forward and say that 'he is the same person who blocked our way on the first day.' He wanted to save himself from that shameful situation by wiping the blackness of his crime with the redness of his blood. Thus, when he insisted a lot, the Imam said, "O Hurr! If you really wish so, you may go."

Conversation between the army of Umar bin Saad and Hurr

Since this brave man was also from Kufa he talked to the Kufan army with reference to the letters people of Kufa had sent to the Imam and said: "O people! Incidentally, I am not of those who called the Imam to Kufa by writing letters to him. However, you and your elders have invited the Imam here after writing to him and you also promised to help him. Hence I ask you people on what basis, principles and religion, are you treating your guest in such an inhuman manner?"

After that, that brave man told something which shows that it was an extremely immoral act and it was against Islam and nature. It was this act which had made the brave man so furious. The history of Islam testifies that it is wrong to treat even an enemy of Islam in this manner. That it is wrong to harass the opponent by straitening his life through cutting the supply of water. Imam Ali bin Abi Talib ☼ was also suggested to cut off water supply to Muawiyah and his army but the Imam did not do so.

Imam Husain ☼ had quenched the thirst of Hurr and his companions on the way even though they were enemies. Hurr certainly remembered this incident. He used to think on whom they had cut off the water supply? He was the one who found them thirsty and quenched their thirst even before they asked for it. Hurr wondered, 'How great and majestic a person Husain was and how mean and lowly we are.' Hence, he said: "O Kufis! Aren't you ashamed that the gushing water of Euphrates should be accessible to every creature including human beings, pets, wild animals but that you cut off its supply to the son of Allah's Messenger?

Imam Husain ﷺ goes to Hurr in his last moments

Ultimately, this brave man fought and got martyred after receiving applause for his bravery. Imam Husain ﷺ did not let him pass away from his world without awarding him. The Chief of the Martyrs reached him quickly and took his head on his blessed thigh and said: "How nice this Hurr, Hurr ar-Riyahi is!"[1] It means what an extraordinary and nice name his mother has selected for him. His mother had called him Hurr ('free') on the very first day and Hurr was actually a free man.

How great Imam Husain ﷺ is! He expressed his concern for his companions as much as possible and took care of them. This is real 'Enjoining good' and 'Forbidding evil' (*Amr bil Maroof* and *Nahi Anil Munkar*). Every companion visited during the last moments by Imam Husain ﷺ was in a different state. Some of them were alive when Imam Husain ﷺ reached them and they even talked to their master while others had passed away even before the Imam could reach them.

May my life be sacrificed for Abbas

None of the companions visited by Imam Husain ﷺ was in such a remorseful state as Imam's younger brother, His Eminence, Abul Fazl al-Abbas who was loved dearly

---

[1] *Luhūf,* Pg. 103; *Biharul Anwār,* Vol. 45, Pg. 13; *Mausuat-e-Kalimat al-Imam al-Husain,* Pg. 437; *Maqtal-e-Husain,* Muqarram, Pg. 236

by Imam Husain ﷺ and who was the inheritor of the bravery of Haider-e-Karrar (Imam Ali). It is mentioned that Imam Husain ﷺ told His Eminence, Abbas: "O Abbas! May I be sacrificed on you!" This statement is so meaningful.[1]

His Eminence, Abbas was about 23 years younger to Imam Husain ﷺ. Imam Husain ﷺ was 57 years old and His Eminence, Abbas was 34 years old. Imam Husain ﷺ was like a father to His Eminence, Abbas as per his age and yet he said: "O Abbas! May I be sacrificed on you!"

Imam goes to the Moon of Bani Hashim

Imam Husain ﷺ was waiting near the tent. Suddenly he heard the roaring voice of His Eminence, Abbas. (It is recorded that the face of His Eminence, Abbas was so good-looking that he was called the Moon of Bani Hashim.[2] His Eminence, Abbas was so tall that it is recorded in some books that he used to mount a sturdy horse and when he inserted his feet inside the stirrups, his toes touched the ground.[3]

I would like to mention the statement of late Shaykh Muhammad Baqir Birjandi, which although somewhat exaggerated, indicates that His Eminence, Abbas was a tall youth. He was so handsome that Imam Husain ﷺ used to feel happy looking at him.

When Imam Husain ﷺ reached this youth in his last moments, he found that both his arms were severed. He was hit on his head by a mace and an eye was pierced with

---

[1] *Irshad*, Shaykh Mufid, Pg. 230; *Maqtal-e-Husain*, Muqarram, Pg. 210
[2] *Biharul Anwār*, Vol. 45, Pg. 39; *Muntahal Amaal*, Pg. 687
[3] *Biharul Anwār*, Vol. 45, Pg. 39; *Al-Abbas*, Muqarram, Pg. 76

an arrow. It is not wrongly said about Imam Husain ※ that when His Eminence, Abbas was martyred, it was seen that the holy face of Imam Husain ※ had also withered.[1]

Imam Husain ※ had himself said: "Brother Abbas! After your martyrdom my back has broken and my determination has decreased."[2]

---

[1] *Qissa Karbala,* Pg. 351; narrated from *Zariat al-Najah,* Pg. 125
[2] *Biharul Anwār,* Vol. 45, Pg. 41

Majlis 23

Imam Husain ﷺ asks for a day's time on Ashura Eve

On 'Tasua' i.e. on the 9th of Muharram at the time of Asr (late afternoon), Umar bin Saad's forces launched the attack as ordered by Ibne Ziyad. They wanted the battle to start on that day. Imam Husain ﷺ sent his brother, Abbas, to them with a message asking for respite for only that night.

Imam Husain ﷺ said: "Dear brother! Ask them for respite of only one night." Then to remove the misunderstanding that he was creating unnecessary delay, Imam Husain ﷺ added: "Brother! Allah knows better how fond I am of praying to Him. I want to spend this night in supplications so that it may be a night of repentance for us."

Ashura Eve was like Meraj Eve for the devotees

Alas! If we can only know how great the Ashura eve was! Actually, it was the night of Meraj. It was night full of joy, happiness and cheerfulness. On that night, the martyrs of Karbala made themselves purest. On that night they decorated each and every part of their existence. The place of decorating their existence was in the tent.

All were inside the tent. Only two persons were outside, guarding it in turns. Apparently, one of them was Burair Hamadani.[1] Perhaps Burair jested with his companion who told him that it was not the night of fun. Burair replied: "Basically, I am not from the humorous people but tonight is a night of fun for us."

Humming of the devotees

When the enemy saw them engrossed in repentance, do you know what they said? When they passed by the camp of Imam Husain 🕮, they said: "They sound like humming of bees at a honeycomb."[2] So loud were the sounds of seeking forgiveness, praying and supplications of Imam Husain 🕮 and his companions (that there was turmoil in the ranks of angels).

Imam Husain 🕮 had said:

"I want tonight to be a night of our repentance and seeking forgiveness." I would say that he wanted it to be the night of his ascension (Meraj). This statement of Imam 🕮 is worth pondering upon. After this statement, can we say that there is no need for us to repent? Was Imam in need of it and we are not? Imam Husain 🕮 spent the entire night of Ashura in divine glorification and worship of the Lord and continued to check the well being of his family members. It was also the night when Imam Husain 🕮 delivered an unforgettable sermon to his companions.

---

[1] It is narrated that Buraira Hamadani was speaking humorously with Abdur Rahman Ansari.
Maqtal-e-Husain, Muqarram, Pg. 216
[2] *Luhūf,* Pg. 94

Repentance Accepted

O mourners!

Here I am going to talk about a repentant of the desert of Karbala and conclude my lecture with it. One of the repentances in Karbala was very important, and it was the repentance of Hurr bin Yazid Riyahi.

Hurr was an extremely brave man. When Ubaidullah Ibne Ziyad dispatched the first unit of his army against Imam Husain ؏, he made Hurr the commander of one thousand strong cavalry. This Hurr had inflicted atrocities on Ahlul Bayt of the Holy Prophet ؐ. I mentioned in one of my speeches that when a person commits a great crime and if his conscience is alive, it surely impels him to make amends. Therefore, you listeners should estimate the reaction of the conscience of a person who had committed a crime against those whose souls were on the highest level.

Hurr had a living conscience

A narrator says that he saw Hurr in the army of Ibne Saad trembling with fear. He came forward and said, "O Hurr! I used to consider you very brave. Were I asked who is the bravest man of Kufa, I would not have mentioned the name of anyone except yours. But at this moment why are you trembling so much?"

Hurr replied: "You have misunderstood. I am not fearing for my life in this battle. In fact, I find myself standing at crossroads. One way leads to Paradise and another to Hell. I am unable to decide where to go and which way to choose." Finally, Hurr selected the path of salvation and began moving his mount on it slowly. He moved in such a manner that no one could realize what he was up to. When he reached a place where no one could have blocked his way, he accelerated his horse and moved swiftly towards the camp of Imam Husain ﷺ.

It is narrated that he inverted his shield to signal that he was not coming to fight but to surrender. He reached the holy Imam, saluted him and said: "Son of the Prophet! Can the repentance of this sinner be accepted?" Imam Husain ﷺ replied: "Why not? Your repentance will indeed be accepted."[1]

Husain's mercy and kindness

O mourners! Look at the mercy and kindness of the merciful son of the merciful Imam. He did not say: "What kind of repentance is this? Now that you have brought us into such perils, you have come to repent?" It was so because the holy Imam did not have such thinking. He had always guided the people. If Ibne Saad's army had repented after killing all his youths, then too he would have said: "I accept the repentance of you all." Because when Yazid had asked Imam Sajjad ﷺ after the tragedy of Karbala, "Will my repentance be accepted, if I do it now?" Imam had replied, "Yes, if you repent with a pure intention, your repentance can be accepted." However Yazid did not repent at that time.[2]

---

[1] *Luhūf,* Pg. 103; *Mausuat-e-Kalimat al-Imam al-Husain,* Pg. 438

[2] Shaykh Sadooq (a.r.) has narrated the tradition from Imam Reḍa through three reliable sources in *Uyun Akhbār al-*Reḍa, Vol. 2, Pg. 47 that the Holy Prophet said that Prophet Musa had prayed to Allah, "O Lord! My brother, Haroon has died. Please forgive him." Eventually, Allah revealed unto him, "O Musa! I would have accepted your repentance for any person from beginning to end except the killers of Husain bin Ali (a.s.) because I am going to take

Hurr said, "Master! Allow me to go to the battlefield and sacrifice myself on you."

Imam said, "Hurr!

You are my guest. Dismount from your horse and sit with me for a while." However, Hurr insisted again and again to permit him to go.

Hurr was very ashamed as long as he remained alive. Why? Because he used to recollect that he was the one who terrorized the friends of the Lord for the first time and intimidated the progeny of the Holy Prophet ﷺ.[1]

Why didn't he like sitting near Imam Husain ؑ? Because he feared that while he sat with the Sayyid, a thirsty child may come out and see him, which would make him die of shame.

---

revenge from them for martyrdom of Husain." Allamah Majlisi has narrated a tradition in *Biharul Anwār,* Vol. 44, Pg. 308 that a person from Bani Israel saw Prophet Musa going somewhere hurriedly. He was pale, trembling and had feeble eyes. The person understood that he is going for supplication. The person asked, "O prophet of Allah! I have committed a great sin. Please pray for my forgiveness to Allah." Thus, when Prophet Musa prayed for his forgiveness and said, "O Lord! You know what I am going to say that so and so servant has committed a sin and he seeks forgiveness from You." Allah replied, "I would forgive whoever seeks repentance from Me except the killers of Husain..." It is written in *Damaatus Sakiba,* Vol. 5, Pg. 194-195 that when Yazid bin Muawiyah met Imam Sajjad (a.s.) he tried to cast on Ibne Ziyad the responsibility for all his crimes and acquit himself.

[1] *Luhūf,* Pg. 103; *Irshad,* Shaykh Mufid, Pg. 235; *Biharul Anwār,* Vol. 45, Pg. 13; *Mausuat-e-Kalimat al-Imam al-Husain,* Pg. 437; *Maqtal-e-Husain,* Muqarram, Pg. 236

Majlis 24

Zuhair bin Qayn

Mourners of the oppressed Imam!

Yesterday I had spoken about the repentance of Hurr. Today you will hear about another companion of the holy Imam, Zuhair bin Qayn because he is also considered among the repentants. However, his repentance was different. He was an Uthmani, a partisan of Uthman bin Affan. He was among those who thought that Imam Ali ﷺ was responsible for Uthman's murder. Hence he did not have a favorable opinion about Imam Ali ﷺ.

Whenever Imam Husain ﷺ confronted an adamant enemy, he used to show such confidence that no power could decrease his honor; leave aside the chance of bowing his head down. Often the Imam used to be in a situation when it was necessary to guide some people; in such cases he even ignored the carelessness of those people.

Zuhair was returning with his caravan from Mecca to Iraq and Imam Husain ﷺ was also traveling on the same route to Iraq. Zuhair was trying not to meet Imam Husain ﷺ face to face somehow. When he used to see that the caravan of Imam Husain ﷺ was getting closer, he used to take his caravan away. Imam knew that Zuhair was keeping away because he was unaware of the facts. In spite of this, Imam ﷺ wanted to remind him of something because the Almighty Allah has said: فَذَكِّرْ إِنَّمَا أَنتَ مُذَكِّرٌ

"Therefore do remind, for you are only a reminder."(Surah Ghashiya 88:21). The Imam wanted Zuhair to come out of ignorance; he didn't want to force him. Even though Zuhair was ignoring the Imam, the latter wanted to guide him because his heart was full of the light of faith.

Zuhair knew that Husain was the son of Allah's beloved; and what his right on Ummah was. He feared that if he met the Imam, the latter may ask for something that he could not fulfill; and it would be a great defect.

At one station, much against his wish, Zuhair had to halt near the Imam. Imam Husain ﷺ had halted at that place and thus, both the caravans halted at the same well. Imam ﷺ sent a messenger to call Zuhair. Zuhair and his companions were having food in one of the tents. Suddenly, the curtain of the tent was lifted and a person said, "O Zuhair! Husain is calling you."[1]

Hearing this, Zuhair's face became pale and he murmured, "This is what I feared." His companions were also aware of the entire situation.

It is mentioned in books that Zuhair and his companions stopped eating because Zuhair was well-aware of the status of Imam Husain ﷺ. Hence, he could neither reject the invitation nor accept it whole-heartedly. He knew that it wasn't proper to reject the invitation of Imam Husain ﷺ. He sat frozen, like the saying goes in Arabic, "As if a bird was sitting on his head". In short, the entire atmosphere became tense.[2]

---

[1] O Zuhair! Aba Abdullah al-Husain has sent me to call you. *Luhūf,* Pg. 72

[2] We were sitting quietly as if we had a bird sitting on our heads and would have flown away if we moved. *Luhūf,* Pg. 72

Suggestion of Zuhair's wife

When Zuhair's wife (Dalham binte Amr) came to know that Imam Husain 🕊 had sent a messenger inviting Zuhair to him but Zuhair has not yet replied to him, she came forward and said: "O Zuhair! The beloved one of Fatima is calling you and you are rejecting the invitation instead of taking it as an honor? Zuhair! You must go to him." Eventually, Zuhair got up helplessly and went to meet the Imam. Sometimes, reminders show their effect in this way also.

Husainite Magnetism

I don't know, that is it is not mentioned in any history and perhaps no one knows what was discussed and how they felt when Zuhair met Imam Husain 🕊 because Zuhair's face was pale when he went to meet the Imam and it looked bright and young when he came out of the meeting.

I don't know how Imam Husain 🕊 transformed Zuhair's thinking. I also don't know what the Imam reminded him of but I certainly know that a revolution had appeared in Zuhair's heart. He was completely transformed. People saw that Zuhair was no longer his old self. When he returned, he ordered his tent to be moved from its place and shifted next to the tent of Imam Husain 🕊. "Now I would live and die with Aba Abdillah only." He also started making a will about how his property should be utilized. He also willed about his sons and daughters. He ordered that his wife should be sent to her father's house after him.

Zuhair spoke and bid farewell in such a manner that everybody understood that he was not going to return.

When he came out of his tent fully armed, his wife caught the tail of his robe and said weeping, "Zuhair! You have chosen martyrdom with the beloved of Fatima so that she may intercede for you on Judgment Day. Zuhair, do not act in such a way that you and I are separated on Judgment Day. I am holding onto you only with the hope that you would ask Lady Zahra to intercede for me on the Judgment Day. Zuhair! Promise me that you would request for my intercession. I want Lady Fatima to intercede for me."[1]

After that, it is this same Zuhair who is seen in the forefront among the rows of the companions of Husain ☙ and the Imam had given him the command of the right wing. How surprising!

Zuhair now topped the list of Imam Husain's companions

Zuhair had displayed such a character that when Imam Husain ☙ was left alone on the Ashura day and none of the companions of Imam Husain ☙ was left, he called out his companions and Zuhair was one of them.

The oppressed Imam said, "O my dear ones! O my brave ones! O Muslim bin Aqeel! O Hani bin Urwah! O Zuhair! Why are you asleep? Get up and safeguard the sanctity of your prophet from those shameless traitors."[2]

---

[1] Zuhair's wife said, "God is your helper. Whatever happened to you has goodness in it. I wish that Husain's grandfather remembers me too at the time of intercession on the Judgment Day." *Luhūf*, Pg. 73; *Maqtal-e-Husain*, Pg. 178; *Biharul Anwār*, Vol. 44, Pg. 372

[2] Imam Husain looked around and saw that all his companions were martyred. His brothers and sons were lying on the earth smeared with their blood. Imam (a.s.) called out aloud, "O Muslim bin Aqeel!

When the battle ended, Zuhair's wife was worried. She thought that others would be shrouded while Zuhair's body would lie unshrouded. Thinking this, she sent her slave ordering him to shroud his master. When the slave came, he saw all the martyrs lying without shroud and felt ashamed. He could not bear to shroud Zuhair and leave his master, Husain, unshrouded.[1]

وَسَيَعْلَمُ الَّذِينَ ظَلَمُوا أَيَّ مُنقَلَبٍ يَنقَلِبُونَ

And they who act unjustly shall know to what final place of turning they shall turn back.[2]

O Hani bin Urwah! O Habib bin Mazahir and O Zuhair bin Qayn! O my true and brave companions! O those who fought alongside me! O honest and honored youths! Wake from your sleep and save the family of your Holy Prophet from those mean traitors." *Mausuat-e-Kalimat al-Imam al-Husain,* Pg. 484

[1] *Luhūf,* Pg. 71; *Maqtal-e-Husain,* Pg. 177; *Mausuat-e-Kalimat al-Imam al-Husain,* Pg. 342; *Tarikh-e-Ashura,* Pg. 198 published by Jame Taalimaat-e-Islami, Pakistan

[2] Surah Shuara 26:227

Majlis 25

Martyrdom of Jaun bin Abi Malik

O mourners!

Imam Husain ﷺ had reached certain companions during their last moments or after their martyrdom in the battle of Karbala. Among them, it is certain about two companions that they were former slaves. They were bought and later on emancipated. One of them was a Roman slave and another Jaun, the Ethiopian, who was freed by His Eminence, Abu Zar Ghiffari.

Apparently he did not leave the Ahlul Bayt even after being freed and continued to serve the family of the Prophet.

Jaun came to Imam Husain ﷺ on Ashura day and said, "Master! Please allow me also to go to the battlefield." Imam ﷺ said, "No, it is not the time for you to leave this world. You should remain alive after this battle also. Whatever service you rendered to our family is enough. We are pleased with you." Jaun insisted again but the Imam refused to permit. Eventually, he fell at the Imam's feet, kissed his feet and said, "Master! Do not deprive me from martyrdom." After that, Jaun made such a statement that the Imam could not restrain him any longer.

Imam Husain ﷺ goes to the Ethiopian Slave

Jaun said, "Master! I know why you are not allowing me. It is so because I am such a lowly person that I do not deserve this honor. How can I get the rank of martyrdom with my black skin, impure blood and smelly body?"

Imam ﷺ replied, "No Jaun, it is not so. The reason behind not permitting you is not what you thought. If you really want to go, you may go." Jaun gave a wide smile on hearing this. He began to rock in joy, recited the war poem and set out towards the battlefield happily. He fought bravely and sacrificed his life on his master.

Imam Husain ﷺ was watching Jaun's fight. As soon as Jaun fell from his horse, The Imam ran towards him and sat near his head. He prayed to the Lord: "O Lord! Make his face bright in this world and the hereafter. Change his body odor into sweet fragrance and resurrect him along with holy men (It must be remembered that the rank of holy men is above the rank of the pious).[1] O Lord! Maintain friendship between him and the progeny of Muhammad in the hereafter."[2]

Martyrdom of the Roman slave

There was another slave in Karbala, and he was Roman and he was also martyred in the company of Imam Husain ﷺ. When he fell from his horse and Imam Husain ﷺ reached near him, a strange thing happened.

---

[1] Surah Mutaffifeen 83:18
[2] *Biharul Anwār,* Vol. 45, Pg. 22; *Maqtal-e-Husain,* Muqarram, Pg. 252; *Muntahal Amaal,* Vol. 1, Pg. 667

Either this slave was unconscious or his eyes were filled with blood. It is narrated that Imam Husain ﷺ took his head in his lap and wiped the blood from his face and eyes. Suddenly this slave regained consciousness. He looked at the holy face of Imam Husain ﷺ and smiled.

Imam ﷺ placed his cheek on the cheek of that slave. It is that gesture which the Imam adopted only with this slave and with his son, Ali Akbar. Such a gesture is not recorded with anyone else; that is "he kept his cheek on his cheek". Seeing this affection, the slave became extremely happy. He just smiled and went on to meet the Lord.[1]

(Master!) If you come near my head as a doctor I would not forgo the tastefulness of illness even in exchange of both the worlds.

The slave's head was in the Imam's lap when his soul flew away from the material cage.

---

[1] *Biharul Anwār,* Vol. 45, Pg. 30; *Muntahal Amaal,* Vol. 1, Pg. 669; *Mausuat-e-Kalimat al-Imam al-Husain,* Pg. 457

Majlis 26

Women who helped Imam Husain

All the aspects of Islam, be they natural, social or related to monotheism, divine recognition and faithfulness or disputes appear complete. Those who played their role in Karbala included a suckling baby as well as an elderly person aged seventy or eighty years old and the ladies. The wife of Abdullah bin Umair Kalbi (Umme Wahab) was one of those elderly people. Three persons had come along to Karbala along with their wives and children to assist Imam Husain . After the martyrdom of these three persons, their families remained with the family of Imam Husain . The other companions were not accompanied by wives and children. The three persons whose wives and children accompanied them in Karbala were Muslim bin Awsaja, Abdullah bin Umair Kalbi and Junada bin Harth Ansari.

Take me along

Abdullah bin Umair was among the companions of the Holy Prophet . He had participated in Islamic battles. It is mentioned that he was not present in Kufa during those days. When he got the news of the disturbed affairs of Kufa that an army was being readied to fight against Imam Husain , he told himself, "By Allah, I fought against the disbelievers for long years for the sake of Islam. However, that jihad cannot be equal in rank to his one where I am getting a chance to defend the people of the house of the Holy Prophet ﷺ. He reached home and told his wife about his decision. His wife said, "May God reward you! You have made a great decision, but I put forward a condition for it." He asked what that condition was. His wife replied, "You should take me along." Thus he took his wife as well as his mother along. What a great thing to do! How great these women were!

Abdullah bin Umair was a valiant fighter. He fought with both the slaves of Umar bin Saad and Ibne Ziyad who had sought their equal and were very strong. He dispatched both to hell.

It is mentioned that when those slaves sought their equal, the choosing eyes of Imam Husain ؏ looked at the body and arms of Abdullah bin Umair and the Imam selected him. He said, "You are the man to fight these two." Thus, he went to the battlefield and became a fitting opponent for both.

First, the slave of Umar bin Saad, Yasar came forward. Abdullah bin Umair defeated him in one stroke. However, before that, a person attacked him from behind. The companions of Imam shouted to alert him but before he could balance himself, he was vigorously attacked with a sword and Abdullah's hand was cut off at his wrist. However, this brave man killed him with his other hand.[1]

He came to Imam Husain ؏ in this state reciting the war poem and asked his mother, "O mother! Are you happy now?" his mother replied, "I would not be pleased with you till you sacrifice yourself for the sake of Fatima's

---

[1] *Mausuat-e-Kalimat al-Imam al-Husain,* Pg. 433 (the topic is related to the companion of the Holy Prophet, Abdullah bin Umair Kalbi till here. After this, it is related to Wahab bin Abdullah bin Habbab Kalbi who was young in age) - Rizwani.

beloved." Abdullah's wife was also present. She clung to him. His mother said, "Beware, don't pay heed to what your wife says. It is not the time to listen to your wife. If you want me to be pleased with you, there's no way for you, except martyrdom."

This stalwart went to the battlefield again and was finally martyred. The enemies severed his head and threw it towards the tents of Husain's family members (Severed heads of some martyrs were thrown at Husain's camp and Abdullah bin Umair's was one of them).

The aged mother of this martyr lifted her son's head, pressed it to her chest, kissed it and said:

"O my dearest one! I am pleased with you now. You have fulfilled your duty." Then she threw his head back to the enemy, saying, "We don't take back whatever we have given in the way of Allah."

After Abdullah bin Umair's mother, who had exceeding love for Ahlul Bayt, picked up a tent pole and attacked the impure enemy saying:

"Even though I am a weak old woman, I would defend the family of Fatima as long as there is strength in my old bones."[1]

In the name of Allah and by Allah and on the religion of the Messenger of Allah ﷺ

---

[1] These verses were not recited by the mother of Abdullah bin Umair Kalbi. Instead they were mentioned by the mother of that child about whom it is written that he was the youth whose father had been killed in the attack.

Biharul Anwār, Vol. 45, Pg. 28; *Mausuat-e-Kalimat al-Imam al-Husain,* Pg. 458

Majlis 27

Martyrdom of Amr bin Qarza bin Kaab Ansari

Amr bin Qarza bin Kaab was from the progeny of Ansar (Helpers) of Medina. He was present in Karbala with Imam Husain 🕮 till the noon of Ashura. He was among those who formed a human shield to protect Imam Husain 🕮 when he offered the Zuhr prayer.

Amr stopped the arrows with his chest as long as the Imam continued to pray. He was hit with so many arrows that he could not bear the injuries and he fell down. When Imam Husain 🕮 came to him after the Prayer, he was in the last moments of his life. He was thinking whether he had fulfilled his duty or not. When Imam Husain 🕮 reached near his head, he asked the Imam only one thing, "O Aba Abdillah! Have I fulfilled the right of loyalty?"[1]

---

[1] It is written in *Maqtal-e-Husain,* Muqarram, Pg. 248, "O son of Messenger! Did I fulfill my duty?"

Majlis 28

Young martyr

O mourners!

In the battle of Karbala where young and old, all inscribed the stories of bravery, the children also did not fall short. It is narrated that nine or ten children sacrificed their lives for Fatima's beloved in this battle. It is narrated that a child whose father had recently got martyred came forward eager for Jihad.[1] (We don't know who that child was or whose son he was)[2] the child kissed Imam Husain's feet and said, "Master! Please permit me to go to the battlefield." The Imam looked at him and said, "No, you shall not go. Your father's martyrdom is enough. Perhaps your mother will not be pleased if you go."

Hearing this, the child replied, "O Aba Abdillah! The fact is that the sword hanging from my waist is tied by my mother only. She told me to go and sacrifice my life, like my father did, for the sake of the Imam." The child insisted so much that Imam Husain ﷺ allowed him to go.

Why can it not be known whether he was the son of Muslim bin Awsaja or Harth bin Junada Ansari? These two were only persons who had taken their family along

---

[1] *Biharul Anwār,* Vol. 45, Pg. 27; *Maqtal-e-Husain,* Muqarram, Pg. 253 and *Mausuat-e-Kalimat al-Imam al-Husain,* Pg. 457
[2] Muqarram writes that the eleven-year-old child was Amr. His father was Junada Ansari who was martyred in the first attack.

with them to Karbala. Although Abdullah bin Umair had also come to Karbala with his family, it is a known fact that this child was not Abdullah's.

When this child came into the battlefield, unlike others who had introduced themselves through the name of their father and grandfather and who recited in Rajaz poetry: 'I am so and so son of so and so', he took a completely different approach. Through his approach he obtained a unique status. On reaching the battlefield he called out in a loud voice:

"My master, Husain; what a good master he is. He is the dearest of the Messenger who was Basheer (brought glad-tidings) and Nadheer (warner)."[1]

---

[1] *Biharul Anwār,* Vol. 45, Pg. 27; *Maqtal-e-Husain,* Muqarram, Pg. 253; *Mausuat-e-Kalimat al-Imam al-Husain,* Pg. 457

Majlis 29

Husain's message permeated the hearts

O dear ones!

It is recorded that many kings and people who wanted to become famous made plates with their name and lineage inscribed on it. The inscription also included names of those who bowed in front of them and obeyed them. Why was this message inscribed on the plates thousands of years ago? It was so that their name is not forgotten. These signs remained buried under tones of soil and nobody knew about them until the modern day European archeologists sought them. Whatever was removed is not significant. There is nothing special about it. Similarly, no one cares about the messages recorded in books. They do not consider them important and don't get attracted towards them because these messages are inscribed on stones and not on hearts. Imam Husain ﷺ did not inscribe his message on stones. Instead whatever he spoke flowed along with the waves of air, reached the human ears and got inscribed on their hearts in such a way that it can never be erased. As the poet Josh has said:

Let man wake up at least,

Every community will announce: Husain is ours

Imam ﷺ himself was well aware of this fact. He had predicted the future correctly that after that day this

Husain would not be killed again. His name would not be erased however someone may try to erase it and Husain shall live forever. Please think upon it. Can it be a mere coincidence? No, absolutely not?

Imam Husain's ﷺ call for help

Imam Husain ﷺ issued a call for help in the final moments on Ashura day. Did Imam Husain ﷺ need any helper at that time also? Did Imam Husain ﷺ want helpers who would come and get killed? No, Imam Husain ﷺ didn't wanted a helper to defend him from the enemies.

Imam Husain ﷺ did not want to remain alive after the martyrdom of his companions, brothers and sons. However the Imam wanted a helper who would have got himself martyred. Therefore, he called out, "Is there anyone to help me?"[1] Imam Husain's ﷺ voice reached his camp and women began wailing aloud.[2] Imam Husain ﷺ sent His Eminence, Abbas and a person from Ahlul Bayt to console the women. They came and comforted the ladies.[3]

---

[1] The famous statement "Hal min nas'irinyans'urna" is recorded in various forms in the books of history as "Is there anyone to protect the sanctity of Holy Prophet? Is there any follower of Monothesim who fears Allah in our matter? Is there anyone to reply our calls for the sake of Allah? Is there any seeker of truth to help us? Is there anyone to protect sanctity of the Holy Prophet (from harm)? Is there anyone to hear our calls for the sake of Allah? Is there any helper to help the holy progeny? (*Firhang-e-Ashura,* Pg. 271)

[2] *Luhūf,* Pg. 116

[3] When Imam Husain (a.s.) had sent His Eminence, Abbas and His Eminence, Ali Akbar to give assurance to women, he was standing with the support of his sword and was introducing himself in a loud voice before the battle on Ashura day.
Luhūf, Pg. 87; *Mausuat-e-Kalimat al-Imam al-Husain,* Pg. 427

Martyrdom of the Little Baby

Then Imam himself turned to the camp of the family members. At that moment Lady Zainab came to Imam Husain ﷺ carrying a little baby. Imam Husain ﷺ took the baby from her but did not ask, "O sister! Why have you come out with this baby in such a dangerous situation where arrows are raining continuously from all sides?" He took the infant in his arms. An arrow came from the enemy and punctured the delicate neck of the baby. What did Imam Husain ﷺ do next? How strange his reaction was! When the baby was martyred in the arms of the father, Imam ﷺ took the blood of his neck in his cupped hand and threw it at the sky saying, "O sky! Look at this cruelty and be a witness to it."[1]

Imam Husain ﷺ applied the blood on his face

Imam Husain ﷺ was broken down because of his injuries during his final moments and fell down on the ground. He used to walk a few steps supported by his hands and then fall down again. He was struck on his neck at that time. Immediately he took his blood in his hands and applied it on his face and said, "I want to meet my Lord in this state only."

This heart-rending story of Karbala immortalized his message, which would live as long as the world exists.

---

[1] *Luhūf,* Pg. 117; *Mausuat-e-Kalimat al-Imam al-Husain,* Pg. 476

Asr of the Ninth Mohurrum

When the enemy attacked in the late afternoon on the ninth of Mohurrum, Imam Husain 🕮 sent his brother His Eminence, Abbas saying, "I want to pray to God tonight, offer Prayer, supplicate and seek repentance. (O brother!) Stop them till tomorrow morning anyhow. Tomorrow we shall definitely fight with them." After a discussion, Ibne Saad's army postponed the war. Imam Husain 🕮 performed some important tasks on Ashura eve, which are recorded in history.

Ashura Eve

First of all, Imam Husain 🕮 ordered everyone to sharpen their spears and swords. Jaun who was an expert in sharpening weapons, was busy polishing the arms of the companions. Imam 🕮 went to him to have a look at his work and inspected the weapons.

Secondly, Imam Husain 🕮 ordered the tents to be brought closer. The tents were brought so close to each other that the tent peg of one tent entered another tent and the space between the tents was not enough for even a man to pass through. Then the Imam ordered the tents to be fixed in such a way that the camp should look like a crescent. A trench was dug behind the tents overnight, which was so wide that no horse could cross it. Thus there was no way for the enemy to attack from behind.

He also ordered that dry leaves and wood be collected so that they could make a fire in the whole trench on the morning of Ashura and ensure that the enemy does not attack from the rear. Now the enemy could attack only from the front, the right and the left sides and they could be sure of safety from the rear.

Imam Husain ﷺ gathered his companions in a tent for the last time that night for exhausting the argument. Firstly, he thanked everybody in an eloquent manner. Then he addressed his family members and his companions, "No Ahlul Bayt in the world is better than my Ahlul Bayt and no companions in the world are better than my companions."

He continued, "You all know that the enemy does not want anything except my life. I am the only target of the enemy. If they get hold of me they would not seek anyone from you. Therefore, you all leave the place in the darkness of the night."

Everyone said, "O Aba Abdillah! How can we do this?" The first one to say this was the Imam's high-ranking brother, His Eminence, Abbas bin Ali.

On this occasion we again hear statements which in fact are historical also and imply the best representation and interpretation of the speaker. Every person speaks according to his thinking. Someone said, "Maula! If I am killed and my body is burnt and my ashes are blown in the air and this process goes on seventy times, then too I would not leave you. Our lowly lives are not worthy of being sacrificed for you." Another companion said, "Even if I am killed a thousand times, I would not leave you."[1]

Muhammad bin Basheer Hazrami's loyalty

Incidentally, Muhammad bin Basheer Hazrami, who was a companion of Imam ﷺ, received the news in Karbala that his adolescent son is taken hostage in a battle. He did

---

[1] *Biharul Anwār,* Vol. 44, Pg. 393; *Mausuat-e-Kalimat al-Imam al-Husain,* Pg. 395-400

not know what his son would go through? He said, "I cannot bear to remain alive while my son is subjected to this." When Imam Husain ﷺ came to know what calamity had befallen on his companion, he called and thanked him. Imam ﷺ praised him and said, "Your son is taken a hostage and it is necessary for someone to bail him out from the clutches of the enemy. There are a few belongings here, which can be sold off to get some money. You take them and bail out your son with the money you get after selling them." Muhammad bin Basheer said, "If I leave you for this, may the wild beasts eat me up alive. Let my son remain a prisoner. Is my son dearer than you?"[1]

His Eminence, Qasim bin Hasan

That night, when Imam Husain ﷺ exhausted the argument and made everyone announce their loyalty in unison clearly and everybody said, "We would not leave you at any cost," The Imam said, "The circumstances are before you. You must know it well that all of us would get martyred." Everybody said, "This news is a cause of joy for us. We thank God for this opportunity."

This success is not due to physical strength.

It is not obtained till God does not bestow it.

A child who was not more than thirteen years old, sat in a corner of the tent. He doubted whether he was included among those who were going to be martyred. The Imam had said that all those who had gathered at that place were going to be martyred the next day. However, the child was a minor and this statement of Imam ﷺ

---

[1] *Biharul Anwār,* Vol. 44, Pg. 393; *Mausuat-e-Kalimat al-Imam al-Husain,* Pg. 403

would have been only for adults. Thus, he asked the Imam, "O uncle! Does my name appear in the list of those who are going to be martyred tomorrow?"

It is recorded that the Imam cried much on hearing this question. He did not give any reply to Qasim. Imam ﷺ said, "Son! Please answer my question first. Then I would answer your question. Tell me, how is death in your view?"

Qasim said, "O uncle! Death is sweeter than honey for me. If you say that I would get martyred tomorrow, it would be great news for me."

Imam ﷺ said, "Yes son, but only after you have borne a great calamity." Qasim said, "Praise be to Allah! A great catastrophe is going to happen."

O mourners of the oppressed one of Karbala!

Hold your hearts and ponder. As per the words of Imam Husain ﷺ, a lot of heart-rending incidents were bound to happen the next day. This thirteen-year-old Qasim comes to the Imam after the martyrdom of His Eminence, Ali Akbar. His body was not well full grown yet, that weapons be hung on it. Armors were made only in adult sizes and even the helmets wouldn't fit the heads of children. The child requested, "Uncle dear! Now it's my turn to go. Please permit me." It should be remembered that no soldier went to the battlefield without the Imam's permission on Ashura day. Everybody used to first salute him, "Peace be upon you, O Aba Abdillah!" Then he used to say, "Master! Please give me permission."

Imam Husain ﷺ did not accord the permission to Qasim easily; instead he began to weep on seeing Qasim.

Qasim and Imam Husain ﷺ hugged each other and wept. It is written that Qasim started kissing the hands and feet of Imam Husain ﷺ.[1] Is it not worth that history should take this into consideration and judge in a better way about the Karbala tragedy? That child was insisting but Imam Husain ﷺ did not permit. Even though Imam Husain ﷺ wanted to allow him, but his tongue did not let him give the permission. Then spreading his hands he said,

"O reminder of my brother! Come, let me embrace and bid farewell to you." Qasim put his arms around Husain ﷺ and the uncle held the nephew in embrace. It is written: After that the two of them cried so much that they lost consciousness. (The companions and Ahlul Bayt of Imam Husain ﷺ were watching this sorrowful scene). Then they separated from each another and Qasim quickly mounted the horse and departed for the battlefield.

"I am the son of Hasan."

A narrator from Umar bin Saad's army narrates that all of a sudden he saw a child astride a horse coming towards them. He wore a turban instead of a helmet and sported normal shoes instead of the thonged ones worn during battles. "He looked like a piece of the moon" – that is he was extremely handsome. Then the narrator says: As Qasim came to the battlefield I saw that tears were flowing from his eyes.

In accordance with custom of Arabs, every soldier was supposed to introduce himself after coming to the battlefield. Everybody was amazed and no one knew who

---

[1] It is written in Karbala narratives: "The child kissed the hands and feet of the Imam until he was granted permission."

this child was. The child reached the battlefield and loudly announced,

"O people! If you don't me; I am the son of Hasan, the grandson of Prophet Mustafa. And this is Husain whom you surrounded and did not give even a sip of water from the flowing Euphrates."

Qasim's head in his Uncle's lap

When Qasim went towards the battlefield, Imam Husain ﷺ stood ready holding the reins of his horse. It looked as if he was waiting to fulfill one of his duties. I don't know what the state of Imam Husain ﷺ was. Imam Husain ﷺ waited. Perhaps he awaited the call of Qasim. Suddenly, Qasim called out, "O uncle! Help me!" The narrator says that he could not understand how quickly Imam Husain ﷺ mounted the horse and attacked the army. According to the narrator, Imam ﷺ went to battlefield like a swift hunter. The people present at the battlefield narrate that Qasim fell from his horse and approximately two hundred horses surrounded him. A person wanted to behead him. As soon as they saw Imam Husain ﷺ coming to the battlefield, they panicked and started running hither and thither. In this process, the person who had come forward to behead Qasim got crushed under the horses' hooves. The enemy soldiers were so terrified that they selfishly crushed one of their fellow soldiers alive in order to save themselves. There was a huge crowd. Horses galloped fast and nothing was visible due to the dust that arose. As Firdausi says,

"In the expanse of that desert, the hooves of horses divided the earth into six parts and the sky into eight."

No one knew what was happening. As soon as the dust settled, people saw Qasim's head in his uncle's lap.[1]

"...do not narrate this part of the sufferings of Qasim."

(I can never forget what a renowned orator of Qum, late Aqa Ishraqi used to narrate, "Once in the presence of Ayatullah Haeri in one of the Majalis I related the calamities exactly as mentioned in history and Karbala tragedy account without alteration of even a single word. Hearing this, the Ayatullah cried so much that he lost consciousness. Later on, he told me: If you find me among the audience do not relate that part of sufferings as I could not bear to hear it).

Now the condition of Qasim was such that he was thrashing his feet due to the severe pain in his last moments. At that time, people heard Imam Husain ﷺ saying, "By God! How unbearable it is for your uncle that you called him for help and but when he reached you he could not do anything for you."[2]

There is no power and might except by Allah the High and the Mighty.

---

[1] The speakers who say that the slender body of Qasim was crushed under hooves are requested to refer to the books of Karbala tragedy and the history of Karbala. (Rizwani)

[2] *Irshad,* Shaykh Mufid, Pg. 239; *Luhūf,* Pg. 114; *Biharul Anwār,* Vol. 45, Pg. 34; *Mausuat-e-Kalimat al-Imam al-Husain,* Pg. 464; *Muntahal Amaal,* Vol. 1, Pg. 680; *Maqtal-e-Husain,* Muqarram, Pg. 264

Majlis 30

Abdullah Ibne Hasan

O mourners!

Today I would like to narrate the sufferings of one of the sons of Imam Hasan ﷺ. Abdullah was the brother of Qasim. (Imam Hasan ﷺ was poisoned ten years before the incident of Karbala. It is narrated that this child was ten years old. Perhaps, this child was born after the martyrdom of Imam Hasan ﷺ. Anyhow, he did not remember his father. He grew up in the house of Imam Husain ﷺ who was his uncle and guardian).

Imam Husain ﷺ had handed over that child (whose name was Abdullah) to his aunt, Lady Zainab who was a special caretaker of children. Abdullah bin Hasan was one of those children who used to try again and again to go to the battlefield but were somehow stopped.

By God, I will not part from my Uncle

I don't know how this ten-year-old managed to come out of the tent and reached the place where Imam Husain ﷺ had fallen fighting. When this child came out of the tent, Lady Zainab ran to stop him, however he managed to free himself and ran away saying, "By God, I would not leave my uncle alone."

This child soon reached the place where Imam Husain lay, about to be martyred, and threw himself on his uncle. When Imam Husain held him in his arms the child started talking to him. At that moment an attacker came forward to attack the Imam. The child cursed him and said, "Have you come to shed my uncle's blood? By God, I would not allow you to do so." As soon as the enemy pulled his sword to behead Aba Abdillah al-Husain, the child covered him with his hands, which got cut off with the sword and just hung from the skin. Now the child started crying, "O uncle! See what this cursed one has done to me."[1]

وَسَيَعْلَمُ الَّذِينَ ظَلَمُوا أَيَّ مُنقَلَبٍ يَنقَلِبُونَ

And they who act unjustly shall know to what final place of turning they shall turn back.[2]

---

[1] *Irshad,* Shaykh Mufid, Pg. 241; *Biharul Anwār,* Vol. 45, Pg. 53; *Mausuat-e-Kalimat al-Imam al-Husain,* Pg. 507
[2] Surah Shuara 26:227

Majlis 31

'Enjoining good' and 'Forbidding evil' – principles of the Husainite Movement

From every aspect, the Jihad of Imam Husain ﷺ in Karbala is a mirror of the miracle, bravery, honesty and nicety of the self. Imam Husain ﷺ also cared about *Amr bil Maroof* and *Nahi Anil Munkar*. Thus the Imam said, "O people! Don't you see that truth is being neglected. Truth is not being followed and no one is stopped from falsehood. Instead falsehood is being made customary. Don't you see that good deeds have been neglected and the poison of wrong deeds is being assimilated into human blood? In such circumstances, an honest person should prefer death over such a life."[1] This should really happen. A believer should desire to meet Allah in such circumstances and shun this world. According to another source, Imam ﷺ said, "Really, I consider death a bounty in such circumstances and consider it a disgrace to remain alive and harassed by the enemy."[2]

Dear brothers!

Think, what kind of feeling a human being has who wants to live with unjust ones and oppressors? It is a life where he was seeing unjust and oppressors everywhere.

---

[1] *Tarikh Tabari,* Vol. 4, Pg. 305; *Biharul Anwār,* Vol. 44, Pg. 381
[2] *Biharul Anwār,* Vol. 44, Pg. 381

Imam Husain 🕮 says, "Should I live with them and become their companions? No, such life is not a life for me. It is a death. It is a cause of disgrace. I wish for death in such circumstances because it would be an honor for me."

The suckling infant separates from Imam Husain 🕮

Imam Husain 🕮 came inside the tent on Ashura day and told Lady Zainab, "O sister! Bring the suckling baby to me so that I bid him farewell."[1] Even though the child's mother was present in Karbala, Imam Husain 🕮 requested his sister so as to signal that Zainab was the leader of the caravan after him. Lady Zainab went inside and taking the child from her sister-in-law, brought it to her brother. Imam 🕮 looked at that delicate baby once; he was looking like a withered flower because he had not been suckled for the past few days. His mother's milk had dried up because of hunger and thirst.

Imam Husain 🕮 took the baby from his sister. When the Imam intended to kiss the baby and grant him fatherly love, the commander told one of his soldiers, "See, what a nice target you have got!" The soldier asked what target he was talking about. The commander pointed to the child in the arms of Imam Husain 🕮.

The baby was in the arms of the Imam and an arrow was shot from the enemy's side. The baby writhed like a slaughtered chicken and passed away but what to say of Husain's 🕮 patience?

---

[1] In some books of Karbala tragedy the words of Imam Husain to Lady Zainab are mentioned as: "Bring my baby so that I bid him farewell." *Luhūf,* Pg. 117; *Muntahal Amaal,* Vol. 1, Pg. 693

Can our mouths praise his patience?

He was praised by prophet and Ali.

(Ghalib)

His steadfastness did not waver. He took the blood of that innocent one in his cupped hand and looked at the sky and said, "O Lord! You are looking at this unjust bloodshed. This is for Your pleasure and hence it is not unbearable for Husain."[1][2]

---

[1] *Luhūf,* Pg. 117; *Mausuat-e-Kalimat al-Imam al-Husain,* Pg. 477
[2] *Biharul Anwār,* Vol. 44, Pg. 381

Majlis 32

Husainite emotions and feelings

My dear friends!

We love our children. So didn't Imam Husain ﷺ love his children? Surely, he loved them more than we love our children.

Prophet Ibrahim ﷺ did not love his son, Ismail less than we love our children. He loved his son very much. The reason is that he was a better person than us. Imam Husain ﷺ also loved his children more than us but he loved God above all the things and did not allow anyone to precede.

It is written that Imam Husain's ﷺ entire family had accompanied him on his journey to Karbala. It is a fact that if a person is traveling with his children he feels responsible and he remains worried about what would happen to them after him.

Recognition of Ali Akbar

It is narrated that Imam Husain ﷺ dozed off during the journey. After sometime he opened his eyes and recited *"Indeed we belong to Allah and to Him we shall return"*. Everybody started asking each other why Imam Husain ﷺ has recited this? They thought perhaps a new issue had arisen. Imam Husain ﷺ loved his son Ali Akbar very much and expressed his love for him often because he looked like the Prophet, Imam Husain's grandfather, (You can imagine what a father goes through when such a son is surrounded by dangers). His Eminence, Ali Akbar comes forward and asks, "O father! Why did you recite the verse of return?" Imam replied, "I heard the voice of the unseen caller in my dream saying: This caravan is being ushered by death. After hearing that voice, I understood that our destination is death. We are moving towards our certain destination of death."[1] Here, the conversation was similar to that between Prophet Ismail and Prophet Ibrahim.[2]

His Eminence, Ali Akbar asked Imam Husain ﷺ, "Are we on the right path?" Imam said, "O son! Why do you ask? The only thing is that we are going where our aim is taking us. Whether we are going towards death or life does not matter." His Eminence, Ali Akbar said, "That is

---

[1] *Irshad,* Shaykh Mufid, Pg. 226

[2] When Prophet Ibrahim had told Ismail that he was having a dream regularly and that he considered it a revelation of God. He said that he was ordered by Allah that he should slaughter Prophet Ismail (even though prophet Ibrahim was not aware of the philosophy of sacrifice, he was sure that it was the order of Allah and a divine will). What could a son say at that time? Did he tell his father that it was just a dream and if someone dreams of death then he gets longevity and that he too would get long life? No, the son said, *"O father! Perform whatever order you have been given. God willing, I would be one of the patient ones."* (Surah Saffat 37:102) When Prophet Ibrahim slaughtered prophet Ismail, he got the revelation, *"...when both of them accepted and father made son lie with his forehead on ground, We said: O Ibrahim! You made your dream come true."* i.e. O Ibrahim! We did not want you to behead your son. It was not at all Our purpose because there was no use in it. The real purpose was to see how obedient you, father and son are to Allah. The real aim was to test your willingness in obeying Allah. You have proved your obedience. Father was ready to sacrifice and the son was ready to get sacrificed and We don't want anything more than that. Hence, do not behead your son.

right but are we on the right path or not?" Imam Husain ﷺ became glad on hearing this. His face lit up with joy. It could be noted from the supplication that he recited at this moment. Imam said, "O son! I do not have anything to reward a responsible son like you at this moment. However, I pray that may God reward you on my behalf whatever you deserve."[1]

Martyrdom of Ali Akbar

O mourners!

Imagine the scene when Ali Akbar returned from the battlefield on Ashura afternoon after facing the enemies bravely. His mouth had dried up so much that he could not fight any more. When this lion-hearted son of Husain came to him, he said, "O father! I am dying of thirst. The weight of armor is causing uneasiness. Can I get some water please?"[2] (As if he meant to say that if he got a little water he would push the enemies far behind).

The reply of Imam Husain ﷺ to his beloved son was, "My dear! I am sure that sooner you attain the rank of martyrdom, sooner you will be satiated by the water-provider of Kauthar."

---

[1] It is mentioned in *Irshad,* Shaykh Mufid, Pg. 226 as follows: "May God give you the best reward a son can get for (his behavior towards) his father."

[2] *Luhūf,* Pg. 113; *Mausuat-e-Kalimat al-Imam al-Husain,* Pg. 461

Majlis 33

Farewell of the Hashimite Youths

Compliers of Karbala tragedy account write that on the Ashura day the enthusiasm of the companions of Husain was obvious. As long as the helpers of Imam Husain 🕮 were alive, they did not allow anyone from the family of the Holy Prophet 🕮 to go to the battlefield. The companions used to say, "Master! Please allow us first so that we fulfill our duty. After we are martyred, it is upto you to decide what to do."

The Ahlul Bayt of the Holy Prophet 🕮 were awaiting their turns. No sooner did the last companion of Imam Husain 🕮 got martyred than a wave of enthusiasm ran among the Hashimite youths. All of them stood in their places. It is recorded that they started bidding farewell to each other.[1] They embraced and kissed each other.

Ali Akbar, the look-alike of the Holy Prophet 🕮

His Eminence, Ali Akbar, the young son of Imam Husain 🕮 was the first to receive permission to go to the battlefield. He was that youth about whom Imam Husain 🕮 had testified that he was an exact copy of the Holy Prophet 🕮 as regards looks, character, speech and

---

[1] *Maqtal-e-Husain,* Muqarram, Pg. 255; *Nafasul Mahmoom,* Pg. 312; *Biharul Anwār,* Vol. 45, Pg. 32

manners. He resembled the Prophet most. When Ali Akbar talked, it appeared as if the Holy Prophet was talking. He looked like the Holy Prophet ﷺ so much that Imam Husain ؑ used to say, "O God! You know that whenever I desire to have a look at my holy grandfather, I look at this young man."

Ali Akbar's departure for the battle

Ali Akbar came to his holy father and said, "O father! Please permit me to go for Jihad." It is recorded about a number of companions especially, the youths, that when they used to come for permission, Imam used to delay by making some excuse as you might have heard in the case of Qasim. However, when Ali Akbar sought permission, Imam bowed his head and the adolescent son left for the battlefield.

It is recorded that Imam Husain ؑ gave a look at that youth with his half-open eyes then looked at him sorrowfully.[1]

Then Ali Akbar moved his horse towards the battlefield and Imam Husain ؑ followed him a few steps and said, "O God! Please bear witness that the youth who is going towards those oppressors, is a facsimile of Your Prophet."

Curse of Imam Husain ؑ

Then Imam said something to Umar bin Saad in such a loud voice that even he could bear it, "O Ibne Saad! May

[1] *Luhūf,* Pg. 113; *Mausuat-e-Kalimat al-Imam al-Husain,* Pg. 460

Allah cut off your generations because you have cut off my generation by martyring this son."[1]

Just two or three years after this curse, Mukhtar killed Umar bin Saad. When Umar bin Saad's son came to Mukhtar to bail out his father, Umar bin Saad's head was brought to Mukhtar in the court covered by a cloth. The son who had come to save his father was asked, "Do you know this person?" He came forward and removed the cloth only to see that it was his father's head. Seeing this, he tried to escape but Mukhtar ordered: "Send him also to his father."[2]

Thirst of Ali Akbar

Historians are unanimous that His Eminence, Ali Akbar fought bravely and then returned to his father. It is a historical puzzle what his aim was and why Ali Akbar had returned to his father?

He came back and said, "O father! I am dying of thirst. If I get a little water I would get a new life and I would be able to go and fight." These words moved his father. The Imam said, "Yes, O son! See that my mouth is drier than yours but I promise you that very soon my grandfather, the Holy Prophet ﷺ will satisfy you (with the drink of Kauthar)." Hearing this, Ali Akbar went to the battlefield again for Jihad.

Hamid bin Muslim who is called a narrator in terminology was present in Karbala as a reporter. He did not participate in the battle but he has narrated a number of incidents. He says that a person was standing near him.

---

[1] *Luhūf,* Pg. 113; *Mausuat-e-Kalimat al-Imam al-Husain,* Pg. 460
[2] *Damaus Sujum,* Pg. 365

Whenever His Eminence, Ali Akbar used to attack, people ran away from him. Seeing this, that person got angry because he was a brave man. He told the reporter, "By God! If he passes by me I would surely injure the heart of his father gravely." Hamid asked him, "What enmity have you got with this youth? After all, those people are going to martyr him." He said, "No" As soon as His Eminence, Ali Akbar passed by his side, the man attacked him with a spear so hard that he could not control himself and hung himself onto the neck of the horse and shouted for help, "O father! Grandfather, the Messenger of Allah ﷺ has come to take me along."[1]

Writers of Karbala tragedy have mentioned a strange statement at this point:

"The horse took him through the army of the enemies and they hit him with the swords cutting his delicate body into pieces."[2]

وَسَيَعْلَمُ الَّذِينَ ظَلَمُوا أَيَّ مُنقَلَبٍ يَنقَلِبُونَ

And they who act unjustly shall know to what final place of turning they shall turn back.[3]

---

[1] *Biharul Anwār,* Vol. 45, Pg. 44; *Mausuat-e-Kalimat al-Imam al-Husain,* Pg. 462; *Maqtal-e-Husain,* Muqarram, Pg. 259
[2] *Biharul Anwār,* Vol. 45, Pg. 44; *Mausuat-e-Kalimat al-Imam al-Husain,* Pg. 462; *Maqtal-e-Husain,* Muqarram, Pg. 259
[3] Surah Shuara 26:227

Majlis 34

Emotions of the perfect human beings

The Holy Prophet ﷺ was a perfect human being and Imam Ali ؑ was also a perfect human being. Imam Husain ؑ was also a perfect human being and Lady Zahra was also a perfect human being. It means that all of them had human qualities. And that too with the point of perfection that is even more than the angels. In other words, they also felt hunger like other human beings and ate food. They also felt thirsty and drank water. They felt sleepy and took rest. They also loved their children. They also had sexual feelings. And that is the reason why they could become the leaders. If it had not been so they could not have become leaders.

If Imam Husain ؑ did not have human feelings and not suffered as a father suffers due to calamities on his son when he was cut into pieces it would not have made a difference between watching a son being cut into pieces or a stone being divided into pieces. This stone-heartedness is nothing great. If I had been such a man even I could have done it.

But the fact is that the emotional and human aspect found in the Imam is much stronger in relation to us. And the Imam is higher than even the angels from the aspect of human perfection. It was on this basis that Husain was made the Imam because he had all human characteristics (to the level of perfection). When his teenaged son came for permission to go to the battlefield, his heart was also hurt badly because the Imam loved his son many times more than we love our sons. It is a different case that when it comes to seeking the pleasure of Allah, the Imam suppresses all his emotions and feelings.

Ali Akbar's Charisma

Ali Akbar came to Imam Husain 🕮 and said, "O father! Please permit me." Imam Husain 🕮 said, "Go, son go."[1] Here, historians have presented some excellent points. They write that Imam Husain 🕮 looked at his son with a look of despair and sorrow. Like a person who has lost hope of the life of the other person.

The psychological and internal effects on a human being are natural facts. If a person hears good news, his face lits up and eyes open wide. However, if a person is sitting near his dear one and is sure that the latter would pass away soon, whenever he glances at the dying person his eyes are only half-open. His eyes appear to be sleepy because his heart does not want him to see the loved one pass away. On the other hand, if a son has achieved an honor or is getting married, the father looks at him with eyes wide open. It is said that when the Imam looked at His Eminence, Ali Akbar, his eyelids were drooping. When Ali Akbar set out, it was the magnetism of the youthful son that impelled Imam Husain 🕮 to follow behind. (As if saying, "Son! It is not you who is going. It is the life of the father that's going.")

---

[1] *Luhūf,* Pg. 113; *Mausuat-e-Kalimat al-Imam al-Husain,* Pg. 260

A lot of different things are said about the soul leaving the body but I have seen with my own eyes my life being taken away from my body.

As Ali Akbar moved ahead Imam Husain ﷺ followed behind for quite a distance. Then he called aloud:

"O Umar bin Saad! May Allah cut off your progeny as you have cut off mine."[1]

---

[1] *Luhūf,* Pg. 113; *Mausuat-e-Kalimat al-Imam al-Husain,* Pg. 260

Majlis 35

The Moon of Bani Hashim – Embodiment of Sacrifice

There could be no better example for sacrifice than the moon of Bani Hashim, His Eminence, Abbas. I present to you an example of sacrifice from early Islam when there were not one but many heroes. A person narrates: "I was passing by injured ones in one of the battles. I saw an injured person lying on the ground taking his final breaths. I knew that excessive blood loss makes a person feel very thirsty. Hence when that injured one looked at me and said something, I immediately thought that he was asking for water. I fetched a glass of water for him but he pointed out that his brother was lying in the same state and asked me to give that water to him first. When I went to that person he pointed to another thirsty person to me and told me to give the water to him first. I went near that person (some narrators have recorded the number of injured ones as three and others have recorded as ten). Before I could reach the last injured, he breathed his last. Then I turned towards the second-last only to find that he too had passed away. Similarly, when I reached the first, he was already dead." Thus, the narrator could not provide water to any of them because whenever he took water to an injured person, he used to ask him to go to the next one. This is called sacrifice, which is the best expression of man's spiritual love.

Have you ever wondered why Surah Hal Ata was revealed? It has the verse:

وَيُطْعِمُونَ الطَّعَامَ عَلَى حُبِّهِ مِسْكِينًا وَيَتِيمًا وَأَسِيرًا O إِنَّمَا نُطْعِمُكُمْ لِوَجْهِ اللّهِ لَا نُرِيدُ مِنكُمْ جَزَاء وَلَا شُكُورًاO

And they give food out of love for Him to the poor and the orphan and the captive: We only feed you for Allah's sake; we desire from you neither reward nor thanks:[1]

(In fact this Surah was revealed to teach the importance of sacrifice).

It has been the duty of the Karbala tragedy to decorate and present human and Islamic spirit of sacrifice. It seems that the responsibility of making this feeling perfect was given to His Eminence, Abbas.

O dear ones!

Abbas attacked fiercely and drove away four thousand soldiers guarding the Euphrates. Now the Euphrates was under Abbas's possession. Abbas went so deep in the river that water reached to the horse's belly and he filled the water-bag without dismounting. After filling the water-bag, he took some water in his cupped hand and brought it near his mouth...The enemy watched from a distance. They say that they saw him taking the water in his cupped hand and then throwing it away; but nobody knows why His Eminence, Abbas did so. It is narrated that he must

---

[1] Surah Insan 76:8-9

177

have remembered that Husain was thirsty.[1] He might have thought that Husain would say: O Abbas! It is not fair than Husain remains thirsty at the camp and you drink water. But when was this thought of Abbas recorded? It came to be known from the couplets recited by His Eminence, Abul Fazl al-Abbas[2] when he came out of the river. He recited a war poem, because of which people came to know why he did not drink that water:

Abbas addressed himself saying, "O self of Abbas! What remains in life after Husain?" Do you want to drink water and stay alive? Do you want to drink cool water and let master Husain remain thirsty at the camp? By God, it is not the manner of a slave. It is not customary from a brother. It is not the custom of the followers of the Imam. It is not the style of loyalty. Indeed, His Eminence, Abbas was an embodiment of loyalty.

There is no power and might except by Allah the High and the Mighty.

---

[1] *Biharul Anwār,* Vol. 45, Pg. 41; *Mausuat-e-Kalimat al-Imam al-Husain,* Pg. 472; *Muntahal Amaal,* Vol. 1, Pg. 688 has the words: Then he remembered the thirst of Husain and his Ahle Bayt.
[2] *Yanabiul Mawaddah,* Vol. 2, Pg. 408; *Biharul Anwār,* Vol. 45, Pg. 41; *Maqtal-e-Husain,* Muqarram, Pg. 268

Majlis 36

Loyalty of Abbas

When Shimr bin Dhiljaushan was departing from Kufa for Karbala, a person in Ibne Ziyad's court said, "Some of my maternal relatives have accompanied Husain bin Ali. Hence I want you to write a letter of pardon for them. Eventually, Ibne Ziyad wrote a letter regarding them.

Shimr's tribe also had a distant relation with the tribe of Ummul Banin. So he also obtained a letter of pardon from Ibne Ziyad and reached Karbala with this letter on the ninth of Muharram in the late afternoon (Asr).

When his filthy one reached near Imam Husain's camp he shouted, "Where are the sons of my sister?"[1] His Eminence, Abbas was sitting near Imam Husain ﷺ along with his brothers. None of them replied. Then Imam Husain ﷺ said, "Give him a reply even if though he may be a transgressor."

When Imam Husain ﷺ gave permission, all of them replied, "What are you trying to say?" He said, "I have brought good news for you. I have brought a letter of pardon for you from the Governor, Ubaidullah Ibne Ziyad. You are free. If you go away now, your lives will be saved."

---

[1] *Luhūf,* Pg. 88; *Biharul Anwār,* Vol. 44, Pg. 391; *Mausuat-e-Kalimat al-Imam al-Husain,* Pg. 389

All of them replied in unison, "May Allah curse you, your Amir and the letter of pardon that you have brought. Shall we leave our Imam and brother only for the sake of saving our lives?"

Bravery of His Eminence, Abbas

The first to announce support to Imam Husain ؏ on the Ashura eve was his brother, His Eminence, Abbas. Even if all exaggerations mentioned about him are ignored, it is well-known in history that His Eminence, Abbas had an excellent character; he was brave, tall and a handsome youth. He had earned the nom-de-plume of 'moon of Bani Hashim'. Now this is such a fact that there is no doubt in it, and there is no exaggeration also. Without any doubt, he was the inheritor of Ali's valor.[1]

It is also a fact that Imam Ali ؏ had told his brother Aqeel, "Find a wife for me who is from the progeny of brave men"[2] and Aqeel had selected Ummul Banin. She proved exactly as desired by Imam Ali ؏. Imam wished that a brave son would be born to her.[3] Everything narrated till here is fact and the wish of Imam Ali ؏ was fulfilled in the form of His Eminence, Abbas.

Moon of Bani Hashim and Equality

According to one or two narrations, His Eminence, Abbas came to Imam Husain ؏ on Ashura day and requested, "Brother dear! Please allow me to go for Jihad. My chest is becoming straitened. I am suffocating. I can

---

[1] *Muntahal Amaal,* Vol. 1, Pg. 687; *Al-Abbas,* Muqarram, Pg. 81; *Damaus Sujum,* Pg. 176
[2] *Absarul Ain,* Pg. 126; *Damaus Sujum,* Pg. 176
[3] *Absarul Ain,* Pg. 26

control no more. I want to sacrifice myself on you as soon as possible." Who knows what was the exigency of Imam Husain ﷺ saying, "Brother! Go if you want, but make some arrangement of water for the children." Imam ﷺ knows the reason better. His Eminence, Abbas had already received the title of 'the water-carrier of the holy household' (Saqqa-e-Haram) because he had brought water for the children during the previous nights tearing through the enemy ranks. [That is why he is also called 'Ghaazi' (victorious)]

From the 7th of Mohurrum, the enemy had cut off water supply to the progeny of the Prophet whose *Kalima* they recited. Anyway, in reply to Imam Husain ﷺ His Eminence, Abbas said: Your command is welcome.

Now see how amazing is the scene. What bravery it is! What valor! What humanity! What a great honor! How great is divine recognition and sacrifice!

The lion of the lion of God attacked a huge army single-handed and drove away four thousand soldiers guarding the river. (After driving them away) he entered the water. (It is also mentioned in books that) first he filled his water-bag and hung it on his shoulder while he is mounted on the horse. The water surface is touching the horse's belly. He is thirsty. It is extremely hot. He has come after fighting a battle. Once he fills a cupped hand with water and takes it to his lips. The enemy saw from far away that after sometime he threw the water back into the Euphrates and came out of the stream thirsty. No one understood why he did not drink the water. However, when he came out of the river and recited the following war poem, people came to know why he had not drunk the water:

"O self of Abbas! I do not want you to remain alive after Husain has passed away. Husain is preparing to drink the cup of death in thirst and you want to drink cool water? What kind of manliness is it? What kind of love and affection is it? Isn't Husain your Imam? Aren't you the follower of Husain? Aren't you the obedient one of Husain? By Allah, neither my religion permits me this nor my loyalty can bear to see that Husain remains thirsty and I drink water."[1]

Abbas, the guardian of Imam Husain's ﷺ camp

When Abbas returned from the river, he changed his route. He had come straight but now he was going through the oases because he was carrying a precious thing with him. He was trying his best to take the water to the camp anyhow and would not risk an arrow that may pierce the water-bag and let all the water get wasted. Abbas was moving forward with extreme care but suddenly something happened and he cried out aloud:

"By Allah, Even if you have cut off my right hand, I would continue to help my religion and the true Imam who is the grandson of the pure and trustworthy prophet."[2]

After some moments, his war poem changed to the following lines:

[1] *Yanabiul Mawaddah,* Vol. 2, Pg. 408
[2] *Biharul Anwār,* Vol. 45, Pg. 40; *Muntahal Amaal,* Vol. 1, Pg. 688; *Maqtal-e-Husain,* Muqarram, Pg. 169

"O self! Do not fear the infidels. Be happy for there is mercy of the Omnipotent God and neighborhood of the Rightful Prophet for you. What is there to worry even if enemies have cut off my left hand also because of their cowardice?"[1]

In this war poem, His Eminence, Abbas stated that his left hand was also cut off. It is written that the water-carrier tried in every way to save the water-bag. He turned it around very skillfully to the front and bent upon it to save it from getting pierced. My tongue does not have the power to narrate this painful incident. This scene is very moving and makes one cry tears of blood.

Normally, sufferings of His Eminence, Abbas are narrated on the eve of the Ninth.

Nauha of Ummul Banin in Baqi

Let me also mention that His Eminence, Abbas' mother, Lady Ummul Banin was alive at the time of Karbala tragedy. However, she was in Medina. When she got the news that all of her four sons were martyred in Karbala, she used to go to Jannatul Baqi and cry. It is narrated that her cries were so remorseful that whoever passed by her used to cry out. Even Marwan bin Hakam, the stone-hearted enemy of Ahlul Bayt used to have tears in his eyes. Sometimes Lady Ummul Banin used to remember all her sons and weep and sometimes she remembered her eldest son and cried.

His Eminence, Abbas was the eldest in age and superior to his brothers in spiritual and physical perfections. I would recite for you one of the two elegies of

---

[1] *Biharul Anwār,* Vol. 45, Pg. 40; *Muntahal Amaal,* Vol. 1, Pg. 688

this lady, which I can recollect. This was recited by the aggrieved mother (Normally, Arabs recite very remorseful elegies):

"O looking eye that was watching the events of Karbala! Narrate to me the scene when my brave Abbas and before him, his (three) lion-hearted sons had attacked the coward army. Is it true that after the hands of my son were cut off, an oppressor hit him on his head with an iron mace?"

"Oh! My brave lion, Abbas, was hit with a mace on his head."

"O my Abbas! O my dearest one! I know that if your hands were all right the cowardly enemy would not have remained in front of you. The impure enemy dared to do this only because your hands were cut off."[1]

In the name of Allah and by Allah and on the religion of the Messenger of Allah ﷺ

---

[1] *Muntahal Amaal*, Vol. 1, Pg. 689

Majlis 37

Misdeeds of the tyrant Yazid

Today is eve of the Ninth. Hence I would narrate the sufferings of that soldier of the right path who is the greatest in fulfilling the duties of enjoining good and forbidding evil. I intend to speak about His Eminence, Abbas, whom the Imam has expressed exceeding pleasure.

When the incident of Karbala occurred, there were no means of communication like we have today. The news of Syria used to reach Kufa and Medina after a long time. At times, people would not even get the news of an incident. The best proof of this fact is this incident of Karbala. Imam Husain ﷺ denied paying allegiance to Yazid and went to Mecca from Medina. After that, a number of incidents occurred and the Imam gets martyred. When the people of Medina got this news, they woke up from a deep slumber, rubbed their eyes and asked, "Is the Imam really martyred? Why was he martyred? They decided to go to Syria to know the exact cause. Seven or eight people went to Syria for this purpose. After making enquiries for some time, they met the caliph and returned after seeing all the conditions. When the people of Medina asked about the real matter, they said, "Please don't ask that. As long as we remained in Syria, we feared that stones will rain from the sky and we would be destroyed.[1] (People are denying the truthfulness of this statement of Imam Husain ﷺ: "I say

---

[1] *Biharul Anwār,* Vol. 44, Pg. 326; *Mausuat-e-Kalimat al-Imam al-Husain,* Pg. 285

farewell to this Islam from a distance, in which an impure ruler, Yazid is inflicting severe atrocities on the people.") When asked further, they said, "We are coming back after meeting a man who openly drinks wine, plays with dogs, keeps monkeys as pets and commits all sins. (Abdullah, son of Hanzala Ghasilul Malaika, used to say that Yazid did not even leave his mother). He fornicated even with his *Mahram* women.[1] That is those people became certain that the prediction of Imam Husain ﷺ was absolutely right because Imam Husain ﷺ was aware of these things since before.

Bani Umayyah Kingdom is shaken

On Ashura day, Imam Husain ﷺ had said, "I know that these people would kill me but they would also be destroyed very soon after my martyrdom. Not only the progeny of Sufyan but the entire Bani Umayyah would be vanquished" and it happened in this way only. Later on, Bani Abbas seized the kingdom from Bani Umayyah and ruled for the next five hundred years. Hence, it can be said that the kingdom of Bani Umayyah was shaken up completely after the incident of Karbala.

Effect of the Husainite movement pervades the enemy's house

What can be a greater impact of the incident of Karbala than the fact that it created differences amongst Bani Umayyah and granted spiritual and moral strength to the incident? Let us take the example of Ibne Ziyad who was famous for his stone-heartedness. His brother Uthman bin Ziyad told him:

---

[1] *Tarikh Khulafa,* Suyuti, Pg. 205

"I wish that entire progeny of Ziyad gets involved in poverty, disgrace and misfortune but does not get defamed because of this crime."[1]

Ibne Ziyad's mother, Marjana was an unchaste woman. However, when her son committed this crime, she said:

"O son! What have you done? Remember, you would not be able to even smell the fragrance of Paradise."[2]

Marwan bin Hakam, the evil-minded one forever, had a brother named Yahya bin Hakam. It is narrated that he got up from his place in the court of Yazid and condemned Yazid saying, "Wow Yazid! The progeny of Sumayya (children of Ziyad's mother) and daughters of Sumayya are worthy of honor in your view, but you are treating the progeny of the Holy Prophet ﷺ in this manner and making them stand like this in the court full of spectators?"[3] Yes, the voice of Husain was being raised from their own houses.

My dear audience!

You might have heard the incident of Yazid's wife, Hinda. She came out of her house and went to the court and condemned Yazid so much that he denied having killed Husain and confessed that he was not pleased with this incident and that this act was committed by Ubaidullah Ibne Ziyad.[4]

---

[1] *Damaus Sujum,* Pg. 230
[2] Ibid. Pg. 372
[3] *Maqtal-e-Husain,* Muqarram, Pg. 354
[4] *Maqtal-e-Husain,* Muqarram, Pg. 355

Yazid's son dissociates from him

Imam Husain's ﷺ last prediction was that Yazid would die soon. Eventually, Yazid ruled for the next two or three years somehow and departed for hell at last. His son, Muawiyah bin Yazid was his heir-apparent. And Muawiyah bin Abi Sufyan had tried all means for these circumstances. He mounted the pulpit forty days after the death of Yazid and said:

"O people! My grandfather Muawiyah fought with Ali bin Abi Talib ﷺ even though he was not on the right path. Instead Ali was on the right path. Then my father, Yazid fought with Husain bin Ali even though my father was not on the right path and Husain was on the right path. Hence I condemn my father and I want to inform you that I consider myself worthy of this caliphate. I don't want to get involved in sins like my father and grandfather. Thus I leave the post of caliph."[1] Saying this, he came down from the pulpit.

Thus, it can be said that this was the result of strength of blood of Husain and the power of truth which influenced the friends as well as the enemies.

Martyrs envy the rank of Abbas

Imam Ja'far Sadiq said, "May Allah have mercy on my uncle, Abbas. He faced the calamities with a smiling countenance. My uncle, Abbas has such a rank near Allah, that it is envied by all the martyrs."[2] By Allah! Such a level

---

[1] *Hayatul Haiwan al-Kubra,* Vol. 1, Pg. 16
[2] *Safinatul Bihar* Vol. 2, Pg. 155 and *Al-Abbas,* Muqarram, Pg. 69. (This tradition is narrated from Imam Zainul Abideen and not from Imam Ja'far Sadiq) (*Nafasul Mahmoom,* Pg. 204)

of bravery, such a pure intention and loyalty! We look at them as embodiment of deeds. We have never examined the spirit of His Eminence, Abbas that we can estimate its importance.

Letter of pardon for the sons of Ummul Banin

His Eminence, Abbas was sitting with Imam Husain ﷺ in a tent on Ashura eve. Suddenly, a commander from the enemy's side calls out, "Send Abbas bin Ali and his brothers to me." His Eminence, Abbas heard this voice but ignored it and continued to sit with the Imam respectfully. Seeing this, the Imam said, "You should reply even though he is a transgressor."

His Eminence, Abbas came out of the tent to see Shimr bin Dhiljaushan standing there. He was a distant relative of His Eminence, Abbas' mother and was related to her tribe.

It is narrated that before departing from Kufa, he had taken a letter of pardon for His Eminence, Abbas and his brothers. He thought that he has done an excellent job for the benefit of his kinsmen. When he told His Eminence, Abbas about the letter of pardon, His Eminence, Abbas snapped at him saying:

"May Allah curse you and one who gave this letter of pardon to you! What do you think I am? What do you think about me? Do you think I would leave my Imam and brother, Husain bin Ali, alone, in order to save my life and come with you? The mother who suckled and brought us up has not trained us like this."[1]

Heart-rending elegies of Ummul Banin

Imam Ali ؏ had four sons from Lady Ummul Banin. Historians have mentioned that Imam Ali ؏ specially requested his brother, Aqeel to find a wife for him[2] who would be from the progeny of the brave having inherited valor "so that I may have a brave son from her."[3]

Even though it is not found in history that Imam Ali ؏ explained his objective, people who have knowledge of Imam Ali's ؏ predictions and believe them, say that Imam Ali ؏ knew about this from the beginning. Aqeel chose Ummul Banin and told Ali ؏, "This is the woman as desired by you." Four children were born to her, among whom His Eminence, Abul Fazl al-Abbas was the eldest. All four were martyred on the side of Imam Husain ؏ in Karbala. When Bani Hashim's turn arrived, His Eminence, Abbas told his brothers, "O brothers! I want you all to go to the battlefield before me because I want to suffer the wound of the martyrdom of brothers." They replied, "We shall do as you order." Thus, all three brothers went to the battlefield and were martyred.[4] After that, His Eminence, Abul Fazl al-Abbas set out.

When Ummul Banin got the news that all her four sons were martyred in Karbala with Imam Husain ؏, she began to mourn for them. She used to go to Jannatul Baqi

---

[1] *Luhūf,* Pg. **88**; *Biharul Anwār,* Vol. 44, Pg. 391; *Mausuat-e-Kalimat al-Imam al-Husain,* Pg. 389

[2] *Absarul Ain,* Pg. 62; *Damaus Sujum,* Pg. 176

[3] *Absarul Ain,* Pg. 62

[4] The names of His Eminence, Abbas's brothers were Uthman, Ja'far and Abdullah. *Malimul Madrasatain,* Vol. 3, Pg. 160

or sit on the road to Iraq and remember and mourn her sons. Other women gathered around her seeing her wail so mournfully.

Marwan bin Hakam, governor of Medina and the bitterest enemy of Ahlul Bayt also used to cry hearing the elegy of lady whenever he passed by the Baqi Cemetery. One of her elegies is as follows:

"O ladies! Do not call me Ummul Banin now. A mother of sons is called Ummul Banin, mother of brave sons. When you address me by this name, I remember my brave sons and my heart shatters. Yes, I was indeed called Ummul Banin once, but now I no more remain the 'mother of sons'.[1]

In a special elegy for His Eminence, Abbas, she says:

"O looking eye that was watching the events of Karbala! Narrate to me the scene when my brave Abbas and before him, his (three) lion-hearted sons had attacked the coward army. Is it true that after the hands of my son were cut off, an oppressor hit him on his head with an iron mace?"

"Oh! My brave lion Abbas was hit with a mace on his head."

"O my Abbas! O my dearest one! I know that if your hands were all right the cowardly enemy would not have remained in front of you. The impure enemy dared to do this only because your hands were cut off."

---

[1] *Muntahal Amaal*, Vol. 1, Pg. 689

In the name of Allah and by Allah and on the religion of the Messenger of Allah ﷺ

Majlis 38

Ashura, the day of martyrs

Why have we gathered here today? What night is it? Today is the night of martyrs. In our present world it is customary to commemorate certain days every year to express devotion and respect. For instance, we celebrate the Mother's Day, Teacher's Day and Labor's Day. However, we have not seen any community commemorating the Martyr's Day. Although the Muslim community commemorates the Ashura day as the Martyr's Day. In this way, tonight is the night of the martyrs.

Logic of Martyrdom

I mentioned in one of my speeches that the logic of a martyr is based on "love of God" on one hand and guidance of society on the other. If the personalities of the reformer and a Gnostic are gathered in one person that person will be called a 'martyr'. One of them might be Muslim bin Awsaja, one Habib bin Mazahir, one of them Zuhair bin Qayn...because the rank of all martyrs is not same and there are different levels in it.

Ashura Eve

Imam Husain ﷺ had testified for the "martyrs of Ashura" the previous night, which displays the rank of those martyrs. Martyrs are seen shining brightly among all virtuous and honored ones while the companions of Husain are seen dazzling among all martyrs.

Do you know what Imam Husain ﷺ said? What did he say about his companions? Those who were not worthy of martyrdom left Imam Husain ﷺ during the journey of Karbala and those who were worthy of that honor held onto the Imam till the end. However, Imam ﷺ tested them for the last time. This time, not one of them parted from the master.

Empty water-bags

What did the Imam do on Ashura eve? Those who have written "He gathered his companions *near the tent of water,*" say that there was one such tent in the camp of Imam Husain ﷺ, which had empty water-bags.[1] Water-bags were kept inside that tent from first the day itself and it was called the tent of water. The Imam gathered his companions and helpers in that tent on Ashura eve. However, I don't know why he did so. Perhaps, he gathered them because there were no filled water-skins in that tent that night.

Even if we consider another version that: "He gathered his companions *as the night fell,*" then too it is consistent with the previous version.[2]

---

[1] *Muntahal Amaal,* Vol. 1, Pg. 625; *Mausuat-e-Kalimat al-Imam al-Husain,* Pg. 395

[2] Some words of Ustad Mutahhari are not included here to avoid repetition because the philosophy of martyrdom of Ustad Shaheed is already published by Jame Talimaat-e-Islami, Pakistan.

Imam Husain's ﷺ address on Ashura eve

Imam Husain ﷺ gathered his loyal companions in one tent and delivered an eloquent sermon. Actually, this sermon was a reaction of the events, which occurred at Asr time on the Ninth.

The time extended by the enemy was going to expire at sunrise on the next Ashura day. Hence the Imam gathered his companions to inform them about the circumstances and test them for the last time. Imam Zainul Abideen ﷺ narrates that Imam Husain ﷺ had gathered his companions in a tent, which was near to his tent. His father glorified Allah and said, "I glorify Allah and thank him during good and bad times. O Allah! I thank you that you gave prophethood to us, taught us the Holy Quran and made us understand the religion."[1]

One who treads the path of truth and reality, in whatever circumstances and condition he might be, all is well for him. The man of truth recognizes well his responsibilities in all circumstances and whatever comes in his way is not bad.

Imam Husain's ﷺ reply to Farazdaq

When Imam Husain ﷺ was heading to Karbala he had uttered a sentence in reply to the renowned poet, Farazdaq, which is worthy of attention. When Farazdaq told the Imam about unsound circumstances of Iraq, the Imam said:

---

[1] *Muntahal Amaal,* Vol. 1, Pg. 625; *Mausuat-e-Kalimat al-Imam al-Husain,* Pg. 395

"If circumstances turn in our favor we would be thankful to Allah for that bounty and seek His help in thanksgiving and if the circumstances are against us; then too we are not at loss because we have good intentions and a clean conscience. Our aim is nothing except rightfulness resulting from piety. Thus, whatever comes in this way is good and not a mischief. We thank Allah in all circumstances, good or bad."[1]

"I was his thanks-giver during the days of comfort as well as the days of suffering." Thus, the Imam wanted to say, "I have seen the days of happiness and peace in my life like those days when I used to sit in the Prophet's lap or mount his shoulders. I have been through those times when I was one of the most loved children in the world of Islam. I thanked Allah for those days as well as for this day when I am surrounded by calamities. I do not consider these circumstances bad for me. Instead I consider them good. O Lord! We thank You for granting the honor of prophethood to our family and that You richened us with the knowledge of Quran. Only we have complete recognition of Holy Quran. O Lord! We thank You for granting us recognition and understanding of religion and for making us reach its depths so that we could understand its soul and inner being, which is the actual reality.

Testimony of Imam Husain ؏ regarding the companions and Ahlul Bayt

Do you know what the Imam said after that? After that, Imam Husain ؏ testified for his companions and

---

[1] *Mausuat-e-Kalimat al-Imam al-Husain,* Pg. 336

Ahlul Bayt and said, "Certainly, I have not seen companions more loyal and better than mine."[1]

In this statement the Imam wanted to say, "O my companions! You are more excellent than the companions of my grandfather, the Holy Prophet ﷺ who got martyred. You are better than the companions of my father, Ali al-Murtada and better than the companions who got martyred in Jamal, Siffeen and Nahrawan, because the circumstances you faced are completely different from those faced by them."

Then the Imam ؑ testified in favor of his Ahlul Bayt and said: "I have also not seen Ahlul Bayt better and more particular in fulfilling the rights of blood relation, than my Ahlul Bayt. The rank and status that my Ahlul Bayt has is not possessed by the Ahlul Bayt of any other person." Thus the Imam certified the status of his loyal companions and Ahlul Bayt and also paid thanks to them at the same time.

Whoever wishes to go is free

After that, the Imam glanced at the gathering and said: "O people! I want to inform all of you that the enemy does not want anyone except me. They want only Husain to pay allegiance to them and I would never do so. They consider only me as a barrier in their way. If they get me, they would not harm you. Hence, I take away allegiance from your necks. Now you are neither under pressure from the enemy nor from my side. You are free. You may happily go wherever you want."

---

[1] *Irshad,* Shaykh Mufid, Pg. 231; *Luhūf,* Pg. 90; *Mausuat-e-Kalimat al-Imam al-Husain,* Pg. 395

After that, the Imam insisted to his companions that each one of them should hold the hand of a child from his family and get out of this trouble.

This is a moment where the rank and honor of the companions of Imam Husain ﷺ can be understood. They were not pressurized by the enemy at that time due to which we could have said that they were already trapped in the clutches of the enemy. And Imam Husain ﷺ also released them from the allegiance he had taken from them.

Imam Husain's ﷺ happiness doubled

Imam Husain's ﷺ happiness had doubled on Ashura eve and Ashura day. The first cause of Imam's happiness was that all companions including the young children as well as the elderly had surrounded him. Secondly, Imam ﷺ did not notice even an iota of weakness in his companions. There was no one among the companions of Imam Husain ﷺ on Ashura day who would have left him or joined the enemy's side. On the contrary, the Imam had attracted many persons from the enemy's side through his magnetic faith. Hurr was one of such persons. It is written that approximately thirty persons joined Imam Husain ﷺ on Ashura eve and this had doubled the happiness of Imam Husain ﷺ.

Companions express their loyalty

After hearing the words of Imam Husain ﷺ, everybody replied one after another saying, "Master! Are you saying that we should leave you alone and go away? No, by God! This life is not sufficient a sacrifice for you. Getting sacrificed for your sake once is nothing much."

Another one said, "I would like to get killed a thousand times continuously and being made alive a thousand times so that I may sacrifice each life for you."

The first to initiate the conversation and express these thoughts was Master Abbas. After him, other companions repeated his words or spoke in the same vein. This was the last test that companions and Ahlul Bayt had to go through.

When they announced their determination and support, Imam Husain 🙼 also started to unveil the events that were to unfold the next day and said: "I would like to inform all of you that you all will be martyred tomorrow." Hearing this, all said, "Thank be to Allah the Lord of the worlds, that tomorrow we would sacrifice our lives for the beloved son of Fatima."[1]

Why Imam Husain 🙼 allowed the companions to remain behind?

Here a points is worthy of note. If the logic of a martyr is not understood, people would say that if Imam Husain 🙼 was going to be martyred in any case what was the use of keeping his companions with him? Except that they too get martyred in the process. Why at all did Imam Husain 🙼 permit his companions to stay with him? Why didn't he compel them to return? Why he didn't say, "The enemy has nothing to do with you and there is not the least benefit in your staying with me. If you stay with me there would be no effect except that you too would get martyred. Hence you should go away. It is obligatory for you to go away and unlawful to stay back."

---

[1] *Luhūf,* Pg. 91; *Mausuat-e-Kalimat al-Imam al-Husain,* Pg. 400; *Muntahal Amaal,* Vol. 1, Pg. 626

If a person like us had been in Imam Husain's position, he would sat on the jurist's chair, picked up the pen and written: "I give a verdict that it is unlawful for the companions to stay here and it is obligatory for them to go away. If you stay here your journey would be considered a journey of sin and it would be obligatory for you to offer complete Prayer instead of Qasr Prayer." However, Imam Husain 🕊 did not do so. Instead he told his companions and Ahlul Bayt to prepare for martyrdom. This proves that the logic of martyr is a different logic.

The martyr's death gives life to the community

Sometimes, some people have to get martyred in order to awaken the spirit of Jihad in a sleeping community or to present a sacrifice to grant it the light of faith or a new life. Such was the situation in Karbala.

Martyrdom is not only for the sake of overpowering the enemy. It includes awakening of the spirit of Jihad. If the companions and Ahlul Bayt of Husain had not been martyred on that day how could the world of the spirit of martyrdom had become inhabited?

Although the pivot of martyrdom is the respected being of Imam Husain 🕊 the companions increased the beauty of his martyrdom. If they had not been martyred the martyrdom of Imam Husain 🕊 would not have got the greatness, which it has till the Judgment Day. People would continue to come and seek inspiration and a fresh spirit from it in the shade of which they may also walk.[1]

---

[1] *Qiyam O Inqilab-e-Mahdi az Deedgah Falsafa-e-Tarikh,* Pg. 124-134

Friends! For the sake of the water of Euphrates

For the sake of thirst of the progeny of the Holy Prophet ﷺ

For the sake of the spirit in the blood of Shabbir

For the sake of the youth of Akbar

Take help from the increasing spirits

Yes, hold unto, hold unto Husain

The beauty of this world is because of struggle

Every moment be a Badr and every breath a Hunain

Move forward in pursuit of capturing the west

Your hearts should be enlightened and tongues should utter: "O Husain!"

You are Haideri; tear the chest of the serpent

Uproot the door of this modern Khaiber

Enquiry of the battle should continue like this

Every attack should be perfect and every stroke shuddering

The unjust army is trying to escape

O blood! Become hotter! O pulse! Tick faster!

The demon of oppression is trembling. May it not find refuge!

The ogre of mischief is trembling. May it not find refuge!

There is no place for delay, O brave ones!

The age is calling, "Move ahead! Move ahead!"

Youth is volleying; move ahead

Roar like thunder and rain after thunder

Yes, roar like an injured lion, O friends!

Clink, clink of Zulfiqar, O friends!

O carriers of burning fire! Move ahead

O conquerors of heavy storms! Move ahead

O those who have God-given strength! Move ahead

Thrust the sword in the chest of today's Shimr

Yes, throw Yazid into hell, throw him.

(A poetic composition by Josh Malihabadi)

Majlis 39

Ninth (*Tasua*) of Imam Husain ﷺ

O mourners!

The ninth of Muharram is a remorseful day for Ahlul Bayt. Imam Ja'far Sadiq ﷺ said, "My grandfather, Imam Husain ﷺ was surrounded from all sides on the 9th of Muharram."[1] Battalions were coming one after another in Karbala to assist Umar bin Saad. However, there was no one to help the Ahlul Bayt of the Holy Prophet ﷺ.

At Asr (late afternoon) of 9th Muharram, Shimr bin Dhiljaushan, the accursed one from start to end, arrived in Karbala and handed over a letter to Umar bin Saad. Shimr had expected that Umar bin Saad will say, "I would not fight with Husain." He would then kill Umar bin Saad as per the order of Ibne Ziyad and take charge of the army. However, Ibne Saad looked at the letter and said, "I think that my letter had an effect on Ibne Ziyad but your presence did not allow him to change his mind." Shimr said, "What is your intention now?" Umar bin Saad said, "By Allah, I would fight in such a way that head and hands would be severed and fly in air." Shimr asked, "What should I do now?"

Umar bin Saad knew that Shimr also held a high position near Ubaidullah Ibne Ziyad because both of them

---

[1] *Kafi*, Vol. 147; *Wasaelush Shia,* Vol. 7, Pg. 339; *Miratul Uqool,* Vol. 16, Pg. 362; *Muntahal Amaal,* Vol. 1, Pg. 624

were of the same type. Those who are more stone-hearted are closer to each other. Umar bin Saad said, "You lead the infantry." The order of Ibne Ziyad was very strict. It was written: "You must start harassing Husain as soon as you receive my letter. Husain should be given two options – pay allegiance or fight. There is no other option."[1]

What happened at the Asr of Ninth?

It is narrated that the sun was beginning to set on the 9th of Muharram. Imam Husain ﷺ sat resting his hands and head on his knees outside a tent. He was feeling drowsy. At that moment, Umar bin Saad read Ibne Ziyad's letter and called out aloud with a firm determination: "O army of Allah! Mount your horses for I give you glad tidings of Paradise."[2] (This statement was used by the Holy Prophet ﷺ while addressing his companions in one of the battles. Note the deceit of Umar bin Saad). It is recorded that the unjust army of thirty thousand soldiers had surrounded the Imam from all the sides. As the waves of ocean become violent in a storm, Umar bin Saad's army was aroused by his call. Suddenly, the entire battlefield became filled with the noise of hooves, slogans of people and clinks of weapons.

State of Lady Zainab on Ashura eve

Lady Zainab was busy tending to Imam Sajjad ﷺ in one of the tents. As soon as she heard these noises, she came running to Imam Husain ﷺ, shook his shoulder and said, "O brother! Can you hear these noises? Look what is wrong out there. Imam Husain ﷺ lifted his head up from his knees and replied without paying attention to the

---

[1] *Irshad,* Shaykh Mufid, Pg. 229
[2] *Irshad,* Shaykh Mufid, Pg. 230; *Biharul Anwār,* Vol. 44, Pg. 391

army, "O sister! I had fallen asleep. I saw grandfather, the Holy Prophet ﷺ in my dream just now. He was saying: O Husain! You would come to us soon."[1] God alone knows what Lady Zainab would have gone through on hearing these words.

Yes, of course, today is Ashura eve. This is such a night that if we take a close look the state of the martyrs of Karbala and the spirit of Jihad in them it would create a commotion in our hearts on one hand and we would feel extremely pained. On the other hand, we would drown in the sea of sorrow. Obviously the Ashura eve was more sorrowful for Lady Zainab than any other night because the spiritual personality of Lady Zainab had gained more strength on Ashura day. It continued to become stronger with the passage of events.

Two calamities on Ashura eve, distressed Lady Zainab a lot and she became extremely depressed. One occurred at the time of Asr on 9th Muharram and another on Ashura eve. Imam Husain ﷺ started making preparations on Ashura eve and ordered his companions to sharpen their weapons.

Jaun, the freed slave of His Eminence, Abu Zar Ghiffari was good in sharpening weapons. He sat in a separate tent and began to polish the weapons of other companions. Imam Husain ﷺ came to have a look at Jaun's work. Imam Sajjad ﷺ was resting in the next tent because of his illness and his aunt, Lady Zainab was tending to him. These two tents were very close to each other because as per the order of Imam Husain ﷺ, the tents were brought so nearer that pegs of one entered the neighboring tent. We shall explain later why it was done.

---

[1] *Malimul Madrasatain,* Vol. 3, Pg. 109

This incident is narrated by Imam Sajjad ﷺ. He says, "My aunt was tending to me when my father came to the tent where weapons were sharpened to survey Jaun work. Suddenly, I heard my father murmuring the following lines, which he repeated twice or thrice:

"Time, shame on you as a friend! At the day's dawning and the suns' setting.

How many a companion or seeker will be a corpse! Time will not be satisfied with any substitute.

The matter will rest with the Mighty One."[1]

In these verses, Imam Husain ﷺ pointed out the disloyalty of this world. He meant that sometimes the world smiles like a merciful friend and people get fascinated and start thinking that it would remain same forever. However, the world turns away its eyes and becomes unkind. Life no longer remains as sweet as honey and it becomes bitter. Reliable friends leave one alone and some become bitter foes. No one knows what is going to happen tomorrow. Honor, power, health etc. are temporary. Is there anyone who did not face failures in life? Is there anyone who did not have to bear disasters?

The Imam is discretely saying that many young men will be martyred the next day.

Imam Sajjad ﷺ says that he understood the purpose of his holy father. He was informing about his own death. Lady Zainab also heard these verses but a meaningful silence continued between us. Imam Sajjad ﷺ was

---

[1] *Irshad,* Shaykh Mufid, Pg. 232; *Biharul Anwār,* Vol. 45, Pg. 1
"The matter will rest with the Mighty One, and every living creature will have to journey along my path."

suffocating but he kept his calm. Lady Zainab's heart also filled with sorrow but she did not cry because Imam Sajjad ؏ was ill. Both controlled their tears till Lady Zainab could hold no more and she burst into tears because she was a woman and women are kind-hearted by nature. She said, "I should not have lived to see this day." She went to Imam Husain ؏ and said, "Yes, O brother! I should have died before seeing this day. You are the memory of those who would go away and you are our support." Imam ؏ consoled her saying, "O sister! Be patient lest the devil would take away patience from you."[1] What are you saying? What is making you sad? Death is a reality. Grandfather, the Holy Prophet ﷺ was better than me. Father Ali, Mother Fatima and brother Hasan were better than me, but all of them went away. I am also going; but O sister! Remember that you have to lead this caravan after me. You would accompany this caravan. You will have to look after my children.

Lady Zainab replied in a broken voice:

"Brother! All these circumstances are fine but whenever someone from the abovementioned personalities passed away from this world, others were present with me. My heart remained happy seeing you after brother Hasan went away. If you also go away leaving Zainab alone, what will remain for Zainab in the world?"

Why did the Imam asked for reprieve?

After narrating his dream at Asr of the Ninth to Lady Zainab, Imam Husain ؏ called His Eminence, Abbas and said, "Brother Abbas! Take along some men with you and

---

[1] *Irshad,* Pg. 232; *Mausuat-e-Kalimat al-Imam al-Husain,* Pg. 403 and *Malimul Madrasatain,* Vol. 3, Pg. 114

immediately go and ask if there is some fresh news. If they intend to fight us, tell them that starting a battle at sunset is against the rules of war (normally, Arabs used to start battles in the morning and return to their camps at sunset). There is certainly something new." His Eminence, Abul Fazl al-Abbas took along some senior companions including Zuhair bin Qayn and Habib Ibne Mazahir to the enemy's army and said, "I have been deputed by my brother to know the reason behind this sudden attack." Umar bin Saad said, "Amir Ubaidullah Ibne Ziyad has ordered that your brother should pay allegiance unconditionally lest we would fight."[1] His Eminence, Abbas said, "Don't be in a hurry. I cannot say anything on my own now. I would go to Abu Abdillah and get a reply."

His Eminence, Abbas returned and narrated the matter to Imam 🕮 who said, "I would not pay allegiance at any cost and would fight with them till the last drop of blood remains in my body. Go to them and if possible, postpone the war till tomorrow morning."[2] Imam Husain 🕮 did not want them to think that he wants to live for one more night and hence, he said, "God knows better that I want one more night's time because I want to talk to God during the last night of my life. I want to spend this night in supplications, worship and recitation of the Holy Quran."[3]

His Eminence, Abbas conveyed the Imam's reply to those people. They were not ready to postpone the battle but later on, differences arose among them. Some of them told others, "You all are very shameless. Even if we had been fighting against infidels we would have given them

---

[1] *Malimul Madrasatain,* Vol. 3, Pg. 109
[2] *Malimul Madrasatain,* Vol. 3, Pg. 110
[3] *Irshad,* Shaykh Mufid, Pg. 230; *Muntahal Amaal,* Vol. 1, Pg. 264; *Malimul Madrasatain,* Vol. 3, Pg. 115

reprieve and you are not ready to give time to the progeny of the Prophet?" Umar bin Saad was forced to end the dispute among his officials. He said, "All right, the battle would start tomorrow morning."[1]

This night was an exceptionally bright one for Imam Husain ﷺ. He spent it in full enthusiasm. People who have interpreted this night as a night of Meraj for Imam Husain ﷺ are absolutely correct. He delivered an eloquent sermon during that night for his companions and Ahlul Bayt. Everyone bid him farewell during this night and the Imam bid them farewell in return. Imam ﷺ said:

"O my companions and O my Ahlul Bayt! I don't know any companions and any Ahlul Bayt better than mine. I thank you all. However, all of you should be aware of a fact. The enemy is in quest of my blood only. They do not want anything except my life. I return the allegiance paid by you all. Now you all are free. Whoever wishes to go may go. Whoever among you is going should take along a person from my Ahlul Bayt, if possible." However, none of the companions of Imam Husain ﷺ went away. The Divine hand had already removed the cowards from the Imam's caravan.

It is recorded that all of them replied in unison, "How is it possible that we leave you alone and go away? May God not bring that day when you get martyred and we are left alive." It is narrated that His Eminence, Abul Fazl al-Abbas was the first to give this reply (Muslim bin Awsaja stood up and said, "If we step back from helping you and leave you alone, what reply would we give to Allah? By God, I would not leave you alone at any cost. I would thrust my spear in the chest of your enemy and continue to quench the thirst of my sword with their blood as long

---

[1] *Muntahal Amaal,* Vol. 1, Pg. 625

as possible. If no weapon is left I would rain stones on them. I swear by Allah, I would not leave you so that He sees that I have fulfilled my duties towards the grandson of the Holy Prophet ﷺ in his absence. If someone kills me and then makes me alive and burns me in fire and blows my ashes in air and repeats this process seventy times then too I would not hesitate in helping you and continue to sacrifice my life on you. Now I know that I would be killed only once and remain happy forever."

After Muslim bin Awsaja, Zuhair bin Qayn got up and said, "I wish I get killed and made alive and this process goes on seventy times but you and your Ahlul Bayt remain safe."

"Others also expressed such zealous thoughts. Imam prayed for their well-being and returned to his tent." The statement of 'Qausain' is taken from Dr. Ibrahim Ayati's book, *History of Ashura*, published by Jame Taalimaat-e-Islami.

Qasim's Cognition

Tonight in order to renew our attachment with Muhammad and Aale Muhammad we would narrate the sufferings of Imam Hasan's ﷺ orphan, Qasim. These sufferings are normally narrated on Ashura eve. When everybody had expressed their loyalty to the Imam, Imam ﷺ modified his way of speech and began to unveil the secrets. Imam ﷺ said, "I want to inform you all that all of you would get martyred tomorrow. None of those gathered in this tent will survive." Everybody exclaimed, "We thank Allah for granting us the honor of martyrdom."

(A friend has reminded that Ayatullah Aqa Hakim and Ayatullah Allamah Mujahid Amini, the author of *Ghadeer* is unwell and is being treated in a foreign country; hence, all believing men and women should pray for him. It is our duty to pray for the well-being of our leaders especially. O Lord! For the sake of Husain bin Ali and for the sake of the pure soul of Qasim, grant good health to the above-mentioned personalities and all others who are unwell.)

A thirteen-year-old child was also present in that tent. When Imam Husain ﷺ announced that everybody present inside the tent would be martyred the next day, this child thought, "Maybe, this statement of Imam ﷺ was meant for only adults and young children like me are not included". Naturally any child of this age would have thought in the same way. The child lifted his head in distress and asked, "O uncle! Am I included among those who will be martyred tomorrow?" The Imam looked at the child sadly and said, "O son! Reply to my question first then I would reply yours." The child asked, "O uncle! Please ask." The Imam said, "Son! How does death taste?" The child replied immediately, "O uncle! Such a death is sweeter than honey for me." (The child has clarified that the reason he asked his uncle was that he feared that he would be kept away from this honor.) The Imam said, "Yes, son! You will also get martyred tomorrow. However, you will have to bear a great calamity before that." Imam did not explain the calamity that he was going to face at that moment but people came to know what that disaster was on the Ashura day.[1]

O uncle! Help me

Qasim left for the battlefield. He was so young that no armor and helmet would fit his body. Then too, the grandson of the lion of God won accolades for his bravery.

---

[1] *Mausuat-e-Kalimat al-Imam al-Husain,* Pg. 402

Suddenly, he was attacked on his head by a sword, because of which he could not balance himself on his horse and fell down. Imam Husain ﷺ was standing near his tent holding the reins of his horse ready to leave any second. Suddenly, a call "O uncle!" was heard. "O uncle! Please help me."

It is narrated that Imam Husain ﷺ moved towards Qasim as swiftly as a hawk moves towards its prey. No one could understand how fast the Imam reached Qasim. It is recorded that after Qasim had fallen, he was surrounded by approximately two hundred mounted foes. One of them moved forward to behead him. Suddenly, they came to know that Husain has attacked them. Seeing this, the soldiers ran here and there like a pack of wolves running away on seeing a lion. The accursed one who had dismounted from his horse to behead Qasim was crushed under the hooves of his own companions and departed for hell. There was so much dust everywhere that no one could understand what was going on. Both friends and enemies watched from a distance. When the dust settled, people saw Qasim's head in Imam Husain's ﷺ lap. People heard Imam Husain ﷺ saying aloud, "My dear! How unbearable it is for your uncle that you called him for help and but when he reached you he could not do anything for you."[1]

---

[1] Ustad Martyr Mutahhari says that there was a famous orator of Qum. He related these calamities while late Ayatollah Haji Shaykh Abdul Karim Haeri was present. (he was a very virtuous person. I have come to know from many sources that he was included among those who had limitless love for Ahle Bayt. I could not meet him because I reached Qum ten months after he passed away. However, the people who had seen him say that this scholar used to have his eyes filled with tears whenever he heard the name of Imam Husain.) He cried so much and slapped his head that he fell unconscious. Later on, he requested the orator not to relate those calamities in his presence because he cannot control himself after hearing them.

O mourners!

It is narrated that Qasim's head was in the Imam's lap and Qasim was having a hard time. Then, Qasim groaned and left for the heavenly abode.[1] People saw Imam Husain ؏ carry the body of Qasim in his arms moving towards the camp. How strange and remorseful this incident is! When Qasim wished to go to the battlefield, Imam Husain ؏ found it difficult to permit him. Then before giving permission, both uncle and nephew cried, embracing each other so much that they fell unconscious. However, the scenario is different now. The Uncle was seen embracing the nephew some time back but now people saw the Imam embracing the nephew's martyred body and Qasim's hands flopped lifelessly, because there was no life in his body.

وَسَيَعْلَمُ الَّذِينَ ظَلَمُوا أَيَّ مُنقَلَبٍ يَنقَلِبُونَ

And they who act unjustly shall know to what final place of turning they shall turn back.[2]

---

[1] *Irshad,* Shaykh Mufid, Pg. 239; *Muntahal Amaal,* Vol. 1, Pg. 680; *Mausuat-e-Kalimat al-Imam al-Husain,* Pg. 463
[2] Surah Shuara 26:227

Majlis 40

Imam Husain ﷺ is Migrant (*Muhajir*) as well as Warrior (*Mujahid*)

From the view of Quranic logic, Imam Husain ﷺ is Muhajir as well as Mujahid. He migrated from his city and country like Prophet Musa. Prophet Musa's homeland was Egypt. He left it and went to Madayn.[1] However Prophet Musa was only a Muhajir and not a Mujahid.

Prophet Ibrahim was also a Muhajir for he had left his homeland, Babel.[2]

However, Imam Husain ﷺ is unique; for he was a Muhajir as well as Mujahid. During the early days of Islam, some people were Muhajir but they were not holy fighters because the commandment of Jihad was not enforced on them. Hence, they were only Muhajirs. Afterwards, the commandment of Jihad was enforced and the Holy fighters also came out of the Muhajirs.

However, Husain is the only one who was a Muhajir as well as Mujahid from the very first day.[1]

---

[1] *So he went forth therefrom, fearing, awaiting, (and) he said: My Lord! deliver me from the unjust people. And when he turned his face towards Madyan, he said: Maybe my Lord will guide me in the right path.* (Surah Qasas 28:21-22)

[2] Surah Saffat: 99

The Holy Prophet ﷺ had advised Imam Husain ؑ in his dream, "O son! The special honor reserved by Allah for you cannot be gained without martyrdom."[2][3]

Imam Husain ؑ lived as an immigrant for approximately 23-24 days i.e. from on 8th Zilhajj when he left from Mecca till he reached Karbala on the 2nd of Muharram and then from the time he entered Karbala till the Ashura day.

Martyrdom is a crown of pride for us

Imam Husain ؑ delivered a famous sermon on the day he departed from Mecca. The Imam discussed about *Hijrat* as well as Jihad in that sermon and said:

"O people! Death has left a mark on the progeny of Adam like a mark of necklace on a virgin's neck. I am as eager to meet my ancestors as Yaqoob was to meet Yusuf. Death is certain for a human being. No one is exempted from death. I do not fear death. Getting martyred in the way of God is a crown of pride on the head of a person. Death is forehead trinket for a martyr like a necklace worn by a virgin. O people! I foresee that wild beasts are tearing my flesh between Karbala and Nawawis. The happiness of we Ahlul Bayt, lies in Allah's pleasure. Whatever is liked by Allah is also liked by us.[4] If He is pleased with our safety, we are pleased with safety and if He is pleased with our illness, we would love illness. If He wants us to keep quiet, we would keep quiet and if He wants us to speak,

---

[1] Surah Nisa 4:100
[2] *Biharul Anwār*, Vol. 44, Pg. 313
[3] Surah Nisa 4:100
[4] *Biharul Anwār*, Vol. 44, Pg. 366; *Mausuat-e-Kalimat al-Imam al-Husain*, Pg. 328

we would speak. If He likes us to rest, we would rest and if He wants us to move, we would move like waves."

Imam concluded his sermon after announcing his intention of migration:

"Whoever wants to sacrifice in the way of Allah like us, whoever wants to join his voice with our voice, whoever wants to migrate in the way of Allah and meet his God should accompany us. God willing, I shall depart tomorrow."[1]

Only the pure ones remained

When Imam Husain 🕮 departed from Mecca, a large number of people accompanied him. In the beginning, many people thought that Husain bin Ali is exaggerating his speech and it is possible that there would be peace everywhere in future. Many people joined him on the way but Imam Husain 🕮 did not want greedy people to accompany him. He used to filter his companions through his words during the journey so that those people who are not worthy of being included in the battle along with him get separated. After filtering out a number of times, whoever passed the test of purity as per the standard remained as a loyal companion of the Imam and others left him.

They were the crown of all martyrs

Now, only those companions were left along with Imam Husain 🕮 about whom the Imam had testified that he had not seen companions better and more loyal than

---

[1] *Luhūf*, Pg. 60; *Biharul Anwār*, Vol. 44, Pg. 366; *Mausuat-e-Kalimat al-Imam al-Husain*, Pg. 328

those. Thus, if a comparison is made between the companions of the Holy Prophet ﷺ in Badr and the companions of the Imam in Karbala, Imam Husain's companions in Karbala will be said to be crown of all martyrs.

Imam Husain ؑ had given permission to his companions on Ashura eve and cancelled their allegiance. Thus, he had made it clear that the enemy wanted to shed only his blood and had nothing to do with his companions. At that time, all said, "We have chosen to get martyred in your way only. Life is nothing compared to your sacrifice. We wish we had a thousand lives and would have sacrificed all on you." The first to say this was the Imam's brother, His Eminence, Abbas.[1]

How happy Imam Husain ؑ would have been when he saw that such companions had accompanied him who agree with his purpose. Hearing this, Imam Husain ؑ told them, "Now that you have taken a decision, I would inform you about the incidents to happen tomorrow. The battle would certainly be fought tomorrow and none of us will remain alive."[2]

Honor for Husain's companions

Imam Husain ؑ granted such an honor to his companions on Ashura day, that it will be remembered in history forever. Those were the final moments and everybody was martyred. None remained except Imam Sajjad ؑ who was lying on his bed in his tent because of his illness. Imam Husain ؑ was standing alone surrounded

---

[1] *Irshad,* Shaykh Mufid, Pg. 231; *Muntahal Amaal,* Vol. 1, Pg. 626
[2] Allamah Majlisi says that Imam Husain (a.s.) made them see their places in Paradise. Thus, they saw their palaces and gardens and bounties of Lord in Paradise. *Muntahal Amaal,* Vol. 1, Pg. 626

by the enemies. The Imam looked to his left and right but found nothing except his martyred companions. Seeing this, the Imam uttered a sentence whose purport was, "I am not seeing any of the bodies lying on the ground alive." Then the Imam said:

"All those buried in the earth and those who sleep on this earth are alive." Then the Imam called out for help (*Istighatha*). The Imam sought help. Who was alive to help the Imam? Who were those living persons? Are they bodies, which were lying dead on the ground? Imam ﷺ called his companions loudly paying homage to them, "O my loyal and courageous ones! O my loyal and brave ones! Wake up from sleep. Get up! Move ahead! These immoral ones want to attack the sanctity of the Holy Prophet ﷺ. These shameless ones are coming forward to rob the tents of the progeny of the Holy Prophet ﷺ."[1] Then he said: "Go to sleep! Go to sleep. I know that your heads have been separated from your bodies."[2]

---

[1] *Mausuat-e-Kalimat al-Imam al-Husain,* Pg. 484 "O martyrs! Wake up. Wake up from your sleep and keep these mischief-mongers from the sanctity of the Holy Prophet."
[2] *Guftar Hai Maanawi,* Pg. 250-255

Majlis 41

Greatness of Imam Husain's soul

Most sayings of Imam Husain ﷺ could not reach us. The main causes of this are the circumstances of that time. We have a huge treasure of sermons and saying of the Commander of the Faithful with us. Especially, sermons delivered by Imam Ali ﷺ during his apparent caliphate are precious wealth. However, Imam Hasan ﷺ and Imam Husain ﷺ had to face restrictions from the rulers of their time. Especially, during the time of Imam Husain ﷺ, Muawiyah had terrorized the people so much that no one dared to approach Imam Husain ﷺ. Even if someone heard something from Imam Husain ﷺ, he dare not quote it to others.

Even though there are not many sayings of Imam Husain ﷺ, I have noticed a characteristic in the sayings of Imam Husain ﷺ during my study that the meanings of Imam Husain's ﷺ words are not only incomparable but basically reflect a combination of Imam Husain's ﷺ soul and greatness. Each and every sentence of the Imam is full of the gems of greatness.

Imam Husain's ﷺ sayings during the last moments

One statement is that which the Imam spoke during his last moments. Imam ﷺ displayed jewels of bravery in the battlefield and fell down injured. The holy body had already lost a lot of blood. The Imam's soul was extremely powerful but his body had become extremely weak. He had no energy to stand up. He could only get up on his knees with the support of his sword. The Imam did not even have the strength to stop the impure steps moving towards his holy camp. Eventually, Imam ﷺ stood up with a great difficulty and said aloud, "O followers of Abu Sufyan! O those who have sold their hearts! Curse be on you! Even if you don't have a religion and fear of the Judgment Day, you should be ashamed like free people of this world."

"I know that you don't have any faith on God and the Judgment Day but at least, you should give way to respectability in your hearts. A respectable person, who emits the smell of respect from his body, does not act like what you are doing." Those oppressors asked, "O son of Fatima! What are you saying? What have we done against liberty?" The Imam replied:

"I am fighting with you and you should confront me. Why do you want to attack the women?"[1]

Glimpses of bravery in the sermons of Husain

If we glance at Imam Husain's sermons from the first one, which he delivered in Mecca till the one delivered during the journey, we find the words of Imam Husain ﷺ filled with respect and greatness.

Imam ﷺ delivered a sermon while departing from Mecca and said, "Death has left a mark on the progeny of

---

[1] *Biharul Anwār,* Vol. 45, Pg. 51; *Mausuat-e-Kalimat al-Imam al-Husain,* Pg. 503

Adam like a mark of necklace on a virgin's neck." He also said, "Whoever wants to give sacrifice in the way of Allah like us, whoever wants to join his voice with our voice, whoever wants to migrate in the way of Allah and meet his God should accompany us. God willing, I shall depart tomorrow."[1] Imam 🕊 wanted to say, "Basically, my soul does not permit me to see the mischief-filled surroundings, remain alive and become a part of it. I prefer death for myself as my well-being in such conditions. My success lies in not remaining alive among you. According to me, living with oppressors is death of the heart and disgrace of life."[2]

Many people met the Imam during the journey and talked to him. Most were careless and tried to deviate others. Someone told the Imam, "Master! The times are bad. Why are you throwing yourself in the clutches of death?"[3] When such a person tried to stop the Imam, he said, "My reply is same as that of a helper fighting alongside the Holy Prophet 🕊, which he gave to his cousin who was trying to stop him from going for battle." Then Imam 🕊 quoted the verses of that helper as follows:

"I am going. Death is not a cause of disgrace for a person who has an intention of fighting in the way of right like a Muslim. Jihad is not a cause of disrespect because this is such a death that makes one meet the virtuous. It is an honor to sacrifice one's life while fighting with the enemies of the right path. Either I would remain alive in this battle

---

[1] *Biharul Anwār,* Vol. 44, Pg. 366; *Mausuat-e-Kalimat al-Imam al-Husain,* Pg. 328
[2] *Luhūf,* Pg. 79
[3] *Biharul Anwār,* Vol. 45, Pg. 238; *Mausuat-e-Kalimat al-Imam al-Husain,* Pg. 358

or die. If I remain alive there is no chance of being disgraced and if I die I would have no worries."[1]

"It is sufficient disgrace for you that you are alive and have got an insulting defeat. I, Husain (who has been suckled by Fatima Zahra), would never bear this. I can get beheaded for the sake of an honorable life but such a life where I have to bow down has no meaning for me."

During the journey, Imam ﷺ discussed with one of his companions that he preferred the life of greatness, honor and respect over a life of disgrace and said, "Don't you see? Aren't your eyes open? Can't you see that the right path is not being followed? Don't you see that mischief and misguidance is spread everywhere and there is no one to stop it? In such circumstances, it is the duty of a believer to wish for death."[2]

Imam Husain ﷺ had inherited respectability and honesty from his father. When Imam Ali ﷺ got news that the forces of Muawiyah had increased plundering the city of Anbar and that they have snatched the earrings of a polytheist woman, the Imam said, "By Allah, if a Muslim dies hearing this news out of sadness and anger, he shall not be condemned by me."[3]

Come, let us go to the Ashura day now. The lamp of Imam Husain's ﷺ life was about to go out. Still, his words

---

[1] Imam Husain had recited these verses in reply to Hurr who was sorry for putting his life in danger.

[2] *Tarikh Tabari,* Vol. 4, Pg. 305; *Biharul Anwār,* Vol. 44, Pg. 381; *Muntahal Amaal,* Vol. 1, Pg. 213; *Maqtal-e-Husain,* Muqarram, Pg. 194; *Mausuat-e-Kalimat al-Imam al-Husain,* Pg. 356

[3] *Nahjul Balagha*, Faizul Islam, Sermon 27, Pg. 85; *Nahjul Balagha,* Subhi Salih, Sermon 27; *Sharh Nahjul Balagha,* Ibne Abil Hadīd, Vol. 2, Pg. 74

were pleasant. Imam ﷺ was still talking about honor and bravery. Here too, the center point of the Imam's conversation was Islamic character and Islamic teachings. When Ibne Ziyad's messenger came to the Imam with a message, Imam ﷺ told him, "Tell your master that I would not give my hand in yours with disgrace. It is impossible that I plead like a slave and seek forgiveness that I had fallen prey to misunderstanding."[1]

There is even more respect in the words of the Imam spoken while fighting his last battle. All his companions and relatives were martyred. Imam ﷺ could see his young son who was martyred. The arms of his brother were cut and he knew that the enemy would soon attack his camp and take his people as hostages. Then too, he was shouting slogans in his battle about his leadership. However, the slogan was not inviting others to start obeying him. He was not asking others to consider him their master and follow him. The meaning of the Imam's slogan was that he was a perfect leader and that his leadership did not permit him to bow down to a lowly person.

"Death is better than a life of degradation. Death is always better and more beloved than disgrace and shame. The apparent defeat in this world is better than entering hell-fire.[2]

This is the meaning of greatness of the soul. This is the difference between a rich man and a respectable personality. Yes, honorable persons may be wealthy but all wealthy persons are not respectable. Every elderly is not honorable. That is why when we stand in front of a great

---

[1] There is slight difference between the text in *Biharul Anwār*, Vol. 44, Pg. 191 and *Biharul Anwār*, Vol. 45, Pg. 7.
[2] *Biharul Anwār*, Vol. 44, Pg. 192; *Mausuat-e-Kalimat al-Imam al-Husain*, Pg. 499

personality who is respected and honored we have to say: *I testify that you established the Prayer, and gave the Zakat and enjoined the good and forbid the evil.*[1]

If we stand in front of Nadir Shah what would we say? Obviously, we would praise him and say that we testify that you went to India and destroyed it and brought the Kohinoor diamond for us from there.

However, when we stand in front of Imam Husain ﷺ we say, "We testify that you established prayer, paid charity and fulfilled the duty of enjoining good and forbidding evil. You strengthened the relationship between a servant and his Lord through Prayer. You struggled in the way of Allah instead of in the way of this world and its wealth. You were not that privileged one who desires property or revenge or evil or wealth. You were that privileged one who did jihad in the way of God. You had forgotten your material desires and had molded yourself in your own oven. Its effects put an end to distance between a servant and his Lord. I testify that you have fulfilled your duty of performing jihad in the way of God as it deserved to be performed."[2]

"You performed jihad but it was not for selfish desires and property or fame; it was for the sake of truth and truthfulness."

---

[1] *Mafaateehul Jinaan,* Ziarat Waritha
[2] *Mafaateehul Jinaan,* Ziarat Waritha

Majlis 42

Prayer – the pillar of religion

It is mentioned in the holy Quran that some of those involved in chastisement of hell would ask each other, "What has brought you here?" They would get a reply, "We did not offer Prayer and did not feed the beggars. Also we used to hear unbelievers speaking against the religion in gatherings or we too used to speak such."[1]

This proves the importance of Prayer in religion. Why did the Holy Prophet ﷺ say that Prayer is the pillar of the tent of religion? It is so because if Prayer is offered correctly all other things would be rectified.

The Imam said in his last will, which begins with the words, "Allah, Allah!" and which is heard by you a number of times, "Allah, Allah! Do not leave Prayer at any time because this is the pillar of your religion."[2]

Imam Husain's ؑ last Prayer

You know that the bloodshed started after the noon (*Zuhr*) of Ashura. Till Zuhr, Imam Husain ؑ, many of his companions and youths of Bani Hashim were alive.[3] Only thirty companions of Imam Husain ؑ were martyred

---

[1] Surah Muddaththir 74:42-45
[2] *Nahjul Balagha*, Faizul Islam, Sermon 47, Pg. 968
[3] The names of persons who were martyred in the first attack are mentioned in *Absarul Ain*.

before Zuhr through arrows and rest of them were alive till Zuhr. When a companion noticed that it was time for the Zuhr Prayer, he requested the Imam,[1] "Master! The time of Prayer has arrived and we wish to offer our last Prayer behind you in congregation."

Imam Husain ﷺ looked at the sky and confirmed that it was the time of Prayer. Then he said, *"You have remembered the Prayer. May Allah include you among those who pray."* Or he said: *"You have remembered Allah. May Allah include you among those who pray."*[2] The Imam is praying for a person whose life is in the clutches of death to be included among those who pray. Thus, see what rank a true worshipper has near Allah?

Of course we offer Prayer. However, we also offer Prayer during the middle of battles. This prayer is called 'prayer of fear' in Islamic jurisprudence. Prayer of fear is like prayer of journey, which comprises of two units instead of four. Hence, even if a person is in his homeland and in the state of war it is necessary for him to offer two units prayer. It is difficult to offer full Prayer during wars and hence, Prayer of fear should be offered there according to the Islamic law. Now if all companions stand in congregation for Prayer their defenses might be disturbed. Hence half the soldiers continue to defend against enemy attack and the other half offer one unit prayer behind the Imam in congregation and one unit on their own and end their prayer. The Imam waits either sitting or standing after the first unit so that they may take their defending positions and other half of the soldiers join

---

[1] The name of that companion was Abu Thamama Amr bin Abdullah Saeed. *Muntahal Amaal,* Vol. 1, Pg. 656

[2] *Biharul Anwār,* Vol. 45, Pg. 21; *Mausuat-e-Kalimat al-Imam al-Husain,* Pg. 444

him in congregation. The rest half of soldiers offer one unit prayer in congregation and another unit on their own.

Imam Husain ۷ also prayed like this but conditions were different at that time. The Imam was not far from his enemies. Hence, the companions defending him stood very close to him but the shameless enemies did not let them pray in peace. The enemy started raining arrows when Imam Husain ۷ was offering the Prayer. They were also taunting orally. The accursed ones were saying, "O Husain! Do not offer Prayer. Your Prayer is useless. You have betrayed the ruler of the time, Yazid and hence, your Prayer is useless."[1]

Saeed bin Abdullah – the martyr of Prayer

One or two companions of Imam Husain ۷ became a shield of Imam Husain ۷ so that they could stop on their bodies arrows shot at Imam Husain ۷ to allow the Imam to complete his Prayer. When both of these companions fell wounded, Imam Husain ۷ had just finished his Prayer. One of them was Saeed bin Abdullah Hanafi. When the Imam reached near him, he was in his last moments. As soon as the Imam took his head in his lap, Saeed asked a strange question. He said, "O Aba Abdillah! Did I fulfill the right of loyalty?"[2] It means, that he was thinking that the right of Husain is so great that such a sacrifice would not be enough for it. Thus was a prayer of Imam Husain ۷ in the desert of Karbala.

[1] *Biharul Anwār*, Vol. 45, Pg. 21
[2] *Maqtal-e-Husain,* Muqarram, Pg. 244

Imam Husain ﷺ bows and prostrates for the last time

Imam Husain ﷺ recited *Takbir* (Allaahu Akbar) as well as *Sub-h'aanallaah* (Glory be to Allah) in this Prayer. He bowed, and prostrated.[1] However, he offered one more Prayer two or three hours later, in which he bowed differently, prostrated differently and recited differently. Imam bowed when he was shot in his holy chest by an arrow. He was forced to bow down then and remove the arrow from his back. Then do you know how the Imam prostrated for the last time? He did not rest his forehead on the ground because when he landed from the horseback, his right cheek touched the hot land of Karbala and he was reciting

Bismillaahi wa billaahi wa a'laa millati rasoolillaah

In the name of Allah and by Allah and on the religion of the Messenger of Allah ﷺ

---

[1] *Muntahal Amaal,* Vol. 1, Pg. 698

Majlis 43

Imam Husain's ؏ words while departing for the last time

If a person surveys the words of Imam Husain ؏ at the time of his last departure from his Ahlul Bayt he gets drowned in the ocean of amazement. He begins to think, "O God! What faith and tranquility did Husain have! From where did he get this faith and tranquility and such kinds of elevated emotions and enthusiasm?

It is mentioned in books that when Imam Husain ؏ came to bid farewell for the second time, he told his Ahlul Bayt, "Be prepared to bear difficulties and know that God is your helper and supporter. Allah will save you from the mischief of the enemies and your end shall be good. Allah will involve your enemies in different kinds of sufferings and you will be rewarded with numerous bounties and honors for the difficulties borne by you. Beware of uttering even a single word of complain and do not say a thing, which would bring down your status."[1]

Imam Husain ؏ was advising his Ahlul Bayt to be patient because of his confidence in his victory, whose source was the following verse of Quran:

$$ وَمَن يَتَّقِ اللَّهَ يَجْعَل لَّهُ مَخْرَجًا $$

---

[1] *Muntahal Amaal,* Vol. 1, Pg. 698; *Mausuat-e-Kalimat al-Imam al-Husain,* Pg. 491

And whoever is careful of (his duty to) Allah, He will make for him an outlet. (Surah Talaq 65:2)

This confidence of Imam came from the holy Quran.[1] It is the same type of faith and tranquility, which was gained by Prophet Yusuf at that time when he succeeded because of his piety and was very happy and pleased at that. He was saying:

إِنَّهُ مَن يَتَّقِ وَيِصْبِرْ فَإِنَّ اللَّهَ لاَ يُضِيعُ أَجْرَ الْمُحْسِنِينَ

Surely he who guards (against evil) and is patient (is rewarded) for surely Allah does not waste the reward of those who do good. (Surah Yusuf 12:90)[2]

However, the greatness of Imam Husain ﷺ is in the fact that he could see the end of an affair and its result before it came to an end and before people could come to a conclusion.

Zainab Kubra speaks in Yazid's court

The words of Imam Husain ﷺ were inscribed on the hearts of Ahlul Bayt. They bore all calamities but did not forgo patience and piety at any moment. At last, the result was same as assured by Imam Husain ﷺ and as guaranteed by God in the Holy Quran. We have seen that a few days later, Lady Zainab Kubra calmly repeated the words of Imam Husain ﷺ in Yazid's court. The soul of Karbala had scratched the face of the kingdom in desert and now it was slapping it openly. Ali's daughter said, "O Yazid! (You have dug your own grave) You may do whatever evil you can and try as much as you can. I swear by God, you will never

---

[1] Surah Talaq 66:2
[2] Surah Yusuf 12:90

be able to wipe our love, which resides in the hearts of people. The revelation, which has got life in our family, cannot be put to the sleep of death by you. There is nothing in this world except disgrace for you."[1]

In the name of Allah and by Allah and on the religion of the Messenger of Allah ﷺ

[1] *Biharul Anwār,* Vol. 45, Pg. 135

Majlis 44

Messenger of Allah ﷺ wept for Khadija

God forbid, the relationship between the Holy Prophet ﷺ and Lady Khadija was not based on lowly animal desires and lust. Thus such points are meaningless. Lady Khadija was fifteen years older to the Prophet (s.a.). Hence, after she passed away, the Prophet (s.a.) used to respect her greatly whenever there was a mention of her. Many a times, he used to have tears in his eyes, which was unbearable to Ayesha.[1] Since Ayesha was young and she was proud of her youth she once told the Prophet (s.a.), "An old woman is not as important as you consider Lady Khadija." The Prophet (s.a.) replied, "What are you saying? Khadija was completely different."[2]

Lady Khadija's will to Asma

Women had gathered behind the room, in which the newly-married Imam Ali ﷺ and Lady Zahra were present on their wedding night like it happens in many rural areas today also. The Holy Prophet ﷺ ordered that no one had the right to sit behind the room and that the women should vacate the place.

After some time, the Holy Prophet ﷺ passed by that place and found Asma binte Umais sitting near the room.

---

[1] *Biharul Anwār*, Vol. 16, Pg. 1-81
[2] *Seerat-e-Halabiya*, Vol. 3, Pg. 313; *Kohlul Basar*, Pg. 70

The Holy Prophet ﷺ said, "Didn't I say that no one should sit here. Why are you sitting here?" Asma said, "Messenger of Allah! Lady Khadija had willed me: 'I am worried about my daughter a lot because she is young. I think she would need me on her wedding night because there are certain circumstances in which every daughter needs her mother on that night. Thus, it is my will to you that you take care of Fatima on her wedding night.'"

Asma says that the eyes of the Prophet (s.a.) were filled with tears on hearing Khadija's name. He told her, "Stay here only." She said, "Messenger of Allah! I will stay here only, so that if Zahra calls out and asks for something I can fulfill her need."[1]

Imam Husain's ﷺ love for Lady Rabab and Sakina

Lady Rabab[2] was one of the wives of Imam Husain ﷺ. Only this lady was present in Karbala. She was the mother of Sakina. Imam Husain ﷺ was so proud of the loyalty of this wife that he used to quote the following verses in her honor:

"I swear by a friend who is dearer than life. I like to live in a house where Rabab and Sakina are present. I love both of them very much. I feel like spending my

---

[1] *Biharul Anwār,* Vol. 43, Pg. 138

[2] Imam Zainul Abideen's mother, Lady Shaharbano had passed away at the time of her delivery. Ali Akbar's mother, Lady Laila was also not present in Karbala. It is not known whether she departed with the caravan in Medina or not. However, it is certain that she was not present in Karbala. (Ustad Mutahhari)

Only Rabab binte Imrul Qais Kalbi was present among the wives of Imam Husain (a.s.) along with him in Karbala. Refer *Tarikh Ashura,* Pg. 199 by Dr. Ibrahim Ayati, published by Jame Taalimaat-e-Islami

entire wealth on them and no one should stop me from doing this."[1]

Did you see how the relations of the people of truth are? It is about such wives that the Holy Quran says:

ادْخُلُوا الْجَنَّةَ أَنتُمْ وَأَزْوَاجُكُمْ تُحْبَرُونَ

Enter the garden, you and your wives; you shall be made happy.[2]

Rabab mourns for Imam Husain ﷺ

Lady Rabab neither sat under shade nor had good food for a long time. She used to cry often. When she was asked why she wasn't sitting in shade, she used to say, "When I saw my husband's body lying in the hot sun[3] (Ustad Mutahhari cries), I vowed never to sit in shade."

There was such a pure bond between this lady and Imam Husain ﷺ that she became the evidence of the verse:

ادْخُلُوا الْجَنَّةَ أَنتُمْ وَأَزْوَاجُكُمْ تُحْبَرُونَ

---

[1] *Damaus Sujum,* Pg. 311; *Mausuat-e-Kalimat al-Imam al-Husain,* Pg. 825

[2] Surah Zukhruf 43:70

[3] *Muntahal Amaal,* Vol. 1, Pg. 819

Enter the garden, you and your wives; you shall be made happy.[1]

"Daughter Sakina, do not make my heart suffer more."

As evident from the abovementioned verses Imam Husain ﷺ loved Sakina very much. This love was two-way. Sakina also loved her father very much. History proves that Sakina's love was a great test for Imam Husain ﷺ. This was a beloved daughter of Imam Husain ﷺ and he could not live without her even for a moment. When Imam Husain ﷺ came to bid farewell and Sakina began to cry, the Imam said:

"Sakina, my dear! Do not cry now. You have to cry a lot after me. Do not shed tears as long as I am alive. Hold your tears to be shed after me. O the dearest one of your father! Don't you know that my heart is filled with sorrow on seeing your tears? So don't make my heart suffer more."[2]

"Of course, it is upto you to cry as much as you want after my soul has departed from my body. However, O daughter! As long as your father is alive, his heart is distressed on seeing your tears. [3] Hence, you are most rightful of crying after me."[4]

---

[1] Surah Zukhruf 43:70
[2] In some books of history "daa'ani" is substituted with "dahaani"
[3] In some books of history "taa-teenahu" is substituted with "taa-teenanee"
[4] *Damaus Sujum*, Pg. 184; *Mausuat-e-Kalimat al-Imam al-Husain*, Pg. 491

Majlis 45

Disgrace is unbearable

The couplets recited by Imam Husain 🕮 on Ashura day were of different types. Some were composed by Imam Husain 🕮 and some were composed by others and recited by Imam Husain 🕮. For example, the couplets composed by Farwa bin Musaik which were filled with enthusiasm and fervor.

Here, are some of the couplets composed by Imam Husain 🕮 Ashura day:

"Death is better than living with disgrace. Death is always better and more beloved than disgrace and shame. The apparent defeat in this world is better than entering hell-fire."[1]

This slogan of Imam Husain 🕮 should be called the slogan of freedom, slogan of respect and slogan of honesty. It means: It is better for a true Muslim to die instead of living a life of disgrace.

The world should know why Imam Husain 🕮 was ready to shed each and every drop of his blood and the blood of his youths. It is so because Imam Husain 🕮 grew up in the lap of prophethood. It is so because the blood of

---

[1] *Biharul Anwār,* Vol. 44, Pg. 192; *Mausuat-e-Kalimat al-Imam al-Husain,* Pg. 499

Ali was flowing in his veins. It is so because he had been suckled by Fatima Zahra (s.a.).[1]

When all hopes were apparently lost on Ashura day, the Imam delivered a sermon, filled with zeal and enthusiasm. It seemed that Imam Husain's ※ tongue was emitting flames of unbearably hot fire. Can these words be a joke? Imam ※ said, "O people! See how this illegitimate person (Ibne Ziyad) is daring to force me to accept one of the two conditions – disgrace or death. Go and tell your master that disgrace is unbearable for Husain."[2]

Blood was dripping from Ibne Ziyad's sword. His tyrant father had oppressed the people of Kufa twenty years ago so much that when they came to know that Ibne Ziyad is appointed the governor of Kufa, they hid themselves in their houses because they knew that he too was a stone-hearted person like his father and would wreak havoc on them.[3]

When this Ibne Ziyad came as the governor of Kufa, the people of Kufa abandoned Muslim bin Aqeel's support due to the awe Ibne Ziyad's father had upon them.

---

[1] *Biharul Anwār*, Vol. 45, Pg. 19 and 83; *Mausuat-e-Kalimat al-Imam al-Husain*, Pg. 423

[2] *Biharul Anwār*, Vol. 45, Pg. 83; *Mausuat-e-Kalimat al-Imam al-Husain*, Pg. 425

[3] Ziyad had arrested Shias of Kufa and Basra. He cut off their hands and legs and thrust iron rods into their eyes and hung them at the door (*Sharh Nahjul Balagha*, Ibne Abil Hadīd, Vol. 11, Pg. 44; *Al-Futuh*, Vol. 4, Pg. 320) This filthy one was the first to start the custom of tying hands and feet and killing in Islam. He buried Abdur Rahman bin Hissan alive for his love of Ali (a.s.) as narrated by Ibne Khaldun and Ibne Athir; *Shifa as-Sudoor*, Vol. 1, Pg. 315

One who is brought up in Fatima's lap cannot bear disgrace

Imam Husain ﷺ addressed the people of Kufa saying, "Do you know what options your ruler has kept before me? He has asked me to either accept disgrace or unsheathe the sword. Go and tell your ruler that Husain says that disgrace is miles away from him. We would not put down our weapons and accept defeat (Ustad Mutahhari cries). God wants Husain to be such but you don't know."

"That illegitimate one does not know in whose lap I was brought up. I was brought up in the lap of prophethood and reared in Ali's lap. I was suckled by the daughter of the Prophet (s.a.), Fatima Zahra (Martyr Mutahhari weeping continuously). Can one suckled by Zahra accept the disgrace of Ibne Ziyad? Disgrace is miles away from me."

The slogans of Imam Husain ﷺ on the Ashura day were of this type only. Hence, I request my brothers, who develop slogans for their friends that they should think whether their slogans are in accordance with those of Husain or not?

Imam Husain's ﷺ thirst on the Ashura day

The thirst of Imam Husain ﷺ, his Ahlul Bayt and his companions was not a matter of jest. The climate was extremely hot at that time (Ashura was in the last days of June and it is an extremely hot season in Iraq, where winters are also hot). There was not a drop of water for the progeny of the Holy Prophet ﷺ for three days at a stretch. It is a fact that when a lot of blood is lost from the body, fresh blood needs to be produced and thirst increases.

God has made the human body in such a way that whenever it feels the need of something, it expresses it. Thus, injured persons feel thirsty because they have lost a lot of blood. The body tries to produce more blood in such a state and needs water. The injured Imam was so thirsty that when he looked at the sky, there was darkness in front of his eyes.[1] This is not a light matter, it is a fact. I have fully searched the books of Karbala Tragedy but could not find these words linked with Imam Husain ﷺ where he said, "Give me a sip of water"[2] because Imam Husain's ﷺ personality is far more elevated than asking for water from those people. Yes, I have found it written that Imam Husain ﷺ was searching for water while fighting in one place.[3] The context shows that Imam Husain ﷺ used to reach water while fighting near Euphrates. However, he never asked them for water.

Nauha and Matam (Elegies)

The greatness of Imam Husain ﷺ is completely different from we people. Imam Husain's ﷺ couplets were also completely different. When we do mourn and recite Nauha, we should try to match verses of our nauhas with those of Imam Husain ﷺ. Reciting nauhas and elegies is a great deed. The Holy Imams used to invite poets to recite the versified sufferings in Majlis of Imam Husain ﷺ. The

---

[1] In *Biharul Anwār,* Vol. 44, Pg. 245 it is mentioned: "…when he looked up to the sky, it was like smoke…"
[2] *Biharul Anwār,* Vol. 45, Pg. 351; *Mausuat-e-Kalimat al-Imam al-Husain,* Pg. 500
[3] *Mausuat-e-Kalimat al-Imam al-Husain,* Pg. 495

poets used to come and recite elegies and the holy Imams used to weep and wail.[1]

I support *nauhas*, breast beating (*matam*) and chain-beating (*zanjir*)[2] but with the condition that the verses that are recited should not be invented by anyone. Instead they should be verses of Husain. For instance, when it is said, "O my young Akbar, O my young Asghar" it is not an elegy of Husain. The elegies of Husain should be of this type: "Don't you see truth is not being followed and the way of falsehood is not being blocked? In such conditions, a believer moves ahead to get martyred in the way of Allah."[3] The Imam did not say 'Husain is one' or 'the Imam is one...' he said, 'a believer is one who prefers to meet his Lord over such a life'.

The slogan of Husain is: "I don't see death but as a success and life with the oppressors, a disgrace."[4] Each and every word of Imam Husain 🕊 is worth writing in golden letters and spreading in entire world so that the world comes to know the secret behind his war. It is not so easy to say, "Death is an honor for me and living with the oppressors is disgrace."

"I feel ashamed to live a life as a slave in spite of being a leader."

The slogans of Imam Husain 🕊 are life-giving:

---

[1] *Damaus Sujum,* Pg. 295; *Maqtal-e-Husain,* Muqarram, Pg. 111

[2] Ustad Mutahhari is talking about that matam with chain, which is practiced in Iran. Blades are not attached to those chains. These chains are not hit on bare back instead it is hit on the back while wearing shirt or coat and blood does not flow because of it. (Rizwani)

[3] *Biharul Anwār,* Vol. 44 Pg. 381; *Muntahal Amaal,* Vol. 1, Pg. 613

[4] *Luhūf,* Pg. 79; *Biharul Anwār,* Vol. 44 Pg. 381

يَا أَيُّهَا الَّذِينَ آمَنُواْ اسْتَجِيبُواْ لِلّهِ وَلِلرَّسُولِ إِذَا دَعَاكُم لِمَا يُحْيِيكُمْ

O you who believe! Answer (the call of) Allah and His Apostle when he calls you to that which gives you life.[1]

Imam Husain ﷺ is a reformer. This word was used by Imam for himself. Imam said, "The purpose of my war is neither oppression nor revolt nor based on selfishness. I do not intend to spread mischief or do injustice to anyone. I am setting out only to reform the Ummah of my grandfather and would follow the way of my ancestors."[2]

The Imam mentioned this in his letter to his brother, Muhammad bin Hanafiyyah, which was also his will. Muhammad bin Hanafiyyah was physically challenged.[3] His hands were paralyzed. He did not have the strength to accompany the Imam in his journey. Hence, Imam ﷺ handed over this will to him so that the world comes to know the purpose of his movement.

Husain is saying, "O people of the world! I am not like others. My revolution is not because I want to reach a good post or gather material wealth. I only want the world to know the truth that my stand is for the sake of reforming the Ummah. I am the reformer of the Ummah of my grandfather (the Imam had written this letter in

---

[1] Surah Anfaal 8:24

[2] *Biharul Anwār,* Vol. 44, Pg. 329; *Mausuat-e-Kalimat al-Imam al-Husain,* Pg. 291

[3] It is written in *Tanqihul Maqal,* Vol. 3, Pg. 112 that Allamah Hilli replied to Muhanna bin Sunan that Muhammad bin Hanafiyyah could not help Imam Husain because he was ill while Ibne Numa Hilli's words at the margin of *Maqtal-e-Husain,* Muqarram, Pg. 135 are: Muhammad bin Hanafiyyah had got such an injury that he could not accompany Imam Husain (a.s.).

Medina). I want to fulfill the duty of enjoining good and forbidding evil. My aim is to give life to the *Sunnah* of the Holy Prophet ﷺ, which has become dead. The *Sunnah* of Ali Murtada has also become dead and I want to enliven it."

Philosophy of keeping Ashura alive

Now we know why the holy Imams emphasized that we consider Ashura as a school and why there is so much reward for the mourners. Is the reward of mourners equal to what good deeds people perform in the memory of their late parents? No, not because our death has no significance. It is so because our death has no reasoning or purpose. Thus, the holy Imams stressed that we should keep Ashura alive so that not only Imam Husain ؏ but his school is also remembered forever. The ideal of this school is Imam Husain ؏. Imam Husain ؏ is alive in the form of a thought. Although Imam Husain ؏ is not apparently present among us, yet the power of his character is alive. Every year when Muharram begins, the voices of this message of Imam Husain ؏ are heard everywhere in the air: *"Don't you see that the truth is being neglected and falsehood made customary. In such circumstances, a believer should wish to meet his Lord."* It is heard everywhere so that the enthusiasm of Shias is enhanced and they begin supporting the truth and enjoin people good and correct all the evils that appear among Muslims.

Ashura is the day of reviving life

If someone asks, "What message do you want to give to the people by calling, O Husain, O Husain and beating your heads and chests? It is necessary to reply that, "We want to make the message of our master reach the people. We vow to revive the spiritual life every year."

يَا أَيُّهَا الَّذِينَ آمَنُواْ اسْتَجِيبُواْ لِلّهِ وَلِلرَّسُولِ إِذَا دَعَاكُم لِمَا يُحْيِيكُمْ

O you who believe! answer (the call of) Allah and His Apostle when he calls you to that which gives you life.[1]

We should reply that Ashura is the day of the revival of the life of a believer. We wash ourselves and our souls in the Kauthar of Imam Husain ﷺ on this day and purify our souls. We learn the fundaments of Islam openly on this day because we do not want to keep ourselves away from enjoining good and refraining from evil or martyrdom or sacrifice in the way of truth. We want to make this feeling unforgettable through Ashura. The philosophy of Ashura is not that we commit sins first and then seek forgiveness through Imam Husain ﷺ. We would get salvation only when our soul is attached to the holy soul of Imam Husain ﷺ. Repentance means that one should not commit a sin after seeking forgiveness for it even by mistake.

Signs of being attached to the soul of Imam Husain ﷺ

The sins of a person are not forgiven by merely saying 'my sins are forgiven' after attending a Majlis of Imam Husain ﷺ. The sins are forgiven only when our soul is attached to the soul of Imam Husain ﷺ. Our sins are certainly forgiven at that time but the condition is that we do not commit that sin again.

However, if we commit sins and attend a Majlis of Husain and then come out and occupy ourselves in

---

[1] Surah Anfaal 8:24

committing sins again, it indicates that our soul has no connection with the soul of Imam Husain 🕮.

Husainite Slogan

The slogans of Imam Husain 🕮 are slogans of the revival of Islam. It is a Husainite slogan that why the wealth of the Muslim treasury is being given to only a particular group? Why is the lawful being prohibited and the unlawful is being permitted? Why is the community divided? Why are the poor involved in difficulties and not getting enough to kill their hunger while others are filled so much that they cannot move from their places?

Imam Husain 🕮 had delivered a famous sermon to the army of one thousand soldiers of Hurr during his journey in which he narrated a tradition[1] of the Holy Prophet 🕮 and said that if such a period comes when the Muslim treasury is being exploited such that what is permitted by God is prohibited and vice versa and Muslims remain quiet; then it is rightful for Allah to send these Muslims to the place where the unjust are destined to go. The Imam

---

[1] O people! The Holy Prophet has said, "If someone sees an oppressor permitting whatever is prohibited by Allah and is breaking the promise made to Allah and going against the Sunnah of the Holy Prophet and having enmity with Allah and the person does not oppose him in spite of having hands and tongue, Allah will put him in hell along with that oppressor.
They are following the Shaitan and disobey the Merciful Lord. They are spreading mischief openly. They have crossed the limits specified by Allah. They are using Muslim treasury unlawfully. They are prohibiting what Allah permitted and permitting what is prohibited by Allah. In such a situation, I am more responsible than others to stand up against him." (*Tarikh Tabari,* Vol. 5, events of 61 A.H.) Rizwani

said that he had an important responsibility[1] in such circumstances and he cares for it. This is the school of Imam Husain ﷺ. This is the soul of Imam Husain's ﷺ slogan. This is the truth behind the slogan of Ashura. Hence, the slogans raised in our gatherings, Husainiyahs and processions must be strong. They should awake and not make people sleep. One who raises meaningless slogans would actually take us away from Imam Husain ﷺ.

Weeping for Imam Husain ﷺ

The heart should be so much filled with the sorrow of Shabbir

That my eyes remain colored with the blood of my heart. *(Ghalib)*

Weeping for Imam Husain ﷺ has a great reward but with a condition that Imam Husain ﷺ is alive in our hearts. It is narrated that the love of Imam Husain ﷺ is hidden in the hearts of the believers.[2]

If there is faith in someone's heart it is not possible that he does not have the love of Imam Husain ﷺ because Imam Husain ﷺ is faith personified.

The slogans raised by the companions of Imam Husain ﷺ area also amazing. The Karbala tragedy occurred in such a way that people were forced to think that the Divine hand had drawn this picture in such a way that it can never be wiped out from the minds of people.

---

[1] *Muntahal Amaal,* Vol. 1, Pg. 68; *Maqtal-e-Husain,* Muqarram, Pg. 183 whereas in *Tarikh Tabari,* Vol. 4, Pg. 266 it is mentioned with a slight difference.
[2] *Khasaisul Husainia,* Pg. 48

How amazing it is that Imam Husain ﷺ introduces himself as follows:

"I am Husain bin Ali. I would not throw away the sword at any cost. I would support my Ahlul Bayt and remain steadfast on the religion of our prophet."[1]

Couplets of Imam Husain ﷺ are of different emphases. When he stood on the battlefield, he recited heavy verses as follows:

"I am the son of Ali, who is from the pure progeny of Hashim and it is enough for my pride that the blood of Ali flows in my veins."[2]

As Josh Malihabadi says:

"In whose veins flows the fire of Badr and Hunain

That brave warrior is named Husain."

Imam Husain's Valor

The valor and calmness of Imam Husain ﷺ shows that he had left everything aside. He displayed such courage that all the brave Arabs were confounded. A narrator from the enemy's side says: "I swear by Allah, I have not seen a person who has suffered so many calamities that all his

---

[1] *Muntahal Amaal,* Vol. 1, Pg. 695; *Mausuat-e-Kalimat al-Imam al-Husain,* Pg. 499
[2] *Biharul Anwār,* Vol. 45, Pg. 49; *Muntahal Amaal,* Vol. 1, Pg. 694; *Mausuat-e-Kalimat al-Imam al-Husain,* Pg. 498

Ahlul Bayt, children and companions are killed in front of him and he remains so calm?"[1]

"I swear by Allah, I am confounded that what a courage he had! What a power he had that his calmness was not affected even after being heart-broken when his loved ones were cut into pieces in front of him! Such a brave heart cannot be found anywhere even though you may search everywhere."

Soul of Ali in the body of Husain

Imam Husain ؏ had selected a spot as his center on the Ashura day. He used to come at that place, stand and address the enemy and then return to his camp. It is a fact recorded by all historians that no one dared to fight Imam Husain ؏ in one-to-one combat. Whoever came in front of Imam Husain ؏ did not return with his head intact. In the beginning a few persons came forward for one-to-one combat and were dispatched to hell. Seeing this, Umar bin Saad shouted, "What are you doing? The heart of his father, Ali, is beating in his chest. You must know whom you are fighting with."[2] After that, one-to-one combat came to an end and those malicious ones started throwing stones and arrows from all sides. Just imagine! An army of thirty thousand had surrounded a lone person from all sides and started raining arrows and stones on him!

---

[1] *Luhūf,* Pg. 119; *Tarikh Tabari,* Vol. 4, Pg. 245; *Muntahal Amaal,* Vol. 1, Pg. 695

[2] ("This is son of Ali who has killed brave Arabs. Attack him from all sides." *Muntahal Amaal,* Vol. 1, Pg. 697; *Maqtal-e-Husain,* Muqarram, Pg. 275

Husainite sense of honor

When Imam Husain ﷺ attacked this army, it started running like a pack of wolves flees on seeing a lion. Imam Husain ﷺ did not chase them long because he did not want to go far from his camp. His honor did not permit that the respect of his household be attacked while he was alive.

Monotheistic Slogan

That is why he used to attack the enemy, drive them away and return to his center. It was a place from where his voice can easily reach the camp. Although his Ahlul Bayt would not be able to see but they could hear him easily. Hence, Imam Husain ﷺ used to recite: *There is no power and might except by Allah the High and the Mighty,* loudly so that Lady Zainab gets calmed, Sakina is assured and his children retain hopes that he would return to them alive. Whenever he reached his center, he used to move his tongue over his dry lips and recite: *There is no power and might except by Allah the High and the Mighty.*[1] Husain wanted to show that the power given to him belonged to Allah.

On one hand the Imam was raising the slogan of monotheism and on the other he was informing Lady Zainab that he was alive. He had instructed his household that no lady should come out of the tent as long as he was alive.

---

[1] *Muntahal Amaal,* Vol. 1, Pg. 295; *Mausuat-e-Kalimat al-Imam al-Husain,* Pg. 496

Imam Husain ﷺ bids farewell

Imam Husain ﷺ came to the camp to bid farewell twice. He bid farewell once before going and then came back when he was successful in reaching the Euphrates. No sooner did Imam Husain ﷺ enter the river that someone shouted, "O Husain! You are drinking water there and the enemy is moving towards your camp." Hearing this, Imam returned from the Euphrates and went to his camp and bid farewell to his household once again.[1]

At that moment, the Imam made an enlightening statement to his Ahlul Bayt: "O my Ahlul Bayt! Remain calm. Do not panic. Look, you would be taken captives after me but do not forget your religious duties in prison. Do not utter a word, which would reduce your reward. Also remember that this is the enemy's last attack. It would be a cause of disgrace and destruction of the enemy. Be calm, for Allah would grant you salvation from the mischief of those unjust and would keep you away from disgrace. After that, there is elevation for you."[2] This is an important statement of Imam Husain ﷺ, "O my Ahlul Bayt! You would surely be taken captives but Allah would not let you be disgraced i.e. prison is not disgrace for you; instead it is a cause of honor and pride."

That is why when people of Kufa offered bread as charity to the hungry children of the captives,[3] Lady Zainab stopped them from taking it. Even though they were prisoners, they did not accept disgrace. If a lion is encaged perpetually then too it is a lion and if a fox is free; even then it is a fox. Thus, when Imam Husain ﷺ came to his camp the second time, his Ahlul Bayt became happy.

---

[1] *Maqtal-e-Husain,* Muqarram, Pg. 276
[2] *Mausuat-e-Kalimat al-Imam al-Husain,* Pg. 491
[3] *Muntahal Amaal,* Vol. 1, Pg. 728

Imam Husain ﷺ bid farewell to everyone and came out of the tent but his household members did not come out in compliance of his orders.

Conversation of Sakina with Zuljanah

After some time Imam Husain's ﷺ horse, Zuljanah, started to neigh and Imam Husain's ﷺ family members thought that he was coming back to bid farewell for the third time (Martyr Mutahhari cries). However, when they came out, they saw Zuljanah standing without its rider (Martyr Mutahhari cries more intensely). Everyone surrounded the Zuljanah and started talking to it. Sakina said, "O Zuljanah! I only ask you whether someone gave water to my father or killed him thirsty?"[1] (Martyr Mutahhari cries aloud).

Nauha of the Imam of the Age (a.t.f.s.)

One of the scenes of Karbala really shatters the heart of the Imam of the Time. The Imam of the Time says:

"Zuljanah swiftly returned to the camp neighing and crying aloud. When the ladies saw Zuljanah without a rider and his saddle hanging, they came out of the tents with unfurled hair and slapping their faces."[2]

The Imam of the Time recites the *Nauha*:

"O holy grandfather! The people of your household did not come out of tents as ordered by you. However, when they saw Zuljanah without a rider,

---

[1] *Masaib al-Masoomeen,* Pg. 320
[2] *Damaus Sujum,* Pg. 200; *Muntahal Amaal,* Vol. 1, Pg. 706

they unfurled their hair and ran towards the battlefield. (Martyr Mutahhari cries).

The calls of 'O Husain' and 'O Muhammad' were heard everywhere.

Majlis 46

Competition between Husainite qualities on Ashura day

Today is Ashura day, a day of Meraj for Imam Husain ﷺ. It is necessary for us today to try to gain inspiration from Imam Husain's ﷺ spirit, honor, steadfastness, bravery and bright thinking. If there is a little feeling of being human in us, it can awaken us.

A renowned writer, Abbas Mahmood Aqqad says that on the Ashura day it seemed that the qualities of Imam Husain ﷺ were having mutual competition between themselves i.e. each quality of Imam Husain ﷺ wanted to move ahead of others. His patience wanted to become better than other qualities. His sincerity wanted to be the best. His bravery wanted to win over every quality.

A poet has aptly said:

The road of life is fragrant to this day

How excellent is the beneficial personality of Husain

On the page of romance and the register of ethics

Even today shines the seal of the rules of Husain.

Imam Husain's ﷺ calmness

I cannot make even the smallest comment about Imam Husain's ﷺ patience because I am smaller than it. Then too I would dare to say that the quality of Imam Husain ﷺ, which was most explicit, was the power of his heart, his calmness, his steadfastness. It is not a thing narrated by me only but it was recognized on the Ashura day. It is the statement of a narrator from the enemy's side which is very meaningful. He says, "I swear by Allah, I am surprised. What a heart he had! What a power he had that his calmness was not affected even when he was heart-broken after his loved ones were cut into pieces in front of him! The power of his heart cannot be found anywhere even though you may search thoroughly. This is really amazing."

Imam Husain's revolution gave rise to other revolutions

It is not an ordinary thing; it is extremely amazing. I was always surprised that Imam Husain ﷺ was moving ahead in a manner on the Ashura day as if marching towards his bright future after seeing the signs of success of his revolution with his own eyes.

He had no doubt that success was destined for him after he is martyred. He had no doubt that the Ashura day was the last day of sowing the crop. Hence he should not grudge about whatever he was facing, because soon it was going to bear fruits. Thus, the fruits of his revolution started coming from the Ashura day. Eventually, we saw that betrayal and revolts against Bani Umayyah started soon after the martyrdom of Imam Husain ﷺ.

First attack on the Umayyad Regime

The first to tear away the veil from the malicious face of Bani Umayyah was a lady from the army of infidels. She played an important part in enlightening the true features of this catastrophe. When that woman saw at the Asr of Ashura that Yazid's army was preparing to attack Imam Husain's camp, she came running, took a tent-pole in her hand and stood in front of the tents guarding them. She was from the tribe of Bakr bin Wail. She shouted, "O progeny of Bakr bin Wail! Are you alive? Come for my help because these people want to even take away the clothes of the ladies of the family of Prophet (s.a.)."[1] Through her few words, this lady made clear the meanness of the enemy.

Imam Husain's sense of honor

In my view, the moment when Imam Husain ﷺ bid farewell to his Ahlul Bayt was a very sorrowful one. There was no one alive except him. This scene of departure was extremely distressing but the reason why Imam Husain ﷺ had come to bid farewell for the second time is very significant. It is narrated that when Imam Husain ﷺ attacked the enemy with ferocity and drove the infidel forces away to reach the Euphrates, the enemy got worried that Husain would drink the water and regain strength. Eventually, someone shouted at that moment, "O Husain! You are drinking water while the army is attacking your camp." Hearing this, the dignified Imam immediately came out of the Euphrates.[2] I don't know whether the statement of that person was right or not or the army of infidels was preparing to attack the camp or not. However, I know that

---

[1] *Muntahal Amaal,* Vol. 1, Pg. 710
[2] *Biharul Anwār,* Vol. 45, Pg. 51

Imam reached his camp from Euphrates within a blink of eye. The camp was not attacked when Imam Husain ﷺ arrived there. The Imam made use of this opportunity and gathered the women and children once again.

Imam Husain's ﷺ glad tidings to his family members

This is the moment when the majesty of Imam Husain's ﷺ soul is displayed. He first said, "O my Ahlul Bayt! Be prepared to bear atrocities." It was as if he wanted his family members to be mentally prepared for this deed. He did not say more. However, he immediately said, "O my Ahlul Bayt! You should have faith that Allah would protect you and grant you salvation from the mischief of the mischief-mongers. He would take you back to the sanctity of your grandfather with respect. After that, the disgrace of your enemy would begin. You should be assured that Allah would make your enemy get involved in different kinds of punishments in this world."[1] It was as if the Imam was looking at the future with his own eyes.

Imam Husain is an expression of the Divine sense of honor

Imam Husain ﷺ had selected a place on the Ashura day as a center during the battle. He used to attack from that place. First he fought in one-to-one combat. The enemy came one by one in groups but the Imam did not leave anyone's head intact. The Imam's attack was such that the enemy was taken aback. Seeing this, Umar bin Saad shouted, "What are you doing? Ali's heart is beating in his chest. He is the son of that person whose sword

---

[1] *Muntahal Amaal,* Vol. 1, Pg. 698; *Mausuat-e-Kalimat al-Imam al-Husain,* Pg. 491

destroyed the pride of the bravest Arabs." In this way, Umar bin Saad was actually trying to rekindle the hatred of Arab tribes for Imam Husain ﷺ. Eventually, the soldiers asked, "What should we do?" He replied, "This is not the right way. If you go one by one, no one would be left alive. You should attack him from all sides."

The enemy used to flee whenever the Imam attacked them but during the entire battle, he made sure that he was not far away from the camp. His sense of honor did not permit that anyone should dare to come near his camp as long as he was alive. He had ordered his family members not to come out of their tents as long as he was alive.

If you have heard somewhere that the Imam's family members were coming out of their tents and shouting *Al-a'tash* ('we are thirsty') repeatedly; it is absolutely wrong.[1]

---

[1] Similarly, a tradition is famously narrated about "disobedience of Allah", in which angel Fitrus had lost his wings. He rubbed himself with Imam Husain's cradle at the time of the Imam's birth. As a result of the blessings of the Imam's presence, he got his wings back. On the other hand, the holy Quran says: يَخَافُونَ رَبَّهُم مِّن فَوْقِهِمْ وَيَفْعَلُونَ مَا يُؤْمَرُونَ Meaning: ***They fear their Lord above them and do what they are commanded.*** (Surah Nahl 16:50). عِبَادٌ مُّكْرَمُونَ Meaning: the angels are respected servants of Allah (Surah Anbiya 21:26). عَلَيْهَا مَلَائِكَةٌ غِلَاظٌ شِدَادٌ لَا يَعْصُونَ اللَّهَ Meaning: ***Over it are angels stern and strong, they do not disobey Allah...***(Surah Tahrim 66:6) Allamah Sayyid Muhammad Tabatabai, author of *Tafseer al-Mizan* had replied to one of the questions saying that the incident of Fitrus is not in accordance with verses of Quran.
Also the holy Quran says: مَن كَانَ عَدُوًّا لِّلَّهِ وَمَلَائِكَتِهِ وَرُسُلِهِ وَجِبْرِيلَ وَمِيكَالَ فَإِنَّ اللَّهَ عَدُوٌّ لِّلْكَافِرِينَ Meaning: ***Whoever is the enemy of Allah and His angels and His apostles and Jibraeel and Mikaeel, so surely Allah is the enemy of the unbelievers.*** (Surah Baqarah 2:98). وَلَـكِنَّ الْبِرَّ مَنْ آمَنَ بِاللَّهِ وَالْيَوْمِ الآخِرِ وَالْمَلَائِكَةِ وَالْكِتَابِ وَالنَّبِيِّينَ Meaning: ***But righteousness is this that one should believe in Allah and the last day and the***

They had come out of their tents only once, when Zuljanah returned without his rider. Whoever came out at that time did not know what was happening. When they heard Zuljanah neighing, they thought that the Imam has come to bid farewell for the third time.

Imam Husain's ﷺ Zuljanah

It is narrated that Imam Husain's ﷺ Zuljanah was well-trained. Not only the Imam's Zuljanah but also horses of enemies were trained so well that whenever their riders fell off they used to sense it immediately. Thus, when Zuljanah saw that Imam Husain ﷺ had fallen and was not getting up from his place, it stained its mane with the holy blood of Imam Husain ﷺ and galloped towards the camp[1] to inform the Imam's family members that he is killed.

On the other hand, the family members thought that the Imam has come to bid farewell for the third time. Hence they came out of their tents. However when they saw the actual circumstances, they began weeping and wailing after surrounding Zuljanah from all sides. The Imam had not permitted them to come out previously. Imam ﷺ had selected a center point for the battle from where his voice could be heard in the camp. In this way, the Imam made sure that their hopes remain alive.

When the Imam used to return to his center point after attacking the enemy, he used to recite: *There is no power and might except by Allah the High and the Mighty,* loudly (I don't know whether it should be called a loud voice because his throat was so parched because of severe thirst; so how could a loud voice come out of it?)

---

angels and the Book and the prophets. (Surah Baqarah 2:177). All these verses prove the elevated status of the angels. (Rizwani)
[1] *Muntahal Amaal,* Vol. 1, Pg. 705

He used to gather all his strength and recite: *"Laa h'aula wa laa quwwata illaa billaahil a'liyyil a'z'eem"* **There is no power and might except by Allah the High and the Mighty.** i.e. "O Lord! Whatever spiritual and physical power Husain possesses is from You only." His family members used to be happy hearing this voice because they got assurance that their master was alive and this kept their hopes alive. On the other hand, whenever the enemies attacked, they tried to surround the Imam in a smaller circle. Those enemies of religion used to shoot arrows on the Imam, hit him with stones while the Imam attacked and drove them away.

A poisonous arrow hits the heart of Imam Husain

You must have heard how Ibne Saad started the battle on the Ashura day. You must also have heard that Imam Husain did not allow staring hostilities from his side. This custom was followed without fail when the opposite army was apparently Muslim. Imam Ali strictly followed this custom. He used to say, "I would never initiate the battle. Let them start the fighting. We would hit them later."

Imam Husain also did not start the battle. Instead Umar bin Saad called for his bow and arrows for seeking the pleasure of Ubaidullah Ibne Ziyad. Umar bin Saad's father was Saad bin Abi Waqqas, a renowned archer during the early days of Islam. He (Umar) placed an arrow in his bow, aimed at the camp of Husain and shouted:

"O people! Bear witness to Amir Ibne Ziyad that I was the first to shoot at Husain's camp to start the battle." The battle of Ashura started with an arrow and also ended with an arrow. The poisonous arrow, which ended the battle, had hit the holy heart of Imam Husain 🕮. It pierced the Imam's chest from front and came out from behind.[1] Thus, the Imam could not take it out from the front. It is written that the Imam pulled it out from his back. After being hit by this arrow, Imam Husain 🕮 could not balance himself on the horseback and he fell down. He did not have enough strength to get up.

Abdullah bin Hasan sacrificed himself for his uncle

It is narrated that a some sons of Imam Hasan 🕮 had accompanied Imam Husain 🕮 on the journey of Karbala. One of them was Qasim. Also, Imam Hasan's 🕮 youngest son, Abdullah was present in Karbala; he was only ten years old. He was only a few months old when Imam Hasan 🕮 was martyred. Imam Husain 🕮 had brought him up. Imam Husain 🕮 loved his nephews very much. Perhaps he loved his nephews more than his sons since they were orphans. Abdullah too loved Imam Husain 🕮 very much. Imam Husain 🕮 had handed him over to his sister, Zainab on the Ashura day and asked her to take special care of him. Lady Zainab was keeping a continuous watch on the children. Suddenly, Abdullah ran out of the tent. Lady Zainab ran after him to catch him but he said, "I swear by Allah, I would not leave my uncle alone."[2] Saying this, the child ran towards the battlefield and threw himself in the bosom of Imam Husain 🕮, whereas the Imam was himself in a bad condition. At that moment, an oppressor moved forward with a sword to behead the

---

[1] *Biharul Anwār,* Vol. 55, Pg. 53
[2] *Irshad,* Shaykh Mufid, Pg. 241; *Biharul Anwār,* Vol. 45, Pg. 53

Imam. As soon as he raised his sword, Abdullah shouted, "O son of an adulteress! Do you want to kill my uncle?"[1]

No sooner did the oppressor attack with his sword than the child put forth his hands to shield the Imam but they got cut off as a result. The child started crying, "O uncle! Look what the oppressors have done to my hands."[2]

I testify that you enjoined the good and forbid evil and performed jihad for Allah as is worth to be performed till you reached certainty.

وَسَيَعْلَمُ الَّذِينَ ظَلَمُوا أَيَّ مُنقَلَبٍ يَنقَلِبُونَ

And they who act unjustly shall know to what final place of turning they shall turn back.[3]

---

[1] *Irshad,* Shaykh Mufid, Pg. 241; *Biharul Anwār,* Vol. 45, Pg. 53
In one version it is mentioned: '*Yabnal lakhnaa-*' and in other it is written as: '*wailaka yabnal khabithati ataqtulu a'mmee*' - (Rizwani)
[2] *Mafaateehul Jinaan,* Ziarat Mutliqa Imam Husain
[3] Surah Shuara 26:227

Majlis 47

The last words of Imam Husain ﷺ

As long as there was life in Imam Husain's ﷺ body on the Ashura day, a fierce battle was fought and the heads of Yazid's men were flying in the air. By Asr time the Imam was exhausted due to the wounds. He began to feel dizzy mounted on his horse. Someone shot an arrow smeared with poison, which hit the Imam's chest and he fell on the ground at once. What did he say at that moment? Did he accept the disgrace by paying allegiance? Did he express any wish at that time? No, absolutely not. After displaying gems of courage in the battle, he faced that Qibla, from which he had never turned away and said, "O Lord! I agree with Your decision. I obey Your order. There is no Lord except You. O the refuge of those who are without refuge!"[1]

This is called true Jihad in the way of Allah and this is true human perfection.

---

[1] *Maqtal-e-Husain,* Muqarram, Pg. 283; it is written in *Mausuat-e-Kalimat al-Imam al-Husain,* Pg. 510 as: "I am steadfast in Your test. O Lord! There is no Lord except You. O Helper of those who seek help! There is no lord except You for me. Nor there is any god except You."

Majlis 48

Death for a brave person

The sayings of Imam Husain ؑ are full of the values of respect, modesty and magnanimity. The reason why this condition is found more in his sayings in comparison to those of the other infallibles is that the Karbala tragedy had occurred so that Imam Husain's ؑ holy spirit could reflect its aspects well.

It is narrated that when the chief of the martyrs was coming towards Karbala, he met numerous people on the way who advised him in different ways against proceeding ahead and informed him about the danger to his life. Eventually, the Imam too replied them in different manners and made clear his aim that he would surely go on.

When one of them told the Imam that the circumstances were bad and it was not advisable for him to go on, the Imam replied, "My reply to you is same that a Prophet's companion gave to one who was stopping him from taking part in Jihad." After that, the chief of martyrs quoted the following verses:

I would surely go. Death is not a cause of disgrace for a brave person (whose intention is to perform Jihad like a true Muslim). If someone fights in the way of truth and gets killed then such a death is not a cause of shame because he has stepped on a path of

virtuous servants of Allah. Supporting virtuous servants, walking with them and getting united with them is not worth condemning. Opposing a sinner is a cause of pride."

After that, the Imam said:

"I am going. Death is not a cause of disgrace for a person who has an intention of fighting in the way of right like a Muslim. Jihad is not a cause of disrespect because this is such a death that makes one meet the virtuous. It is an honor to sacrifice one's life while fighting with the enemies of the right path. Either I would remain alive in this battle or die. If I remain alive there is no chance of being disgraced and if I die I would have no worries."[1]

"Either I would remain alive or get martyred. There is no third possibility. The path I have chosen has reward on both ends. If I remain alive it is not a cause of shame because I have embraced death. If I get killed, then too I would not regret. A life free from fear of death is one, which is not a cause of disgrace. If I get killed my death would not taunt at all. (The other lines mention the same point that is said in the first two lines.) "It is sufficient disgrace for you that you are alive and have got an insulting defeat. I would never bear this."

"A prisoner of this world is unaware of other worlds."

There are a few more couplets, which are either composed by Imam Husain 🕮 or his holy father, the

---

[1] Imam Husain (a.s.) recited these verses in reply to Hurr who was sorry for endangering the Imam's life.

Commander of the Faithful, Imam Ali ☩, which are quoted from the Collection of Amirul Mu'minīn ☩. Regarding them also it is narrated that these couplets were also recited by Imam Husain ☩:[1]

"The world seems so beautiful that man is enamored by it but the world of Hereafter is far better and greater than this world. A prisoner of this world is unaware of other worlds."

"If a person has to leave behind all his wealth before going away from this world, is it not better that he helps others with it as long as he is alive?"

"If one has to die, what difference does it make whether he dies on his bed or in the battlefield or due to fever? But how nice it would be for a man to die a good death! Getting martyred in the way of Allah with sword is not only good but also best for a human being."[2]

Feeling of being broken into pieces in the way of Allah

You should estimate the spiritual state and ecstasy of the person who has recited the above verses. I am sure that only one personality would come to your mind who handed over his self to such an abode where he would be beautified even more.

How pleased Imam Husain ☩ would have been on seeing that his blood, which was destined to flow on the earth was flowing in the way of Allah, his forehead split in

---

[1] *Diwan Imam Ali,* Pg. 312
[2] *Tarikh Ibne Asakir,* Pg. 123; *Biharul Anwār,* Vol. 44, Pg. 374

Allah's way and arrows hitting his chest in the way of Allah!

It is narrated that Imam Husain's ﷺ body had one thousand nine hundred fifty-one injuries.

If you can feel the pleasure of being broken into pieces in the way of Allah, the injuries on Imam Husain's ﷺ chest would seem like medals, which increase his honor.

Low-land of martyrdom

During the last moments, Imam Husain ﷺ lay in a depression of land. He had no energy to stand up. The place where Imam Husain ﷺ was martyred was a sort of lowland. It was called "Low-land of martyrdom". If Imam Husain ﷺ had been a little away from this place his family members would not have been able to see him. Imam Husain's ﷺ body had so many injuries and so much blood had flowed from his body during last moments that he could not bear his thirst and his vision became blurred. In this state also, the enemies could not dare to attack his family members. They thought that Imam Husain ﷺ would trap them by acting like that. The enemies were sure that the Imam would attack them fiercely as long as there is life in his body.

A mercenary moved forward to behead the Imam but could not dare to go near him. Narrators of this scene say that Imam Husain ﷺ was a dignified person. He was the dignified one of Allah. It was impossible for him to bear that enemies attack his camp as long as there was life in his body.

Thus, when the enemies thought that Husain has become lifeless, they marched towards his camp. When the

Imam sensed this move, he gathered all this energy and stood up with the support of his sword and called out condemning his enemies:

"O followers of the progeny of Abu Sufyan! O those who have sold their consciences to the progeny of Abu Sufyan! I am fighting you and you must fight me. What harm have those women and children done to you? If you don't recognize God, if you don't fear the hereafter, what has happened to your human respect and nobility?"[1][2]

---

[1] *Luhūf,* Pg. 120
[2] *Falsafa Akhlaq,* Pg. 160-161

Majlis 49

Delight of Imam Husain ﷺ at the time of his martyrdom

It is mentioned that as soon as the Imam finished his Morning Prayer with his companions on the Ashura day,[1] he told his companions:

"O brave companions! Be prepared for death. Remember that death is a bridge, which takes you from this world to another. This bridge would take you from this world of atrocities to a lofty, noble and kind world."[2]

This was a part of Imam's speech. Now let us look at his actions in this matter.

The point I am going to mention was not told by Imam Husain ﷺ. It is recorded by the narrators. Hilal bin Nafe, a correspondent of Umar bin Saad, has narrated this incident. He says that he was surprised at the determination of Husain bin Ali. As the time of his martyrdom approached and as his calamities increased, his face was becoming brighter like a person approaching the

---

[1] It is narrated from Imam Sajjad (a.s.) in *Mani al-Akhbār*, Pg. 288 that this conversation took place when Imam Husain (a.s.) and his companions were facing a tough situation. Except Imam Husain (a.s.) and his selected companions whose strong faith was matchless, all others had turned pale and were terrified. Then Imam Husain (a.s.) developed their confidence and faith through these words.
[2] *Maani al-Akhbār*, Pg. 288

time of his meeting. The accursed one from start to end who had come to behead him was so much terrified by the reverence of the Imam's bright face that he could not move his dagger. He says, "When I reached Husain bin Ali and looked at his face, I was lost in the brightness of light glowing from his face and was so frightened that I stopped from the intention of killing him."[1]

Guarding the camp till the last moments

It is narrated that Imam Husain ﷺ had selected a place for his battle, which was very near to his camp. There were two reasons for doing so. Firstly, he knew that the enemy was very coward and would not remember that he had enmity only with Husain and would not leave the women and children inside the camp unharmed. Secondly, he did not want anyone to touch his tents as long as there was the last drop of blood in his body and as long as his nerves were ticking. Eventually, during the battle, if the enemy ran away from him, he did not chase them long and would return to his place to ensure that no one attacked his camp.

"No one should come out of the tents as long as I am alive."

He wanted that his Ahlul Bayt should be informed that he was alive. Therefore, he had selected a place as a center point from where his voice could easily reach his camp. He used to attack the enemy and return to that center and recite loudly: "Laa h'aula wa laa quwwata illaa billaahil a'liyyil a'z'eem." *There is no power and might except by Allah the High and the Mighty.* Hearing this

---

[1] *Luhūf,* Pg. 128; *Mausuat-e-Kalimat al-Imam al-Husain,* Pg. 513

voice of Imam Husain 🕮, ladies used to heave a sigh of relief that their master was alive.

The Imam had ordered his family members that no lady was to come out of the tents as long as he was alive. You must not believe that any lady came out of tents as long as the Imam was alive as is commonly narrated. It never happened thus. It was the Imam's order that no lady would come out as long as he was alive. Imam had even told his family members, "Look, you should not utter anything, which would decrease your reward. Be patient. Your end is very good. You shall be protected from the mischief of the mischief-mongers. Allah would soon chastise your enemy.[1]

The ladies were not permitted to come outside. Also, they would not have come out on their own. As the Imam's dignity did not permit any lady to come out, the infallibility of those ladies too stopped them from stepping out of the tents.

Hence, when the Imam's family members used to hear him reciting, "Laa h'aula wa laa quwwata illaa billaahil a'liyyil a'z'eem", *There is no power and might except by Allah the High and the Mighty,* they used to heave a sigh of relief.

As the Imam had come to the camp once or twice even after bidding farewell, his family members waited for him to return.

---

[1] *Muntahal Amaal,* Vol. 1, Pg. 298

Imam's family members recite Eulogies around Zuljanah

In those days, the Arabs trained their horses well for the battles because the horse is an animal that can be trained well. As soon as its rider used to get killed, it displayed a special reaction.

The Imam's family members were waiting to hear some voice or to have a look at Imam ﷺ outside. Suddenly they heard Zuljanah neighing. They came to the entrance of the tent thinking that the Imam had arrived but instead saw Zuljanah alone with his saddle sagging. They started shouting: "O Husaina, O Muhammada" and surrounded Zuljanah from all sides. (Wailing is a part of human nature. When a human being wants to express his sorrow, he wails, addresses the sky, animals or other human beings) and all of them started wailing in some way or other.[1]

The Imam had ordered his family members not to cry but he had permitted them to cry after his martyrdom. Thus, they started crying aloud.

Sakina's grievous question to Zuljanah

It is narrated that Husain loved his daughter Sakina very much. Later on, this daughter became extremely accomplished and knowledgeable and all scholars speak

---

[1] *Biharul Anwār,* Vol. 45, Pg. 60

about her respectfully.[1] Imam Husain ﷺ loved Sakina very much and she too loved her father very much.

It is recorded that Sakina used to recite such heart-rending elegies that everybody was moved. When all the family members surrounded Zuljanah and were mourning, Sakina addressed Zuljanah and said, "O father's loyal horse! Tell me whether my father was given water or killed thirsty?"[2]

When did it happen? It happened when the Imam fell off from the back of his horse.

$$وَسَيَعْلَمُ الَّذِينَ ظَلَمُوا أَيَّ مُنقَلَبٍ يَنقَلِبُونَ$$

And they who act unjustly shall know to what final place of turning they shall turn back.[3]

---

[1] Most scholars of India and Pakistan narrate that Imam Husain's four-year-old daughter, Sakina passed away in the prison of Syria and is buried there. (Rizwani)

[2] *Masaib al-Masoomeen,* Pg. 320

[3] Surah Shuara 26:227

Majlis 50

The toughest time for the Imam's Ahlul Bayt

The 11th of Muharram was the most difficult day for the Ahlul Bayt of Imam Husain ﷺ. If we analyse both positive and negative aspects of the incident of Karbala, we would feel that the incident of Karbala is picturing the conversation between the angels and God Almighty at the time of the creation of Prophet Adam and the reply that Allah gave to them. The angels had said:

أَتَجْعَلُ فِيهَا مَن يُفْسِدُ فِيهَا وَيَسْفِكُ الدِّمَاء وَنَحْنُ نُسَبِّحُ بِحَمْدِكَ وَنُقَدِّسُ لَكَ قَالَ إِنِّي أَعْلَمُ مَا لاَ تَعْلَمُونَ

What! Wilt Thou place in it such as shall make mischief in it and shed blood, and we celebrate Thy praise and extol Thy holiness? He said: Surely I know what you do not know.[1]

The angels had predicted many evils at the time of the creation of human beings in their essence and all of them were displayed in Karbala. On the other hand, the Almighty Allah had said, "O My angels! You are seeing one side of the coin and not the brighter side, which depicts the greatness of a human being." This human excellence became explicit in Karbala.

---

[1] Surah Baqarah 2:30

Thus, the battlefield of Karbala was very amazing and a testing ground.

Callousness of the enemy

Yazid committed such callous deeds in Karbala, which were hardly committed by anyone or by very few. On the whole we can say that there is no match for such callous deeds. One of them was martyring a youth or a child in front of their mothers. In Karbala, eight persons were martyred in front of their mothers or beheaded or cut into pieces. Out of them, three were youths and five were children.[1]

Martyrdom of Ali Asghar

Out of those eight martyrs, one of them is Abdullah, who is mostly known to as Ali Asghar. The mothers of those eight martyrs were present in Karbala. According to reliable books of history, this baby of Imam Husain ﷺ was martyred outside the tent. Imam Husain ﷺ came inside and said, "Sister Zainab! Bring my suckling child so that I bid him farewell."[2]

It is narrated that Lady Zainab brought the baby to the Imam. He took him in his arms and wanted to kiss him. The mother of that baby stood at the entrance of the tent watching this scene when an arrow was shot on the order of Umar bin Saad; which penetrated the neck of the little one.

---

[1] *Absarul Ain*, Pg. 130
[2] *Muntahal Amaal*, Vol. 1, Pg. 693

Another such martyr was Qasim, who had a face as lovely as moon. His mother was also present in Karbala.[1] However, His Eminence, Ali Akbar's mother, Laila, was not present in Karbala. Although it is generally narrated that Laila was present in Karbala, the fact is that her name is nowhere mentioned in the events of Karbala.[2]

Zainab felt indebted to Husain 🕮

Zainab had seen her son, Aun bin Abdullah bin Ja'far Tayyar being martyred in front of her eyes in Karbala.

Two sons of Abdullah bin Ja'far Tayyar had accompanied Imam Husain 🕮 to Karbala and both were martyred. One of them was Lady Zainab's son.[3] It is a proven fact that only one son of Lady Zainab was martyred in Karbala. The elevated character of Lady Zainab is worth noticing that none of the books of history have recorded that she cried before or after the martyrdom of her beloved son in his remembrance. It seemed that whenever she wished to call out the name of her son, she used to stop thinking that it would be a cause of disrespect of her brother, Husain. It means, she used to think that her son was not enough as a sacrifice on Brother Husain. For instance, Lady Zainab ran out of the tent at the martyrdom of Ali Akbar and cried, "O my brother! O my nephew!"[4] However, no one saw Lady Zainab expressing such grief at the martyrdom of her son.

---

[1] The name of Qasim's mother was Ramla. She was Umme Walad. *Maqtal-e-Husain,* Muqarram, Pg. 263

[2] *Muntahal Amaal,* Vol. 1, Pg. 675

[3] The second son of Abdullah bin Ja'far was Muhammad whose mother's name was 'Khausa'. *Maqtal-e-Husain,* Muqarram, Pg. 262

[4] It is written as follows in *Irshad,* Shaykh Mufid, Pg. 239 and *Muntahal Amaal,* Vol. 1, Pg. 674: *'Yaa ukhayyaah wabna ukhayyaah.'*

One of the youths from the sons of Muslim bin Aqeel was also martyred in front of his mother. That mother was Ruqayya, daughter of Imam Ali ﷺ.[1]

(All those martyrs were from the progeny of His Eminence, Abu Talib)

Two or three martyrs were from the companions of Imam Husain ﷺ. One of them was Abdullah bin Umair Kalbi[2] while it is not known the sons of which companions the others were.[3] These two youths were also martyred in front of their mothers. I have already spoken about them in my previous mourning speeches (*Majalis*).

A mother whose young son was beheaded in front of her

A ten-year-old child from Ahlul Bayt was martyred after the martyrdom of Imam Husain ﷺ. I do not remember his name. When there was chaos in the camp after the martyrdom of Imam Husain ﷺ, this child ran out. It is written in books of Karbala tragedy that the child could not understand what was going on and he came out confused. The narrator says that he cannot forget that there were earrings in that child's ears and his mother was also standing near him when suddenly an oppressor came forward and beheaded that child.[4]

---

[1] The name of this son of Muslim was Abdullah. *Absarul Ain,* Pg. 130

[2] This youth was Wahab bin Abdullah bin Habbab Kalbi who was newly married. (Rizwani)

[3] The name of this child was Amr bin Junada Ansari. *Maqtal-e-Husain,* Muqarram, Pg. 253

[4] The name of this child was Muhammad bin Abi Saeed bin Aqeel. *Maqtal-e-Husain,* Muqarram, Pg. 280

The martyrdom of one more child, which became a cause of grief for Imam Husain ﷺ was Abdullah bin Hasan. This son of Imam Hasan ﷺ was ten years old. His mother was present in Karbala.[1] He was brought up under the care of Imam Husain ﷺ. Imam Husain ﷺ loved this memento of his brother very much. It is narrated that when Imam Husain ﷺ was lying in the downs of martyrdom during his last moments, this child came out of the tents and ran towards the battlefield. Lady Zainab caught hold of him but the child managed to free himself and ran away saying, "I swear by Allah that I would not leave my uncle alone". Reaching the low-land he fell on Imam Husain ﷺ. Glory be to Allah! How majestic this patience is! How great the patience of Husain is! How calm the heart of Husain is! Imam Husain ﷺ took the child in his arms. The child began talking to him. A killer came forward with his sword to behead the Imam. The child said, "O illegitimate one! Do you want to martyr my uncle?"[2] As soon as the oppressor struck with his sword, the child put forth his hands and they got cut as a result. The child cried for help, "O Uncle! Help me." Imam Husain ﷺ sighed, "O memento of my brother! Be patient. You would soon meet your father and grandfather."

In the name of Allah and by Allah and on the religion of the Messenger of Allah ﷺ

---

[1] *Absarul Ain,* Pg. 130

[2] *Irshad,* Shaykh Mufid, Pg. 241; *Biharul Anwār,* Vol. 45, Pg. 153; It is written as follows in *Muntahal Amaal,* Vol. 1, Pg. 700: "O son of a dirty person! May Allah curse you! Do you want to kill my uncle?"

Majlis 51

Lady Zainab leads the caravan

The history of Karbala is a history in which both men and women have played important roles. In this history each have their own roles but with the difference that the men kept to their limits and the ladies their own. And this is the miracle of Islam because it does not want one to become the buyer of hell. The world of today should also accept that men and women have their own limits. If not today, this fact would be accepted in the future.

Imam Husain ﷺ had taken his family members along to Karbala because he wanted that the character of women should also be adorned and displayed in this permanent history. He wanted Lady Zainab to play the role of a leader in the making of this history, remaining in the limits of female gender and not to cross the limits at any point.

Lady Zainab's character began to show soon after the Asr of Ashura. Now she was seen as the leader of the Imam's family members because Imam Sajjad ﷺ, the only man alive, was severely ill and she was taking care of him. It was Ibne Ziyad's order that no male members of Imam Husain's ﷺ progeny should be left alive. Thus, a number of attempts were made to slay Imam Sajjad ﷺ but the enemy said, "He would die on his own. Why to kill him?"[1] It was Divine will, which wanted to keep the progeny of Imam Husain ﷺ alive forever.

---

[1] *Irshad,* Shaykh Mufid, Pg. 242; *Biharul Anwār,* Vol. 45, Pg. 61

"Take us through the battle ground."

Imam Husain's ﷺ family members were taken captives on the 11th of Muharram and made to mount animals (camels or donkeys or both) with wooden saddles. They were not allowed to keep a cloth on that saddle because the army of the oppressors wanted to make them suffer the most. The family members said, "For the sake of Allah, take us through the battle ground (so that we may bid farewell to our dear ones who are martyred)."[1]

Lady Zainab mourns at the body of her brother

Only Imam Sajjad's legs were tied to the abdomen of his mount because he was ill while others sat loose on their mounts. When the reached the battle ground they all let themselves fall from their mounts. When Lady Zainab reached the body of Imam Husain ﷺ, she saw him in a state she had never seen before. She saw that her brother's body was lying unshrouded and he was beheaded. Eventually, she addressed the beheaded body, "May I be sacrificed for you, O brother! You suffered calamities and departed from this world. You passed away from this world thirsty." After that she wept so much that by Allah the enemies as well as the friends cried.[2]

Responsibility of Lady Zainab

Even though the first mourning assembly (*Majlis*) in memory of Imam Husain ﷺ was established by Lady Zainab, she was never careless about her responsibilities.

---

[1] *Luhūf,* Pg. 132; *Biharul Anwār,* Vol. 45, Pg. 58
[2] *Luhūf,* Pg. 134; *Biharul Anwār,* Vol. 45, Pg. 58; *Maqtal-e-Husain,* Muqarram, Pg. 307

Looking after Imam Sajjad ﷺ was one of her responsibilities. Thus, she used to glance at his face occasionally. When she saw that Imam Sajjad ﷺ was not able to control himself seeing the beheaded body of Imam Husain ﷺ unshrouded, she felt that he too would depart from this world out of pain. She immediately left the body of her brother, came to him and said, "O son of brother! Why are you in such a state? It seems that your soul would depart from the body." Imam Sajjad ﷺ replied in a thin voice, "Auntie! Why wouldn't I feel pain seeing my near and dear ones lying martyred?" Lady Zainab then consoled Imam Sajjad ﷺ.[1]

A tradition narrated by Umme Aiman

Umme Aiman was a great lady. She was apparently a slave-girl of Lady Khadija and was freed later on. After being freed, she lived in the Prophet's house. The Holy Prophet ﷺ used to respect her much. She spent a long time in the house of the Holy Prophet ﷺ. She narrated a tradition of the Holy Prophet ﷺ to Lady Zainab. Hearing this tradition, Lady Zainab went to her father, the Commander of the Faithful to confirm it. These were the last days of he caliphate of the Commander of the Faithful. Lady Zainab said, "O father! I have heard this tradition from Umme Aiman." Then she repeated that tradition to her father. Hearing the tradition, the Commander of the Faithful said that Umme Aiman had narrated correctly.[2]

Lady Zainab comforted Imam Sajjad ﷺ and narrated this tradition to him when he could not control himself seeing the martyred bodies of his near and dear ones. In that tradition it is mentioned that the incident of Karbala

---

[1] *Biharul Anwār,* Vol. 45, Pg. 179; *Muntahal Amaal,* Vol. 1, Pg. 718
[2] *Biharul Anwār,* Vol. 45, Pg. 183

has a significance associated with it. Hence, seeing the circumstances, he should not think that his father is killed and it is all over. 'No my nephew, no. It is the tradition of our grandfather that the place where Imam Husain ۩ is lying martyred[1] would be the grave of Husain tomorrow, which would be circumambulated by our followers.'

If the philosophy of martyrdom is explained

Husain's mausoleum would become the Qibla of Muslims.

Caravan of the prisoners in Kufa

Just like today, it was the 11th of Muharram in Karbala. Ibne Saad stayed back in Karbala to have his dead soldiers buried but the bodies of Imam Husain ۩ and his companions were left unshrouded. The Imam's family members were arrested (i.e. on the eve of the 12th Muharram) in Karbala and taken to Kufa. The distance between Karbala and Kufa was about twelve parasang (approx. 36 miles). They had planned that the prisoners should be made to enter Kufa accompanied by beating of drums of victory of Yazid to display his power. In this way, their mean minds had planned to deliver the last strike to Ahlul Bayt of the Prophet (s.a.).

They are being taken in such a condition that Lady Zainab had not slept since the Ashura eve. The holy severed heads of the martyrs mounted on spears were sent to Kufa in advance.[2] I don't know what time of the day it was (according to a tradition, two or three hours had passed since the sunrise of 12th Muharram). As soon as the

---

[1] *Biharul Anwār,* Vol. 45, Pg. 179; *Kamiluz Ziaraat,* Pg. 259
[2] *Muntahal Amaal,* Vol. 1, Pg. 718

prisoners entered the city, the heads of the martyrs were brought forward to welcome them.[1] The state of the Imam's family at this moment cannot be described in words.

Lady Zainab's sermon reminded one of Ali

O mourners!

Just imagine! The daughters of Ali and Fatima are seen at the gates of Kufa. People are watching the events. This is the same Kufa which was ruled by Imam Ali ﷺ. Ali's daughter, Zainab had a distinctiveness and individuality (Zainab in the market of Kufa?!) as proved by her eloquent sermon.

It is narrated that the aggrieved Lady Zainab selected a suitable time for her speech and signaled. It is recorded that there was so much noise everywhere that one could not hear a word. However, as soon as she signaled, there was pin drop silence as if people had stopped breathing and clock-bells stopped ringing.[2] Even riders stopped by (obviously, if the riders stop the mounts would stop automatically).

Dignity and Modesty of Lady Zainab

Lady Zainab delivered a sermon regarding which the narrator says: "By Allah, I have not seen a woman (Khafra)

---

[1] Ibid. Pg. 728
[2] *Amali,* Shaykh Mufid, Pg. 198; *Luhūf,* Pg. 146; *Biharul Anwār,* Vol. 45, Pg. 108-162

who has greatness of womanhood and dignity overflowing from her speech".[1]

The word 'Khafrah' is most important in this statement, which means a dignified woman. As it was told about her speech, it means, "By Allah, I have not seen a woman who has greatness of womanhood and dignity overflowing from her speech." It would not be an exaggeration to say that Lady Zainab had a mixture of Imam Ali's ﷺ courage and dignity of womanhood in her speech.

Imam Ali ﷺ was called the Commander of the Faithful twenty years before in Kufa and ruled there for about five years. Imam Ali ﷺ had delivered numerous sermons from the pulpit of Kufa. The people had not forgotten the way of Ali's speech because it was matchless. Thus, the narrator says that when Lady Zainab delivered a sermon, it seemed as if Ali has come to life once again and Ali's soul was speaking from Zainab's body.

The narrator says that when Lady Zainab's brief sermon[2] was over, he saw that everybody was biting their nails.

It was as if Lady Zainab had displayed the character of women as desired by Islam. That is, Islam wants a woman to have her personality full of dignity, chastity and purity.

On the basis of this, women have also fulfilled their responsibility remaining within their limits as much as the effective role played by men in making the history of

---

[1] *Amali,* Shaykh Mufid, Pg. 198; *Luhūf,* Pg. 146; *Biharul Anwār,* Vol. 45, Pg. 108-162

[2] The translation of this eloquent sermon of Lady Zainab is present elsewhere in this book.

Karbala. As if the history of Karbala, which has passed through the stages of human perfection has come into being through the partnership of both, men and women.

There is no power and might except by Allah the High and the Mighty.

Majlis 52

Lady Zainab in the court of Ibne Ziyad

You must have heard a number of times that the holy personalities of Imam Husain ﷺ, his companions and Ahlul Bayt are distinguished because of their determination of not accepting disgrace in the Karbala tragedy. They could be made captives, shackled in chains, made to wear heavy iron collars, get wounded, get martyred but they cannot bear the load of disgrace even if women have to become captives.

It is narrated that when the Imam's family members were made captives and brought to the court of Ibne Ziyad, women, including those from the Ahlul Bayt as well as wives and slave-girls of the companions of Imam Husain ﷺ encircled Lady Zainab and kept her veiled from the view. Lady Zainab was tall; therefore she was visible even after being surrounded by other women. She did not greet the ruler upon entering the court.

Ibne Ziyad used to think that he has taken away all the strength of Ahlul Bayt after the Karbala tragedy. His mean thinking was that he had made Ahlul Bayt helpless and was expecting them to fall at his feet and seek forgiveness. Thus, he had expected that at least Lady Zainab would greet him even if based on some Divine Will. However, the determined daughter of Ali shattered all his expectations. He was enraged at this act of disrespect for him. Perhaps he was not aware that the souls of the family of the Prophet (s.a.) were not going to be intimidated. When Lady Zainab sat down,[1] he proudly asked, "Who is this haughty woman?" Or he asked, "Why didn't she greet me?" or asked, "Who is this woman careless about others?" (Both versions are found. One of them has the word *Mutakabbir* and other *Munkir*) No one replied to Ibne Ziyad's question. He repeated his question once again but did not get any reply. When he repeated it for the third or fourth time, a woman said, "This is Zainab, the daughter of Ali bin Abi Talib ﷺ".

Ibne Ziyad tried to deceive the people. He said, "Praise be to Allah for He disgraced you. He killed you and exposed your lie." The accursed one continued to taunt Lady Zainab with his words.

Lady Zainab had a great responsibility on her shoulders at this moment. Hearing his words, the determined Lady Zainab spoke in a defying manner, "All thanks is for the Lord Who gave prophethood to Muhammad Mustafa and honor to us and granted the miracle of infallibility to our household. What you are saying is wrong." Then she said,

"O Ibne Ziyad! Disgraced is one that is a sinner and a liar. We are not such! We have dignity. Falsehood is not the practice of truthful ones. Falsehood is far away from us. O son of Marjana! May God destroy you!"[2]

---

[1] Normally, prisoners of war cannot sit without the permission of the commander of the victorious army but Lady Zainab took her seat in Ibne Ziyad's court without his permission and broke his pride. She made it clear that she was the actual victor and not he. (Rizwani)

[2] *Irshad,* Shaykh Mufid, Pg. 243; *Luhūf,* Pg. 160; *Biharul Anwār,* Vol. 45, Pg. 115-117; *Muntahal Amaal,* Vol. 1, Pg. 735; *Maqtal-e-Husain,* Muqarram, Pg. 324

Ibne Ziyad's eyes were red in anger on hearing this. He hissed like a desert snake and said, "Do you still have strength left? Are you talking in the same way even after suffering so much? Are you still focused on your aim?"

Although "son of Marjana" are three words, they describe a story, which unveiled the lowly character of Ibne Ziyad. Ibne Ziyad's mother, Marjana was an unchaste woman. Lady Zainab directed the attention of everyone present in the court towards this fact by calling him "son of Marjana".

Ibne Ziyad ordered his executioner to "behead that woman" (Lady Zainab).

Similarly, when he addressed Imam Sajjad 🕮, he also replied without hesitation. Thus, Ibne Ziyad ordered the executioner to behead that youth also. Hearing this, Lady Zainab got up from her place, held Imam Sajjad 🕮 near her and said,

"By Allah, you cannot kill him unless you behead me."[1]

It is written that Ibne Ziyad looked at them for some time and then said: "What a strange thing blood relation is!"

"I can see that if I want to kill this youth, I will have to kill this woman first."[2]

There is no power and might except by Allah the High and the Mighty.

---

[1] *Irshad,* Shaykh Mufīd, Pg. 244; *Biharul Anwār,* Vol. 45, Pg. 117; *Maqtal-e-Husain,* Muqarram, Pg. 325
[2] *Falsafa Akhlaq,* Pg. 57-59

Majlis 53

Imam Husain's ﷺ Killers gave a religious hue to their crime

Every system is in needs of ideological and religious support for it survival. Thus, every system wants its support to be based on some philosophy or thought, even if it be a religious thought, inscribed on the hearts of people, so that no one objects to it. Yazid's regime also could not survive without the support of some beliefs.

You should not think that they were so foolish and thinking that everything has come to an end after the battle of Karbala and there was no need of doing anything about it. It wasn't so. After this tragic event, the regime was always busy planning how to keep the people occupied in an issue so that they are forced to think that whatever was happening was in favor of that regime. For seeking the pleasure of religious class, it is necessary for the regime to give a religious look to their moves. Therefore, Qadi Shuraih's help was sought so that people may be satisfied intellectually and their way of thinking could be changed. This thinking was successful till the Asr of Ashura day in Karbala.

Imam Baqir ﷺ says that thirty thousand people had gathered in Karbala to slay the grandson of the Holy Prophet ﷺ. Why? They wanted to seek the nearness of God after shedding the blood of the son of the Holy

Prophet ﷺ.[1] They used to attack Imam Husain ؏ with swords in order to earn Paradise. The leaders of those people were bribed with bags of gold for this, as Farazdaq has said; while people were completely unaware of this fact. The leaders who deviated people from their paths were those who had filled their pockets with bribes. The peculiarity of Ibne Ziyad's regime was that he had given his crimes a religious look in order to deceive people.

On the other hand Yazid had a stigma because of his drinking habit. When he got heated up after being intoxicated, his self spoke. Then he would not be able to control himself and used to speak the truth. He had said that he would not accept anything. This habit left him nowhere. Otherwise, Yazid too would have misguided the people through such intellectual attacks.

After the great martyrdom, Ibne Ziyad gathered the people in the great mosque of Kufa to inform them about the matter. He tried to give a religious look to the martyrdom of Imam Husain ؏ at that time also. He wore the veil of purity and said, "I thank Allah Who granted victory to truth and the truthful ones and killed a liar, son of a liar who used to deceive people."[2] Ibne Ziyad wanted the people to thank Allah and hundreds of people did so. However there was a blind man in the gathering who though unable to see with his physical eyes was very farsighted. He thwarted Ibne Ziyad's plan.

---

[1] *Biharul Anwār,* Vol. 44, Pg. 298
[2] *Irshad,* Shaykh Mufid, Pg. 244; *Luhūf,* Pg. 163; *Biharul Anwār,* Vol. 45, Pg. 119
The words of Ibne Ziyad in Masjid Kufa are recorded as follows in *Maalimul Madarasatain,* Vol. 3, Pg. 186: "Praise be to Allah for He made truth and people of truth triumph and helped the master of faithful, Yazid bin Muawiyah and his group and killed liar Husain bin Ali and his supporters." (Rizwani)

The blind man did not let Ibne Ziyad's trick to succeed

There was a gentleman called Abdullah Ibne Afif.[1] May God bless him. Sometimes, it happens that people dare to lay down their lives and save the entire world by sacrificing themselves. The case of Abdullah bin Afif is similar. He could not see from his eyes. He had lost one eye in Jamal and another in Siffeen fighting alongside Imam Ali 🕮. He could not work because of his blindness and could not even participate in Jihad because of his handicap. Hence he used to spend most of his time in worship. On that day, he was praying in the Kufa mosque. As soon as he heard the words of Ibne Ziyad, he got up from his place and said, "O Ibne Ziyad! You are a liar and your father was a liar."[2] After that, Abdullah bin Afif continued to speak till people pushed him down and he fell. He was arrested and got martyred but the veil of Ibne Ziyad was already torn.[3]

Ibne Ziyad's logic based on force

Ibne Ziyad illegitimate in both senses i.e. he was illegitimate by birth and also had a devilish character. Normally, in societies where people are inclined to religion, despotic rulers use a logic based on force in order to justify their oppression. They associate every move with Allah. They say that everything was because of the Divine Will. If it had not been so the incident would not have occurred. Whatever happens is because of the Will of

---

[1] Abdullah bin Afif Azudi
[2] "O enemy of God! Certainly you are a liar and your father was a liar and the person who made you governor is also a liar and his father was also a liar. O son of Marjana!"
[3] *Irshad,* Shaykh Mufid, Pg. 244; *Luhūf,* Pg. 164; *Biharul Anwār,* Vol. 45, Pg. 119

God. This logic of forcefulness is the logic of Ibne Ziyad. When he faced Lady Zainab, he associated the course of events to Allah and said, "Praise be to Allah..."

These statements have lot of meaning hidden in them. "I thank Allah for He disgraced you. He killed you and unveiled your lie. i.e. you had spread a strange mischief among the Muslims."[1]

---

[1] After a thorough research in this matter, one concludes that the autocratic rulers propagated belief in compulsion because through it they could be acquitted of all crimes. People consider their crimes as one's destiny and keep quiet and consider it as a part of their faith. Unjust rulers of Bani Umayyah played an important role in spreading the belief of compulsion.

When Imam's family members were taken captives to Kufa in the court of Ibne Ziyad after incident of Karbala, he told Lady Zainab: "Praise be to Allah Who has disgraced you, killed you and revealed the false nature of your claims." Lady Zainab opposed him saying: "Praise be to God Who has favored us with His Prophet, Muhammad, may God bless him and his family. And He has purified us completely from sin. He only disgraces the great sinner and reveals the false nature of the profligate. Such men are not among us, praise be to God. Ibne Ziyad said, "How do you consider God has treated your House?"

"God decreed death for them and they went forward (bravely) to their resting-places," Zainab replied, "God will gather you and us together. You will plead your excuses to Him and we will be your opponents before Him."

Then Ibne Ziyad asked Imam Sajjad (a.s.): "What is your name?" he replied, "Ali bin Husain" Ibne Ziyad said, "Didn't Allah kill Ali bin Husain in Karbala?" Imam Sajjad (a.s.) said, "My brother, Ali, was martyred by the people." Ibne Ziyad said, "Indeed Allah killed him." Imam Sajjad (a.s.) said: اللَّهُ يَتَوَفَّى الْأَنفُسَ حِينَ مَوْتِهَا وَالَّتِي لَمْ تَمُتْ فِي مَنَامِهَا Meaning: *Allah takes the souls at the time of their death, and those that die not during their sleep.* (Surah Zumar 39:42) And: وَمَا كَانَ لِنَفْسٍ أَنْ تَمُوتَ إِلاَّ بِإِذْنِ الله كِتَابًا Meaning: *And a soul will not die but with the permission of Allah.* (Surah Aale Imran 3:145)

Just think upon it! A person who has apparently lost a battle is disgraced according to Ibne Ziyad's logic. It means, a person who is killed in a battle is like a defeated one. The defeat disgraces and finishes him. In other words, he cannot be said to be following the right path. If he had

---

Yazid told Imam Sajjad (a.s.) regarding oppression in Karbala, "Your father broke relations with me and denied my right and fought against me in my rule. Whatever Allah did to him in return is in front of your eyes." Imam Sajjad (a.s.) said:

مَا أَصَابَ مِن مُصِيبَةٍ فِي الْأَرْضِ وَلَا فِي أَنفُسِكُمْ إِلَّا فِي كِتَابٍ مِّن قَبْلِ أَن نَّبْرَأَهَا

Meaning: *No evil befalls on the earth nor in your own souls, but it is in a book before We bring it into existence.* (Surah Hadīd 57:22)

Yazid told his son, Khalid reply but he could not. Yazid said, "Tell him: وَمَا أَصَابَكُم مِّن مُّصِيبَةٍ فَبِمَا كَسَبَتْ أَيْدِيكُمْ Meaning: *And whatever affliction befalls you, it is on account of what your hands have wrought* . (Surah Shura 42:30)

Ibne Ziyad and Yazid related the incident of Karbala to Allah and said that all injustice in Karbala was done by Allah. However, Imam Sajjad and Lady Zainab rejected their logic and said, "God did not do injustice to us. You and your companions have done it."

Narrators who supported the three caliphs have narrated traditions of the Holy Prophet to prove the validity of belief in compulsion. It is narrated from Abu Huraira that the Holy Prophet said, "Ask me." However, everyone kept quiet because of his awe. Then a person came and sat near the Holy Prophet. He asked, "O Messenger of Allah! What is Islam?" Holy Prophet said, "Not holding anyone as a partner of God, offering prayer, paying Zakat and observing fast in the holy month of Ramadan." He said, "You are right." Then he asked, "What is faith?" The Holy Prophet said, "Believing in Allah, His angels, His books, gathering in front of him, His messengers, resurrection and complete destiny is faith." He said, "You are right."

The conclusion of the first nine traditions of *Sahih Muslim,* "Kitab al-Qadr" is that as soon as a fetus is formed inside the womb, Allah orders His angels to destine is earning, character and habits. He also orders to note down whether the child would be fortunate or not. Whenever a person is still in the womb, it is decided that he would enter Paradise or Hell and this decision never changes. Thus, a human being is compelled in his actions. (Allamah Sayyid Murtadha Askari, *Ahya-e-din mein Ahle Bayt ka kirdar,* Vol. 2, Pg. 387) - Rizwani

been on the right path he would have won. He meant to say that since he was able to overpower the Ahlul Bayt, it was a proof that they were on the wrong path.

Standard of disgrace according to Lady Zainab's words

Lady Zainab replied to Ibne Ziyad saying, "I thank Allah for He granted us honor of prophethood and because we are from the family of the Holy Prophet ."[1]

"Whoever dies in the battlefield is not disgraced because the standard of disgrace is something else."[2]

"The standard of dishonor is dependent on the search of truth and reality. Whoever sacrifices his life in the way of Allah is not dishonored. Disgraced is one who oppresses, and one who turns away from the truth. The standard of being disgraced or not is being on the right path or going astray respectively. On the basis of dishonor, whoever is killed is not necessarily a liar. The standard of truth or falsehood is a person himself, his goals and his words and deeds. Although my brother, Husain has been martyred, he would be called truthful. If he had remained alive then too he would have been called truthful. However, even if you are killed, you will remain a liar. If you remain alive then too you will be a liar." After this crushing reply, Lady Zainab attacked Ibne Ziyad severely with her statement and he was dumbstruck. She said, "O son of Marjana!" Marjana was Ibne Ziyad's mother and he

---

[1] It is written as follows in *Irshad,* Shaykh Mufid and *Biharul Anwār*: "Praise be to Allah Who honored us by His Prophet."
[2] *Irshad,* Shaykh Mufid, Pg. 244; *Luhūf,* Pg. 160; *Biharul Anwār,* Vol. 45, Pg. 117

did not like anyone calling him by her name because she was well known for her unchastity."[1]

Ibne Ziyad ordered Lady Zainab to be killed

Ibne Ziyad had no reply for statements like: "O son of Marjana! O son of an unchaste woman! Disgrace is for the son of Marjana because it is in his destiny."

Thus, he became furious and ordered his executioner to behead that woman. A Khariji (enemy of Ali) was present in the court at that time. When he heard Ibne Ziyad's order, his Arabian sense of honor surged up and he told Ibne Ziyad,[2] "O Amir! Are you in your senses? You are talking to a woman and that too, one who has borne infinite sorrows. Her brothers are killed and she has lost her near and dear ones."

Ali's name offends the enemy

Imam Sajjad ؏ was presented before Ibne Ziyad. He shouted at Imam ؏ loudly like Firon, "Who are you?" The Imam said, "I am Ali, son of Husain."

Ibne Ziyad asked, "Didn't Allah kill Ali bin Husain in Karbala?" (Again the act was associated with Allah) so that people are assured that Yazid was right. Imam Sajjad ؏ replied, "Certainly, capturing the souls of everyone is in the hands of Allah but my brother was martyred by the people (and not Allah)."

---

[1] *Luhūf,* Pg. 160; *Biharul Anwār,* Vol. 45, Pg. 116
[2] The name of this person is mentioned as Amr bin Harith in *Irshad,* Shaykh Mufid, Pg. 244; *Biharul Anwār,* Vol. 45, Pg. 116

Ibne Ziyad said, "One Ali and another Ali?[1] What is all this? Did your father name all his sons Ali? Is your name and your brother's name Ali? Wasn't there any other name?" Imam Sajjad 🕮 replied, "My father loved his father very much. He liked to name his sons after his father while you consider your father a disgrace for yourself."

Shield of Imam Sajjad 🕮

Ibne Ziyad had expected Imam Sajjad 🕮 not speak a word in front of him because in his view no prisoner could dare to speak up. He had expected Imam Sajjad 🕮 to agree with him when he said that it was the work of Allah and accept their fate. However when he saw that Imam Sajjad 🕮 dared to speak freely in spite of being a captive, he said, "How dare you reply me like this?"[2] He hissed like a desert reptile in fury and ordered his executioner, "Go on and behead this youth."

It is narrated that when this order was given to the executioner, Lady Zainab stood up from her place and held Imam Sajjad 🕮 near her. She said, "I swear by Allah, you cannot kill him unless you kill me."

It is narrated that Ibne Ziyad looked at them for some time and then said, "I can see that if I want to kill this

---

[1] It is written in *Damaus Sujum,* Pg. 251 that it is narrated from Yahya bin Hasan in Manaqib that Yazid told Imam Sajjad (a.s.), "How strange it is that your father has named both his sons Ali!" Imam (a.s.) replied, "My father loved his father and wanted to name all his sons Ali."

[2] *Irshad,* Shaykh Mufid, Pg. 244; *Luhūf,* Pg. 162; *Biharul Anwār,* Vol. 45, Pg. 117

youth, I will have to kill this woman first."[1] Thus he refrained from killing Imam Sajjad 🕮.

Yes, it is an important characteristic of Ahlul Bayt that they fought against the belief of predestination, which is prevalent even today and is being interpreted as justice. In other words, Ahlul Bayt of the Holy Prophet 🕮 proved that statements like "there is no responsibility on a human being" or "It is not the duty of a human being to try to bring change in the society" or "whatever is happening was bound to happen" i.e. "there is no role to be played by a human being in this society" were practically wrong and fought against them.

---

[1] *Irshad,* Shaykh Mufid, Pg. 244; *Luhūf,* Pg. 162; *Biharul Anwār,* Vol. 45, Pg. 117

Majlis 54

Our souls cannot be shackled

It is narrated that when the Imam's family members were brought in Ibne Ziyad's court, the ladies of the Imam's family and slave-girls surrounded Lady Zainab who was tall in stature and was thus visible in the center like a jewel surrounded by its protectors.

Ibne Ziyad knew Lady Zainab as much as he knew the chiefs of his court. He had expected her to greet him upon entering the palace (as per the custom). However, Ali's daughter did not greet him.

Zainab wanted to prove and she proved effectively that Ibne Ziyad should not think that he would be able to arrest their souls like he had shackled their bodies and arrested them. Not at all! She proved that their souls were perfected human souls, not made on their own but they were divine souls. Hence, their souls could neither be controlled nor given death. Therefore, Lady Zainab did not greet him.

This infuriated Ibne Ziyad and he said, "Who is this haughty woman?" No one replied. He repeated his question two or three times and got a reply at last, "She is Zainab, the daughter of Ali bin Abi Talib ﷺ."[1] Then Lady

---

[1] *Irshad,* Shaykh Mufid, Pg. 243; *Luhūf,* Pg. 160; *Biharul Anwār,* Vol. 45, Pg. 115-117; *Muntahal Amaal,* Vol. 1, Pg. 735; *Maqtal-e-Husain,* Muqarram, Pg. 324

Zainab condemned Ibne Ziyad so much that he could not speak a word. He was compelled to order his executioner to 'behead that woman'.

Lady Zainab in Yazid's court

When Lady Zainab was brought in Yazid's court in the Green Palace, she displayed the same majesty over there also. Even after passing through imprisonment and forty stages of the journey, her determination was not affected. Her soul had not broken down and her determination and patience was more explicit in Yazid's court.

The sermon of Lady Zainab in Yazid's court has no match in this world. I would like to narrate only one statement of that sermon here. Lady Zainab said, "O Muawiyah's son! You may try all means to attack but remember that you would not be able to extinguish this "light of revelation" that has descended in our house. You and your kingdom would be destroyed in this world. Your name would become a word of abuse but the name and the message of my brother would remain forever.[1] The field grown by him would remain green forever. My brother, Husain, is a source of inspiration for the pious. The whole world would become a fan of my brother."

Why was Lady Zainab confident that Yazid's name would be demeaned and Husain's message would spread everywhere? It was so because she was confident about human nature. Allah has created men with the "love for truth". As said by the famous poet, Iqbal:

Musa and Firon and Shabbir and Yazid

---

[1] *Biharul Anwār*, Vol. 45, Pg. 135

These two opposing powers come into being since the
beginning of creation.

Enlivening of truth is from the power of Shabbir

And falsehood finally ends in despair and death.

When the relationship of the Caliphate was cut off
from the Quran.

Poison was dissolved in the mouth of freedom.

When the leader of the best of the nations wanted

To spread greenery like a cloud gives rain.

These rained on the land of Karbala and went away

Leaving behind a field of red flowers they went away.

So that tyranny is destroyed forever

The waves of his blood created a garden.

"The Prophet used to kiss those lips."

Although Yazid was considered among the eloquent
poets of Arabia, he remained speechless in front of Lady
Zainab's logic. The representatives of non-Muslim
countries and top military officials were present in the
court. Hence, he had to face a lot of humiliation.[1] Yazid
tried much to silence Lady Zainab but could not succeed
and then he committed a serious crime in order to do so.
He told himself that it was necessary to control this lady in

---

[1] *Maqtal-e-Husain,* Muqarram, Pg. 355

such a way that it is not known to others that she had been silenced. Actually, Lady Zainab's words had changed his state. Thus, he committed a crime, which I cannot narrate in detail. I would only say that this act of Yazid was not liked by one of his courtiers.[1] He shouted:

"O Yazid! Hold your cane. By Allah, I have seen with my own eyes that the Holy Prophet ﷺ used to kiss these lips."[2]

---

[1] Abu Barza Salami

[2] *Maqtal-e-Husain,* Muqarram, Pg. 354; *Falsafa Akhlaq,* Pg. 220-221

Majlis 55

Zainab – inheritor of the greatness of Ali and Fatima

The greatness of Lady Zainab is a fact. That she achieved it through being brought up in the lap of Lady Zahra and Imam Ali ☀ is also a decided matter. However, after the Karbala tragedy, Zainab had changed a lot i.e. the greatness she achieved after Karbala was much more.

We have seen that Lady Zainab could not control herself two or three times on the Ashura eve. Once she cried so much that she fell unconscious in the lap of Imam Husain ☀ who consoled her through his words later on. Imam Husain ☀ said, "I fear Shaitan would overcome you and snatch away your patience."[1]

When Imam Husain ☀ asked Lady Zainab, "Why do you do like this? When the Holy Prophet ☀ could not live forever, who would? Didn't you see grandfather, the Holy Prophet ☀ pass away? My grandfather was better than me, my father was also better than me and my brother Hasan and mother Fatima were also better than me." Lady Zainab replied, "O brother! When they all passed away you were my last refuge but after you go away there would be no refuge for me."

---

[1] *Irshad,* Shaykh Mufid, Pg. 232; *Biharul Anwār,* Vol. 45, Pg. 2

However, as soon as the sun arose on the Ashura day and she saw Imam Husain ﷺ moving towards his goal with a strong determination; such a change occurred in her personality that even the least personality did not remain for one who opposed her. Imam Sajjad ﷺ says, "We were twelve persons in all, and we were all tied with a single rope. One end of this rope was tied to my arm and the other to the arm of my aunt, Zainab."[1]

Prisoners in the palace of Yazid

It is narrated that the prisoners, tethered in a rope reached Damascus on the 2nd of Safar.[2] Thus, Lady Zainab had remained captive for twenty-two days. She was suffering constant harassment and hardships for twenty-two days. The prisoners were brought into Yazid's court in a very bad condition. Yazid's palace was named as 'Qasr-e-Khazra' (Green Palace), and it was built by his father, Muawiyah. The grandeur of the palace dazzled the eyes of the onlookers.

Some historians have mentioned that people had to pass through seven huge courtyards to reach the last one where Yazid was seated on a gem-studded throne. Apart from the rich, representatives of other countries used to sit on gold or silver chairs.[3] The situation was same on the day the prisoners were brought to his palace.

When the grief-stricken Zainab reached this magnificent palace, a storm brewed up in her soul as a

---

[1] *Luhūf,* Pg. 178; *Damaus Sujum,* Pg. 247-248; *Muntahal Amaal,* Vol. 1, Pg. 764

[2] It is written as follows in *Maqtal-e-Husain,* Muqarram, Pg. 248: They entered Damascus on 1st of Safar and were stopped at Baabus Saa'at.

[3] *Muntahal Amaal,* Vol. 1, Pg. 759

result of which she delivered a sermon that created so much tumult that Yazid was taken aback and could not speak a word in spite of being famous for his eloquence.

Lady Zainab's sermon in Yazid's court

When Yazid had no reply for Lady Zainab, he began to humming the verses of Abdullah bin Zibari Sahmi,[1] which were full of polytheism and he had composed them when he was a polytheist. He was proud of his apparent victory. Suddenly, Lady Zainab raised her voice,

"O Yazid! Do you think that you have closed for us the paths of the earth and heaven by making us roam here and there like ordinary prisoners? Do you think that your honor would increase and our dignity would decrease because of this?"[2]

"O Yazid! You have filled some more air in your brain.[3] You think that you have closed all the paths for us by imprisoning us and we are in the custody of your servants. By Allah, at this moment you are an extremely immoral and lowly person in my view. I don't even consider you worthy enough to speak to."

Lady Zainab brings a revolution in Syria

Look, these people have sacrificed everything in the way of Allah except their faith and spiritual personality. Even after knowing this, can't you believe that such a paragon personality can create such fervor in the people

---

[1] *Muntahal Amaal,* Vol. 1, Pg. 766
[2] *Biharul Anwār,* Vol. 45, Pg. 133
[3] *Biharul Anwār,* Vol. 45, Pg. 133; *Maqtal-e-Husain,* Muqarram, Pg. 358

that they bring a revolution, like she brought a revolution in Syria? The speech of Lady Zainab had shaken the people so much that Yazid feared public reaction and was forced to change his ways and send the prisoners back to Medina respectfully. Then he tried to dissociate himself from this heinous crime by saying, "May Allah curse Ibne Marjana. All this happened because of him. I didn't order him this." Whose handiwork is it? Who compelled Yazid to say this? It was the achievement of Ali's daughter.

Lady Zainab said at the end of her speech: "O Yazid! So scheme whatever you wish to scheme, and carry out your plots, and intensify your efforts, for, by Allah, you shall never be able to obliterate our mention, nor will you ever be able to kill the revelation (that was revealed to us)."[1] Lady Zainab had dared to speak in front of that unjust ruler whom people feared for a thousand reasons and called him "the Commander of the Faithful".

"O Yazid! Use all the deceit you have to your heart's content. Try all the means. Increase the speed of your struggle and fulfill your wishes. However, remember that in spite of all this, you would neither be able to destroy our name from this world nor would be able to decrease our dignity or stop our views from spreading. It is you who is going to be destroyed."

As the poet Iqbal says:

The tradition of love consists of two chapters: Karbala and Damascus.

One was written by Husain and the other by Zainab.

---

[1] *Luhūf,* Pg. 185; *Biharul Anwār,* Vol. 45, Pg. 135

Lady Zainab delivered such a sermon in the court that Yazid was at his wit's end and the air of pride filled inside his head was removed. He became enraged. He committed a very cowardly and shameless act in order to silence Lady Zainab; he lifted his cane started misbehaving with the holy lips and teeth of Imam Husain's ﷺ.[1]

In the name of Allah and by Allah and on the religion of the Messenger of Allah ﷺ

---

[1] *Maqtal-e-Husain*, Muqarram, Pg. 354

Majlis 56

Imam's family in the prison of Syria

O mourners!

Since these are the days of mourning, I would like to mention a few sentences of the sufferings of Imam Husain's ﷺ family. These are days when the Imam's family was taken to Syria, though it cannot be said with certainty how many days had passed since they were brought to Syria, but according to a reliable tradition, they had arrived in Damascus on 2nd Safar.[1] Also according to whatever is mentioned in the books of Karbala tragedy, the Imam's family was confined within a four-walled place during these days.

The prison where the Imam's family members were lodged neither shaded them from the sun during the day, nor the cold at night. It was only a four-walled enclosure in which they were, so that they may not escape.

The above is the description given by the writers of Karbala account.[2] Now the question arises as to how much time did the Imam's family members spend in the prison? There is no perfect answer for this, whether it was a few days, a few weeks or a few months. It is recorded in the

---

[1] It is written as follows in *Maqtal-e-Husain,* Muqarram, Pg. 348: They entered Damascus on 1st of Safar and were halted at Baabus Saa'at

[2] *Luhūf,* Pg. 188; *Muntahal Amaal,* Vol. 1, Pg. 771

books of Karbala tragedy regarding this, that a person saw Imam Sajjad ﷺ sitting at the gate of the prison one day. Seeing his worn-out facial skin, he asked Imam ﷺ the reason for this. The Imam replied, "We were kept in such a prison where there was no protection against sun and cold."[1]

The stay of Imam's family in Syria was most torturous for them. It is narrated by Imam Sajjad ﷺ himself because he was once asked, "O master! Which was the most torturous stage for you? Was it the journey from Karbala to Kufa? Or from Kufa to Syria? Or the journey from Syria to Medina?" The Imam replied, "Ash-Shaam, Ash-Shaam, Ash-Shaam".[2] The journey to Syria was the toughest for them of all the places. The main cause of this was that the Imam's family had to enter Yazid's court where there was no stone left unturned to humiliate them.

Imam Sajjad ﷺ says, "Twelve of us were tied with a single rope. One end of the rope was tied to my arm and the other to my aunt, Zainab's arm. We were brought in Yazid's court in this state where Yazid was sitting on his throne surrounded by his courtiers." In this state also, Imam Sajjad ﷺ issued such a statement that Yazid was humiliated in front of everybody. Yazid had not at all expected that a prisoner would talk to him in this manner.

Imam Sajjad ﷺ addressed Yazid and said, "Do you permit me to say something?"[3]

Yazid gave the permission but with a condition that he should not speak anything obscene. The Imam said, "It

---

[1] *Anwār-e-Nomaniya,* Vol. 3, Pg. 252; *Muntahal Amaal,* Vol. 1, Pg. 277

[2] *Tazkiratush Shuhada,* Pg. 412

[3] *Muntahal Amaal,* Vol. 1, Pg. 764; *Damaus Sujum,* Pg. 247

is not possible for a person like me to speak anything obscene in such a court. I am going to speak logic." (The Imam certainly said this so that people become aware of the fact and wake up from their slumber of ignorance). "Yazid is sitting on his throne as the caliph of the Prophet (s.a.). What if the Holy Prophet ﷺ comes here and sees us who are his progeny, in this state?"[1]

In the name of Allah and by Allah and on the religion of the Messenger of Allah ﷺ

---

[1] *Ashnai ba Quran,* Vol. 5, Pg. 57

Majlis 57

Prisoners who enlivened the history of Karbala

The history of Karbala was revived by the prisoners of Karbala i.e. they are the protectors of the greatness of Karbala. The greatest foolishness of the Umayyad rulers was to take the Imam's family as captives through the bazaars of Kufa and Syria. If they had not done so, perhaps they could have succeeded in distorting the Karbala event or at least they could have veiled its truth to some extent. However, they dug their graves with their own hands and committed such an act that the Imam's family got an opportunity to revive the history of Karbala forever.

The Umayyad regime had not expected that distressed women and children could take full advantage of this opportunity. How could they have thought this? They had made a false propaganda to achieve their aim.

Imam Sajjad ☺ addresses the congregation during Friday prayer

It was Friday in Syria and people were getting ready for prayers. Yazid was forced to attend the prayer because perhaps he had to lead the prayer (at present I cannot be certain about it). It is necessary that two beneficial sermons be given before Friday Prayer. After that Prayer should start because these two sermons substitute for two units of Zuhr prayer and Friday Prayer consists of only two units.

At first, the government speaker mounted the pulpit. He praised Yazid and Muawiyah as usual and associated goodness with them. Then he spoke ill of Imam Ali and Husain ﷺ and cursed them as if God forbid, they had given up the religion and committed such acts.

Imam Sajjad ﷺ called out aloud, "O speaker! You are selling the pleasure of the Creator for the sake of gaining the pleasure of a creature."[1] Then he said, "O Yazid! Can I stand on these pieces of wood and speak?" How strange is this! The Ahlul Bayt of the Holy Prophet ﷺ kept even minute things in mind. For instance, Yazid was called 'the Commander of the Faithful' in his court but Ahlul Bayt did not call him so and did not even call him by is agnomen. They called him by his name i.e. 'Yazid'.[2] Both Imam Sajjad ﷺ as well as Lady Zainab followed the same practice. At that time, Imam Sajjad ﷺ did not called the pulpit 'a pulpit' but called it 'pieces of wood'. The three step wood seen from that place had such a lowly speaker mounted on it. Imam ﷺ asked whether he was permitted to mount those pieces of wood and speak a few words.

Yazid denied the permission to him. The people gathered there supported Imam Sajjad ﷺ because he was from Hijaz and they knew that the conversation of the people of Hijaz was very interesting. They also insisted Yazid to permit him because they wanted to see the Imam's style of speaking, but Yazid did not allow. His son said, "Father! Please permit him. We want to hear this youth from Hijaz." Yazid said, "I fear these people." However, the people insisted so much that Yazid was

---

[1] *Luhūf,* Pg. 188; *Biharul Anwār,* Vol. 45, Pg. 137
[2] *Biharul Anwār,* Vol. 45, Pg. 137

forced to allow him.[1] He also realized that if he asked for more justification, it would further expose his helplessness and fear; so he gave the permission.

Look, Imam Sajjad ﷺ was ill and a captive at that time because of Divine Will (after that, he did not remain ill and led a normal life like other Imams). Also, as commonly narrated from the pulpits, the Imam was tied in chains and had a heavy iron collar put around his neck. He had traveled forty stages in such a state to reach Syria. In spite of this, when he mounted the pulpit, what did he do? He created such an enthusiasm in the people that Yazid began to regret his mistake.

O Muezzin! Keep quiet

He began to feel that people would soon pounce upon him and kill him. Thus, he thought of a way to save himself. The time of prayer had arrived. He ordered the Muezzin to recite the Azaan (call for prayer) as the prayer was getting delayed. As soon as the Muezzin raised his voice the Imam became silent. The Muezzin called out, "Allah is the greatest, Allah is the greatest". Then he said, "I bear witness that there is no god except Allah" and the Imam repeated those words. When the Muezzin said, "I bear witness that Muhammad is the Messenger of Allah", the Imam took off his turban and said, "O Muezzin! For the sake of Muhammad, keep quiet." Then he turned towards Yazid and said, "O Yazid! Who is this messenger whose testimony is being given? Is he your grandfather or mine?" Then the Imam turned towards the people and said, "O

---

[1] *Biharul Anwār,* Vol. 45, Pg. 138; *Maqtal-e-Husain,* Muqarram, Pg. 352

people! Do you know who we are? Whom you have held captives? Who is my father, Husain who is martyred?"[1]

The people were unaware of truth till that time. You must have heard that Yazid released the family members of Imam Husain 🕮 and sent them back to Medina with all respect.

Noman bin Basheer was a mild and a friendly person. He was given the responsibility of accompanying the Imam's family to Medina and taking care of their needs and maintaining their honor. Did you ever wonder why it happened thus? Did Yazid suddenly transform into a good person? Did his thinking change suddenly? No, absolutely not. In reality, the society of Damascus had changed. You must have heard that Yazid used to curse Ibne Ziyad later on and accuse him of all the crimes. He used to say that he never ordered the killing of Imam Husain 🕮[2] and that Ibne Ziyad did all that on his own.

How did all this happen? All this happened because Imam Sajjad 🕮 and Lady Zainab had turned the flow of circumstances.

---

[1] *Biharul Anwār,* Vol. 45, Pg. 139; *Maqtal-e-Husain,* Muqarram, Pg. 353

[2] *Irshad,* Shaykh Mufid, Pg. 247; *Muntahal Amaal,* Vol. 1, Pg. 784

Majlis 58

Prison of Syria

Historians have mentioned that in the beginning the Imam's family had to bear a lot of difficulties in the prison of Syria were they were lodged. The four-walled prison where they were kept had no protection against sun and cold. Thus, they had to suffer day and night.[1] However, not much time had passed when Yazid regretted his political move. We cannot say that he had repented for his sins; but he realized that his mistakes in politics would prove dangerous for his power.

After that he used to abuse Ibne Ziyad often. He used to say, "May Allah curse the son of Marjana! I never told him to smear his hands with Husain's blood. I had told him to snatch his turban and bring it to me but he cut the head and brought it to me. I did not order him to kill Husain bin Ali ﷺ. Ibne Ziyad killed him of his own will."

Yazid repeated all this many times. However, they were all lies. He wanted to dissociate himself from this crime by talking in such a way and he tried to transfer his crime to Ibne Ziyad's account in order to ensure the safety of his regime.[2] In order to save his regime, he tried to shift the prisoners to a better place. If he had kept them in the same place, people would have said, "All right, we understand that Ibne Ziyad was behind everything in

---

[1] *Luhūf,* Pg. 188; *Muntahal Amaal,* Vol. 1, Pg. 771
[2] *Irshad,* Shaykh Mufid, Pg. 244; *Muntahal Amaal,* Vol. 1, Pg. 784

Karbala but he is not present here and you have all the power. Then why are you treating the prisoners so badly?" Thus, he ordered the prisoners to be shifted to a house near his palace. After that he released Imam Sajjad ؏ and permitted him to go anywhere in Syria. He invited Imam Sajjad ؏ many a times to join him for lunch or dinner.[1] He even asked the Imam one day, "Would my repentance be accepted if I repent?"[2]

There is no power and might except by Allah the High and the Mighty.

---

[1] *Irshad,* Shaykh Mufid, Pg. 244; *Muntahal Amaal,* Vol. 1, Pg. 783; *Damaus Sujum,* Pg. 265
The lecture could not be recorded further because it was end of the cassette.
[2] *Ashnai ba Quran,* Vol. 5, Pg. 249-250

Majlis 59

Imam Sajjad ﷺ – the embodiment of love

The personality of Imam Sajjad ﷺ was a perfect embodiment of love. He was love personified in all aspects. Whenever he saw a newcomer on the way, who was helpless, poor and destitute, he used to comfort him and take him to his house and take care of him.[1]

One day he saw a group of lepers (normally, people shun them fearing that they too would get that disease),[2] and brought them to his house and looked after them well.[3] The blessed house of Imam Sajjad ﷺ was a refuge of the poor, the orphans and the helpless.

Serving the caravan going for Hajj

He is the son of Allah's Messenger. However, he did not travel with a caravan, in which people knew him well. He used to wait for a caravan coming from far off place in

---

[1] *Muntahal Amaal,* Vol. 2, Pg. 15

[2] In ancient days, people used to consider leprosy a contagious disease. Imam Sajjad's grandfather Imam Ali (a.s.) also took care of lepers. This proves that this disease is not contagious. When this fact was mentioned in one of the books of Ustad Mutahhari, he got a call from a leprosy center managed by Christian missionaries. They asked him, "Did Imam Ali and Imam Sajjad really take care of lepers?" He replied them with proofs and they were impressed by the knowledge and helpful character of our Imams and asked for reference, which was given to them. - (Rizwani)

[3] *Biharul Anwār,* Vol. 46, Pg. 55; *Kafi,* Vol. 2, Pg. 13

which no one recognized him and he joined that caravan as a traveler. Eventually, such a caravan arrived and the Imam was permitted to join it. During those days, it took ten to twelve days traveling on horses or camels to reach the destination. Imam ﷺ served that caravan for this period and continued to travel for Hajj. During the journey, a person joined the caravan and he recognized the Imam. When he saw the Imam serving the people of caravan, he asked the people, "Do you know who the person serving you is?"

The people replied that they did not know who he was. They only knew that the youth belonged to Medina and was a nice man. That man said, "You are right that you don't know him. If you had recognized him you would not have ordered him and let him serve you." The people asked worriedly, "Do you know him?" The man replied, "Yes, he is son of Allah's Messenger, Ali, the son of Husain."

No sooner did the people come to know that he was Imam Sajjad ﷺ that they came running and fell at his feet. They said, "O son Allah's Messenger! Why are you making us sin? If we had dared to disregard you at any point, Divine chastisement would have befallen us. You are our master. You be seated here. We would serve you. The Imam said, "No, whenever I join a caravan in which people know me, they do not allow me to serve them. They say that they would serve me; but I want to travel with a caravan where people do not recognize me so that I get a chance to serve the pilgrims."[1]

---

[1] *Biharul Anwār,* Vol. 46, Pg. 69; *Muntahal Amaal,* Vol. 2, Pg. 13

Weeping and Supplications of Imam Sajjad 🕮

Imam Sajjad did not get as much opportunity as his father, Imam Husain 🕮 or Imam Ja'far Sadiq 🕮 because political conditions were not favorable during his time. However, a person who has desire to serve Islam, the conditions are always favorable for him except that the way is different.

We can estimate this from the fact that Imam Sajjad 🕮 had left behind a treasure of guidance for Shias in the form of supplications. He performed his duty nicely through these supplications. Some people are of the opinion that for whatever period Imam Sajjad 🕮 lived after his father, since he did not fight with the sword he ignored most matters related to the movement of Karbala. However, it is not true. Imam Sajjad 🕮 actually used every moment to enliven the Karbala movement.

Imam Zainul Abideen 🕮 mourned regularly. In whose memory he did thus? Was the Imam's state like that of a person who starts crying aimlessly when his feelings are hurt? Didn't this mourning mean that the Imam wanted to keep the memories of the Karbala tragedy alive? Didn't he want that people should never forget why Imam Husain 🕮 sacrificed his life and who all got martyred alongside him? This was the actual reason why the Imam mourned; and sometimes he used to mourn intensely.

One day a servant asked the Imam, "O master! How long would you keep mourning?" (He used to think that the Imam was mourning for his relatives) Imam 🕮 said, "What are you saying? Yaqoob was aggrieved only for one Yusuf and the holy Quran narrates his feelings that: "His eyes became white due to grief".[1] While I have seen eighteen Yusufs being martyred before my own eyes, who all fell on the land of Karbala one after another."[2]

[1] Surah Yusuf 12:84
[2] *Biharul Anwār,* Vol. 45, Pg. 149; *Seeri dar Seerat-e-Aimma-e-Athaar,* Pg. 112-114

Majlis 60

Martyrdom of Imam Musa Kaḍim ﷺ

As is well known, today is the night of the martyrdom of our seventh Imam, Imam Musa Kaḍim ﷺ. He was born in 128 A.H. It was the time when the Umayyad rule was at its peak while he was martyred in the prison of the Abbasid caliph, Harūn Rashid in 183 A.H. He was aged fifty-five years at that time. He spent the last years of his life in prison and he was poisoned and martyred in the prison itself.[1]

An Arab poet says:

"People taunt me that I was imprisoned. I say that it is not a defect. Is there any sharp sword that is not kept inside a sheath?

Don't you see that when a lion grows old, it gets into the habit of living in his den while lowly animals run here and there?"

Maulana Rumi had narrated an incident in the first section of his *Mathnawi*. After Prophet Yusuf ﷺ bore the calamities, falling into the well, becoming a slave and living in prison for many years, one of his childhood friends came to him. Maulana Rumi says:

---

[1] *Muntahal Amaal,* Vol. 2, Pg. 287 and 366

'One day a childhood friend of Prophet Yusuf ؑ paid him a visit. He reminded him of the oppression and jealousy of his brothers. Yusuf ؑ replied, "We are lions and those incidents were chains. Even if a lion is tied with a chain then too its dignity would not be affected. Even if the lion's neck is chained, it would be better than other chained ones."

His friend asked, "What was your state when you were in prison and in the well?"

He replied, "My state was like a moon, which reduces its phases and finally disappears but becomes a full moon again and reappears. Wheat is buried inside the earth but it grows out once again. Then it is ground to make flour in a mill but its value increases and it becomes bread later on. When this wheat is crushed under teeth, it becomes life, intellect and perception."

Since a good part of his life was spent in prison, Imam Musa Kaḍim's condition is similar to that of Prophet Yusuf ؑ. It is mentioned in the holy Quran that the ladies of Egypt tried to seduce Yusuf ؑ but he opted for imprisonment in order to save his faith and to keep the clothes of piety from being stained.

Prophet Yusuf ؑ said:

قَالَ رَبِّ السِّجْنُ أَحَبُّ إِلَيَّ مِمَّا يَدْعُونَنِي إِلَيْهِ وَإِلاَّ تَصْرِفْ عَنِّي كَيْدَهُنَّ أَصْبُ إِلَيْهِنَّ وَأَكُن مِّنَ الْجَاهِلِينَ {33}فَاسْتَجَابَ لَهُ رَبُّهُ فَصَرَفَ عَنْهُ كَيْدَهُنَّ إِنَّهُ هُوَ السَّمِيعُ الْعَلِيمُ {34} ثُمَّ بَدَا لَهُم مِّن بَعْدِ مَا رَأَوُاْ الآيَاتِ لَيَسْجُنُنَّهُ حَتَّى حِينٍ {35}

He said: My Lord! the prison house is dearer to me than that to which they invite me; and if Thou turn not away their device from me, I will yearn towards them and become (one) of the ignorant. Thereupon his Lord accepted his prayer and turned away their guile from him; surely He is the Hearing, the Knowing. Then it occurred to them after they had seen the signs that they should imprison him till a time.[1]

---

[1] Surah Yusuf 12:33-35

Iblis had told God that he would present evil as good to the people and would lead everyone astray but his tricks would not work on the virtuous servants of Allah. Allah replied him saying, "Certainly, you would not have power over My virtuous servants. Only those who are misguided would obey you."

God presented the example of Prophet Yusuf as a virtuous servant saying:

وَلَقَدْ هَمَّتْ بِهِ وَهَمَّ بِهَا لَوْلَا أَن رَّأَى بُرْهَانَ رَبِّهِ كَذَلِكَ لِنَصْرِفَ عَنْهُ السُّوءَ وَالْفَحْشَاء إِنَّهُ مِنْ عِبَادِنَا الْمُخْلَصِينَ

And certainly she made for him, and he would have made for her, were it not that he had seen the manifest evidence of his Lord; thus (it was) that We might turn away from him evil and indecency, surely he was one of Our sincere servants. (Surah Yusuf 12:24)

Zulaikha intended to commit an evil act in a room where there was no one except her and Prophet Yusuf. In such a situation, if Prophet Yusuf had not seen the manifestation of his Lord he would have killed Zulaikha or would have fulfilled her wish because she was an embodiment of beauty and prophet Yusuf was the owner of God-given elegance. Also, Prophet Yusuf was young and unmarried and the environment of a closed room encourages evil activities. In spite of all this, prophet Yusuf did not commit an evil deed because he had already seen the proof of his Lord. He was the selected one of Allah and from the group of the virtuous. Hence Allah kept him away from evil. The proof seen by Prophet Yusuf was a result of the good deed of a person and the bad deed of a person. (*Islami Aqaid – Quran ki nazar mein,* Sayyid Murtadha Askari, published by Jame Taalimaat-e-Islami, Pakistan) - Rizwani.

Jealousy of brothers cast Prophet Yusuf in the well and the unacceptable lust of the ladies of Egypt sent him to prison. He remained imprisoned for many years.

فَلَبِثَ فِي السِّجْنِ بِضْعَ سِنِينَ

...so he remained in the prison a few years.[1]

He got prophethood in the prison and came out purer, more perfect and more determined.

Yusuf ☘ was a prophet, who was thrown into a well because of the fault that he was loved by his father and was imprisoned for recognition of truth, purity and piety. From the progeny of the Holy Prophet ☘, Imam Musa Kadim ☘ was imprisoned for many years because people loved him and considered him more worthy of leadership than Harūn Rashid. The only difference is that Yusuf ☘ was released from the prison while Harūn Rashid poisoned and martyred the Imam in the prison itself.

أَمْ يَحْسُدُونَ النَّاسَ عَلَى مَا آتَاهُمُ اللّهُ مِن فَضْلِهِ

"Or do they envy the people for what Allah has given them of His grace?"[2]

Of course, whenever jealous people see Allah's pleasure on someone's favor, they become jealous and start troubling that person.

The two Arabic couplets that I quoted in the beginning of the lecture also mean the same: That, **"People taunt me that I was imprisoned. I say that it**

---

[1] Surah Yusuf 12:42
[2] Surah Nisa 4:54

is not a defect. Is there any sharp sword that is not kept inside a sheath? Don't you see that when a lion grows old, it gets into the habit of living in his den while lowly animals run here and there?"

After that the poet says:

"Small stars are not visible till the sun disappears from sight.

Fire remains hidden inside stones and cannot be used till it is scratched out with a tool."

If the imprisonment is not due to some moral crime, prison is not a bad place."

If someone has committed a theft, murder, cheating, spread mischief and the court charged him and imprisoned him; it is really a cause of disgrace. It is a cause of indignity and even if he is not imprisoned because of these crimes, it is shameful. However, if someone goes to prison for a right cause and to fight against injustice, it is a cause of pride.

A prison is a place where the honor of a fair person increases. People go there to meet him and feel proud to meet him. He need not go to the people.

Then the poet says:

"When tears were flowing from the eyes and the fire of interest was ignited in the heart, I told the helpless not to worry for his feet shackled in chains. These chains are adornment for men."

Effects of prison for the crime of loving freedom

Two points are worth mention here. Firstly, the tortures borne by a person for supporting truth are not a cause of sorrow. Instead they are cause of pride. It is necessary for this point that we glance at history which is full of such incidents, in which great people gave their lives with honor; they were imprisoned and they suffered pains and atrocities. These sufferings are not only a cause of pride for those leaders but also for the entire humanity.

Another point is that bearing such injustice is a way of perfecting the soul of humanity. The life of worldly comforts is a cause of bad character and reduces courage. Nothing can reduce courage, give birth to bad character and destroy one's life more than a life of worldly comforts.

The soul is energized through hardships and difficulties. It gets strengthened. The gold of human existence becomes purer and strong. So long as a person does not face calamities and difficulties, his personality is not perfected. Evolution does not take place without breaking up of a personality. Maulana Rumi says that the grain of wheat gets trapped when buried inside the earth. It bursts there and its existence comes to an end. After that, it moves towards the highest stage. After a few days, it comes out in the form of a plant having many offshoots holding grains inside them. When the wheat gets mixed in earth, it marks the beginning of its evolution. Then this wheat is ground in the mill to become flour. Wheat flour turns into bread. When bread is chewed with teeth, it is dissolved and wheat is converted into intelligence and understanding after going through different stages.

Law of opposites and conflicts

A law of nature is called 'the law of conflicts'. According to philosophy, if there is no contradiction there would be no possibility of continuity of benefits from the fountainhead of bounties. It is a fact that there is some kind of evolution in everyone.[1]

If we look at the other side we see that every existing thing comes across certain things at different stages of evolution, which are necessary and beneficial for it at that stage. For instance, a peel of a fruit provides warmth to it or the shell of an egg, which protects the egg-yolk and albumen. These skins are necessary and beneficial as long as warmth is warmth and egg remains an egg. If the seed of a fruit wants to progress and become a tree or the egg wants to become a chick and then finally an adult hen, there is no way for it but to break the bounds of shell and free itself.

These boundaries and walls collapse as a result of natural contradiction and barriers are destroyed and the fountain of divine grace starts flowing.

As a result of these difficulties, brave ones and extraordinarily intelligent persons and ideal personalities are born. Strength and power reappears. Great leaders had to bear a lot of pain and difficulties and only later on they could lead the world to great revolutions.

---

[1] *Al-Hikmatul Mutaliyyah fil Asfaar al-Aqliyyatur Rabaahu,* Vol. 7, Pg. 77

Lady Zainab Kubra

Our religious history has numerous such examples. Lady Zainab Kubra is one such woman who is a cause of pride for Islam. History narrates that the deadly calamities and atrocities of Karbala had made Lady Zainab stronger. Lady Zainab was not same when she returned to Medina as she was when she departed from there. She had evolved a lot after returning from Syria. The feats she achieved during the period she was held captive were completely different from the events of Karbala when her great brother was alive and she had little responsibility on her shoulders.

Dr. Ayesha binte al-Shati is one of the qualified Arab women of our time. She has written a book titled, *Batlatu Karbala* (Great woman of Karbala). This book is translated into Persian and was published a number of times. She writes that the causes of the greatness of Lady Zainab are calamities of Karbala. The events of Karbala were the cause of her fiery sermon in the court of Yazid, which you all have heard.[1]

An Arabic poet Abu Tamaam says:

If aloe wood is not burnt with fire no one would become aware of its fragrance.

Saadi has also presented this saying as:

The natural word emerges only when the heart is full of sorrow.

---

[1] *Biharul Anwār*, Vol. 45, Pg. 133

Like aloe wood which does not emit fragrance till it is burned.

Rudaki says:

Severe hardships give birth to

Excellence, greatness and leadership.

Speaking and desiring truth

Imam Musa Kaḍim ﷺ was imprisoned for the 'crime' that he spoke the truth and had faith and piety. There is a saying of the Imam, which he told to one of his Shias: "Look, fear Allah's anger. Always speak truth even if it seems to result in destruction because your salvation lies in it; and remembrance of truth never leads to destruction. Instead, truth is the ultimate salvation. Always keep away from falsehood even if there is apparent salvation in it, remember that falsehood would never give you salvation."[1]

Shaykh Mufeed writes that Imam Musa Kaḍim ﷺ was the greatest worshipper, jurist, graceful and elegant one of his time.[2] He always used to submit himself to the Lord and express his humility. He used to supplicate often: "O Allah! I seek comfort at the time of death and forgiveness at the time of the accounting of deeds."[3]

He used to be on lookout for beggars. He used to fill cash, flour and dates in a container and distribute among

---

[1] *Biharul Anwār,* Vol. 78, Pg. 319
[2] *Irshad,* Shaykh Mufid, Pg. 292
[3] *Irshad,* Shaykh Mufid, Pg. 296

the poor people of Medina in different ways. Those poor ones did not even know who their benefactor was.[1]

He was a matchless *hafiz* of the holy Quran who knew the divine book by heart. He used to recite the Quran so sweetly that it touched the hearts of the people. The listeners cried on hearing his recitation. The people of Medina had given him the title of 'Zain al-Mutahajjidin' (the best of those who worship at night)'.[2]

Prison of Basra

In 179 A.H. Harūn set out for Hajj from Baghdad. He went to Medina first and summoned the Imam there. The people of Medina were shocked. There was a turmoil among the people. Harūn ordered that the Imam should be sent to Basra immediately in the darkness of night after veiling him on his mount. He ordered that the Imam should be handed over to Isa bin Ja'far, the Abbaside in Basra. He was the governor of Basra and a paternal cousin of Harūn. Imam 🕮 was taken there and imprisoned. Harūn ordered that one more mount should be veiled and sent towards Kufa so that people believe that the Imam is sent to Kufa. Thus, they would not worry as Kufa was the center of the Imam's lovers and Shias and the Imam would not be harmed there. Even if some people try to bring the Imam back, they would go to Kufa.[3]

Imam Musa Kaḍim 🕮 remained imprisoned for a year in Basra. Harūn told Isa to eliminate the Imam in the prison itself but he did not agree. He wrote in reply, "I have always found this person engrossed in worship for

---

[1] *Irshad,* Shaykh Mufid, Pg. 296
[2] *Irshad,* Shaykh Mufid, Pg. 298
[3] *Irshad,* Shaykh Mufid, Pg. 300; *Biharul Anwār,* Vol. 48, Pg. 207-221; *Muntahal Amaal,* Vol. 2, Pg. 337

the past one year. He does not fall short in worship. I appointed some persons to watch him whether he curses me in his supplications or not? I got to know that he does not speak anything except seeking mercy from the Almighty Allah for himself. I am not ready to participate in the murder of such a person. I don't even want to keep him in the prison any more. So you take him back or I would release him."[1]

Prison of Baghdad

Harūn ordered that the Imam be brought to Baghdad and imprisoned in the prison of Fazl bin Rabi. Harūn ordered Fazl bin Rabi also to murder the Imam but he did not agree. Then, Harūn handed over the Imam to Fazl bin Yahya Barmiki so that he remains under his captivity.[2] Fazl bin Yahya reserved a room in his house for the holy Imam and also ordered that a close watch be kept on the Imam. He was informed that the Imam worships, supplicates and recites the holy Quran day and night and observes fasts on most days. He does not get involved in any activity except worship. Fazl bin Yahya ordered that the Imam should be respected and he took care of his comforts.

Reporters informed Harūn about this. Harūn was not in Baghdad when he got this news. Harūn immediately wrote a letter reprimanding him and ordered that the Imam should be eliminated. However, Fazl was not ready to do so. Harūn was displeased much. He wrote separate letters to Sindi bin Shahik and Abbas bin Muhammad and sent them through his personal servant, Masrur. Also, he ordered Masrur to investigate secretly and if Musa bin

---

[1] *Irshad,* Shaykh Mufid, Pg. 300; *Biharul Anwār,* Vol. 48, Pg. 233; *Muntahal Amaal,* Vol. 2, Pg. 338
[2] *Irshad,* Shaykh Mufid, Pg. 300

Ja'far was staying comfortably in the house of Fazl bin Yahya the latter should be whipped. The order was obeyed and Fazl bin Yahya was whipped. Masrur wrote down all the details of this operation and sent them to Harūn.[1]

Harūn ordered that the Imam should be handed over to Sindi bin Shahik from the custody of Fazl bin Yahya.

Sindi was a non-Muslim and a stone-hearted person. Also, Harūn had once announced publicly that Fazl bin Yahya had disobeyed his orders, sent curses on him and asked people to curse him. Eventually, the heartless people cursed Fazl bin Yahya in order to please Harūn.[2] When Fazl bin Yahya Barmiki's father, Yahya bin Khalid Barmiki got this news, he mounted his horse and went to apologize on behalf of his son. Harūn accepted this apology.[3] Finally the Holy Imam ﷺ was poisoned and martyred in the prison of Sindi.[4]

A high official visits Imam

One day Harūn sent a person to visit the Imam in the prison of Sindi. Sindi accompanied this high official. When this envoy met the Imam, the latter asked, "What do you want?"

He replied, "The Caliph has sent me to visit you."

Imam ﷺ said, "Go and tell your caliph that every single day of torture for me reduces a day of comfort for him. A time will come when both of us will be at one

---

[1] *Irshad,* Shaykh Mufid, Pg. 301; *Muntahal Amaal,* Vol. 2, Pg. 341
[2] *Muntahal Amaal,* Vol. 2, Pg. 341
[3] *Muntahal Amaal,* Vol. 2, Pg. 341
[4] *Biharul Anwār,* Vol. 48, Pg. 247

place. The unjust would be punished for their deeds there."[1]

Contentment of Imam Musa Kadim ﷺ

During the time when he was in the prison of Harūn, Harūn sent a message to the Imam through Fazl bin Rabi. Fazl says that when he reached the prison, the Imam was occupied in Prayer. He did not dare to sit because of the Imam's awe. He stood leaning on his sword. Imam did not pay attention to him even after completing his Prayer. He started offering the next Prayer. After that, the Imam was about to start his third Prayer when he interrupted him and said:

"The Caliph has ordered me to come to you and convey his regards to you. He has asked me not to prefix the title of Commander of the Faithful before his name and mention his name as your brother, Harūn. He wants to inform you that there was a misunderstanding because of wrong news. It is now known that you are not at fault but he wishes that you stay near him all the time and not return to Medina. Now it is decided that you shall stay near him, he wants to know what kind of food is liked by you. I am appointed to take care of your comforts."

Hearing this, the Imam replied to Fazl in two sentences. Imam ﷺ said, "I don't have my own money that I can use and I don't have the habit of asking for it that I may ask you for it."[2]

Imam ﷺ expressed his independence and contentment in these two words and proved that prisons cannot

---

[1] *Al-Muntazim*, Vol. 9, Pg. 88
[2] *Muntahal Amaal*, Vol. 2, Pg. 339

diminish his enthusiasm. Saying this, the Imam got up and started another Prayer with a *Takbir* (Allaahu Akbar).

"O Lord! Shower blessings on Musa bin Ja'far who was a virtuous successor, a leader of pious, owner of secrets of Divine Light, a dignified personality and owner of a calm heart. He is owner of wisdom and effects of knowledge. Peace be upon that chief who used to remain awake whole night till morning and worship Allah and seek repentance continuously."[1]

---

[1] *Mafaateehul Jinaan*, Ziarat Imam Musa bin Ja'far
Beest Guftar, Pg. 161-173

Majlis 61

Martyrdom of Imam Reḍa

Today is the anniversary of the martyrdom of Imam Ali Reḍa 🕮, therefore I shall quote a tradition in order to connect ourselves to the bounties of his holy presence. This tradition is called *Hadith Tauheed* and *Hadith Silsilatuz Zahab* i.e. A tradition whose chain of narrators consists of narrators who are as pure as gold.

Hadith Silsilatuz Zahab

For instance, if a tradition is narrated by a narrator from Ahmad from Mahmood from Khalid from Zurarah from Muhammad bin Muslim till it reaches an infallible Imam, the narrators present in between are called chain (*silsila*) i.e. chain of narrators.

The tradition, which I am going to narrate here, is named *Hadith Silsilatuz Zahab* - A tradition whose chain is golden. It is a comparison made by others. Why? Because it is tradition narrating which Imam Reḍa 🕮 had said:

"I narrate this tradition from my holy father, Musa bin Ja'far from his holy father, Ja'far bin Muhammad from his holy father, Muhammad bin Ali from his holy father, Ali bin Husain from his holy father, Husain bin Ali from his holy father, Ali bin Abi Talib 🕮 from the Holy Prophet 🕮 from archangel Gabriel from the tablet and pen from the

Almighty Allah."[1] Now, which chain of narrators can be more golden than this? 'Golden' is used for something about which nothing better can be imagined.

Imam Reḍa ﷺ should not be made to pass through areas populated by Shias

This incident took place in Nishapur, which proves how much people, especially the people of Iran loved the holy Imams ﷺ. Even after many efforts of the supporters of the Abbasid caliphate, it is amazing that Mamoon made Imam Reḍa ﷺ depart from Medina with all respects to show diplomacy, which cannot be discussed in detail here.[2] However, he had given secret orders that the Imam should not taken through cities populated by Shias. Hence, he was made to pass through areas not populated by Shias and where the people did not know him. Look at the apparent respect given to Imam Reḍa ﷺ by Mamoon and his political move, which was veiled. That is why the Imam was not taken to Qum, which was the center of Shias. Apart from this, Baghdad, the capital of caliphate was not the center of a single group. It was populated by all groups. It was possible to bring the Imam there but he was not made to pass through there fearing an atmosphere of enmity against Mamoon because of his presence. Similarly, he was not made to pass through Kufa also and was taken through unknown routes to Nishapur. The reason was that they had not expected that they would come across such exuberance and people would come out of their houses in such large numbers in this remote town of Khorasan to welcome the Imam.

---

[1] *Biharul Anwār,* Vol. 49, Pg. 126; *Muntahal Amaal,* Vol. 2, Pg. 453
[2] Interested persons should read Ustad Mutahhari's book, *Seerat Aimma Athar*

Imam Reḍa 🕮 in Nishapur

When the Imam's mount reached Nishapur, a flood of people gathered to welcome him. Men, women, young and elderly, everyone gave him a warm welcome.[1] The

---

[1] In those days, Nishapur was the center of Khorasan. It was also called central Khorasan or south Khorasan. (It did not include the cities of Mawaraun Nahr, which are to the north of Khorasan) There were big cities like Balkh, Bukhara and Merv but the center of current Khorasan was Nishapur. Tus is four farsangs away in the west of holy Mashad. There is tomb of Firdausi in Tus. In those days, Tus was a small hamlet. The place of holy Mashad today used to have two small hamlets. One of them was called Sanabad. Imam Reḍa is buried at this place only. Another hamlet was called Naughan, which is famous as locality of Naughan even today. It is at the end of the city of Mashad. The historical significance of this place is that Haroon fell sick at this place on his journey to Khorasan. Then his illness increased so much that he died and was buried in Sanabad.

We know that Haroon is buried in the mausoleum of Imam Reḍa at the feet of his grave exactly in the center of the dome.

The grave of Imam Reḍa (a.s.) is not in the center of dome. There is very little place above the head of Imam's grave. The reason is that Haroon's grave is in the center of dome and Mamoon wanted that Imam Reḍa should be buried at the feet of his father's grave. However, as narrated in many traditions, some unusual circumstances led them to bury the Imam at the head of his grave. Earlier this dome was called "Baq-a'h haruniyyah"

Dibil Khuzai was an amazing poet. In modern terminology, he can be called a revolutionary poet. According to me, a poet like Dibil has not been born in our age. He used to say that he roamed carrying his crucifix on his shoulders for fifty years. It means, Dibil quoted such verses continuously for fifty years, which could have caused his death anytime. Dibil was a poet who enraged the Abbasids. For example:

There are two graves in Tus. One is of the best creature and another of worst creature and this fact is a good lesson.

Can that impure benefit from that purest? Can that purest be affected by the impurity of that impure one? Absolutely not.

scholars of the city also gathered in his love. The city's greatest scholar requested that he be given the honour of holding the reins of Imam Reḍa's mount. Thus, the greatest scholar of Nishapur was given this honour.

Imam ؏ was not permitted to halt at any place by the people of Harūn. He was supposed to go through every area as soon as possible. On the other hand, the people desperately wanted that the Imam's mount should be halted for some time. However, the armed soldiers denied permission, saying they were in a hurry as Mamoon awaited them. If they delayed, they could be punished.

Fortress of Tauheed

The people requested the holy Imam, "O master! We want you to leave a memento, which would remain with us forever. Hence, we request you gift us something as you pass through and the best gift would be to narrate a tradition for us, which we can write down and keep with us forever."

The popular saying that twelve thousand people had gathered with golden pen and paper to note down the tradition and hence, it is called *Hadith Silsilatuz Zahab* is absolutely baseless. It is called *Hadith Silsilatuz Zahab* because each of its narrators is infallible. This place was a center of traditionalists and hence, the Imam was requested to narrate a tradition.

It is mentioned that when the Imam peeped out from the curtain of his mount and the people saw him, they immediately exclaimed, "It seems as if we are looking at

---

Naturally, these verses would have infuriated the Abbasids much. (Ustad Mutahhari)

the Holy Prophet ﷺ."[1] The enthusiasm of people increased. Then the Imam said:

"I narrate this tradition from my holy father from his holy father and so on till it reaches the Holy Prophet ﷺ and then from there till the tablet and pen and finally the Almighty Allah said, "The statement, 'there is no God except Allah', is My fortress and whoever enters My fortress shall be safe from My chastisement."[2] When a person enters the fortress of monotheism, everything follows after that much in the same way as all letters are followed by A. The basis of religion is monotheism.

The first and the last praise be to Allah
And may Allah bless Muhammad and his pure and
chaste progeny
And curse be on all their enemies from now till the
Judgment Day

---

[1] *Muntahal Amaal,* Vol. 2, Pg. 451
[2] *Tauheed,* Sadooq, Pg. 25; *Biharul Anwār,* Vol. 49, Pg. 127

Sermon of Lady Zainab Kubra in the market of Kufa

"Praise be to Allah and divine blessings be on my father Muhammad and his good and exemplary descendants.

O people of Kufa, O you who are deceitful and treacherous:[1] Do you shed tears? May your tears never dry up and your loud lamentations never cease.[2] You are like the woman that unravels to bits the thread which she has firmly spun. Your faith is nothing but deceit and betrayal. Are there any among you but the immodest, disgraced, proud, spiteful, adulator, enemy and reviler? There are among you those who are as guileful as a beautiful plant growing in filth, or the silver on a grave. Certainly evil is that which your souls have sent before for you. Allah is displeased with you and in punishment shall you abide.

Are you crying and wailing? Indeed, by Allah. Do cry endlessly and laugh but little, for your deed was so horrendously disgraceful that you will never be able to atone for it. How can you wash away the crime of murdering the scion of the Seal of the Prophets, the essence of the message, the lord of the youth of Paradise, the refuge of your nobles, the refuge for whom you resorted during affliction, the bright divine proof of yours, your master who defended the Prophet's tradition.

What an awful sin you did commit! Away with you, there will be no forgiveness for you. Certainly your efforts

---

[1] In a version it says: "Breaking of Pledge"
[2] In a version it says: "Your tears will not cease and your lamentations will not fall quiet."

failed, your hands suffered loss and your bargain is brought to naught. You have made yourselves deserving of the wrath of Allah. Abasement and humiliation have been brought down upon you.

Woe to you! Do you know how you tore the liver of the Apostle of Allah? Whom of his womenfolk you exposed? What blood of his you shed? What honor of his you defamed?

Your deed is most certainly so dangerously ugly and foul, that it filled the earth and sky with its putridness. Are you surprised that it rained blood? Certainly the punishment of the Hereafter is infinitely more abasing, and you shall not be helped. Don't make light of the delay of punishment in that it is not hastened by the fear of missing the taking of revenge. Most surely Allah is watching." The she recited the following couplets:

O Kufians! What reply would you give at that time when the Holy Prophet ﷺ asks you, "What did you do? You were the last Ummah. Why did you treat my family, my progeny and my sanctity like this? Why did you hold some of them as captives while made others bathe in blood?

Was it the reward for my service as a messenger that you behaved like this with my relatives? I fear that you do not become rightful to that chastisement and it befalls on you like the one revealed on the community of Aad.[1] (Rizwani)

---

[1] *Maqtal-e-Husain,* Muqarram, Pg. 387; *Noorul Absaar,* Shablanji, Pg. 167

Quoted from: *Hayatul Imam al-Husain bin Ali,* Baqir Sharif Qarashi, Vol. 3, Pg. 335

Bibliography

1) *The Holy Quran*
2) *Absaarul Ain Fee Ansaarul Husain*
3) Muhammad bin Tahir as-Samawi
4) Manshoorat Maktabe Baseerati
5) *Al-Irshad*
6) Shaykh Mufeed
7) Mausisal Ilmi Lil Matibooaat, Beirut
8) *Irshad al-Quloob*
9) Abi Muhammad al-Hasan bin Abil Hasan Muhammad ad-Dailami
10) Marka Nashr Kitab
11) *Usud al-Ghaba Fee Marifat Sahaba*
12) Abil Hasan Ali bin Abil Kiraam, Ibne Athir
13) Intisharat Ismailiyan
14) *Al-Aghani*
15) Abil Faraj Isfahani
16) Intisharat Darul Fikr, Beirut
17) *Al-Amali*
18) Shaykh Sadooq
19) Intisharat Islamiya
20) *Al-Amali*
21) Shaykh Mufeed
22) Matba Haidariya, An-Najaf al-Ashraf
23) *Anwar Nomaniya*
24) Sayyid Nimatullah Jazaeri
25) Shirkat Chaap
26) *Biharul Anwar*
27) Allamah Muhammad Baqir Majlisi
28) Intisharat Islamiya
29) *Barrasi Tarikh Ashura*
30) Muhammad Ibrahim Ayati
31) Kitab Khana Sadooq
32) *al-Bayan wat Tibiyyin*
33) Jahiz
34) Manshoorat Dar-O-Maktab Hilal
35) *Baitul Ahzan Fee Masaib Sayyidatun Niswan*
36) Shaykh Abbas Qummi
37) Nashir Mausise Naba
38) *Tarikh Ibne Asakir*
39) Abul Qasim Ali bin al-Hasan bin Hibtullah as-Shafei
40) Mausise Mahmoodi, Beirut
41) *Tarikh Khulafa*
42) Jalaluddin Suyuti
43) Manshoorat Darul Qalam Arabi, Halab, Shaam
44) *Tarikh Tabari*
45) Abi Ja'far Muhammad bin Jurair Rabari
46) Manshoorat Al-Ilmi Lil Matbooaat, Beirut, Lebanon
47) *Tarikh Payambar Islam*
48) Muhammad Ibrahim Ayati
49) Intisharaat Danishgah Tehran
50) *Tatmatul Muntaha Dar Tarikh Khulafa*

51) Shaykh Abbas Qummi
52) Intisharaat Dawari, Qum
53) *Tohafful Uqool An Aale Rasool*
54) Ibne Shoba Bahrani
55) Intisharaat Jame Madrasatain
56) *Tazkeratush Shohada*
57) Mulla Habibullah Shareef Kashani
58) Old Edition
59) *At-Tauheed*
60) Shaykh Sadooq
61) Maktabe Sadooq
62) *Tanqihul Maqal Fee Ilmur Rijal*
63) Allamah Shaykh Abdullah Mamqani
64) Tabatul Murtazviya, an-Najaf al-Ashraf
65) *Al-Hikmatul Mutaliyyah fil Asfaar al-Aqliyyatur Rabaahu*
66) Hakeem Ilaahi Sadruddin Shirazi
67) Dar Ahya Turath al-Arabi, Beirut
68) *Hayatul Haiwan al-Kubra*
69) Kamaluddin Damiri
70) Intisharaat Darul Fikr, Beirut
71) *Khasais al-Husainia*
72) Shaykh Ja'far Tustari
73) Mausisa Darul Kitab Littaba-a wan Nashr
74) *Damatus Sujum*
75) Allamah Mirza Abul Hasan Sherani
76) Intisharaat Ilmiya Islamiya
77) *Damatus Sakiba*
78) Muhammad Baqir bin Abdul Kareem Bahbani
79) Mausisa Al-Ilmi Lil Matbooaat, Beirut, Lebanon
80) *Diwan Imam Ali* ﷺ ﷺ
81) Translation: Mustafa Zamani
82) Intisharaat Payam Islam
83) *Diwan Hafiz*
84) Calligrahy Abbas Mazoori
85) Iqbal Printers
86) *Riyaheen ash-Shariah*
87) Shaykh Zabihullah Mahallati
88) Intisharaat Islamiya
89) *Safinatul Bihar*
90) Al-Muhaddith al-Hajj ash-Shaykh Abbas Qummi
91) Intisharaat Farahani
92) *As-Seerat-e-Halabiya*
93) Ali bin Burhanuddin Halabi Shafei
94) Maktabe Islamiya Beirut, Lebanon
95) *Sharh Nahjul Balagha*
96) Ibne Abil Hadid
97) Manshooraat Maktabe Ayatullah Uzma Marashi Najafi
98) *Shifa as-Suddor Fee Sharh Ziarat Ashoor*
99) Mirza Abul Fazl Tehrani
100) Published by: Sayyid Ali Mauhad Abtahi

101) *As-Sawarim al-Mohreqa*
102) Al-Qadi Noorullah Tustari
103) Musawi Printers, Tehran
104) *Al-Abbas*
105) Sayyid Abdur Razzaq Muqarram
106) Baseerati Booksellers
107) *Al-Iqdul Farid*
108) Abi Umar Ibne Abde Rabb Andalusi
109) Kitab Khana Ismailiyan
110) *Uyun Akhbaar* Reḍa
111) Shaykh Sadooq
112) Manshooraat Al-Ilmi, Tehran
113) *Al-Ghadeer*
114) Allamah Amini
115) Darul Kitab al-Arbi, Beirut
116) *Al-Futuh*
117) Abi Muhammad Ahmad bin Asim Kufi
118) Darul Kutub Ilmiya, Beirut, Lebanon
119) *Firhang Ashura*
120) Jawad Muhaddithi
121) Nashr Maroof
122) *Qissa Karbala*
123) Ali Nazari Munfarid
124) Intisharaat Sarwar
125) *Kamiluz Ziaraat*
126) Ibne Quluwahy
127) Matba Murtzviyah an-Najaf al-Ashraf
128) *Al-Kamil Fee Tarikh*
129) Ibne Athir
130) Dar Sadir, Beirut
131) *Al-Kafi*
132) Abi Ja'far Muhammad bin Yaqoob Kulaini
133) Kitab Faroshi Islamiyah
134) *Kohlul Basar Fee Seerat Sayyidul Bashar*
135) Shaykh Abbas Qummi
136) Mausisa al-Wafa, Beirut, Lebanon
137) *Kashful Ghumma Fee Marifatul Aaimma*
138) Abul Hasan Ali bin Isa Irbili
139) Darul Kitab al-Islamiyah, Beirut
140) *Al-Lohoof Alaa Qatli Tafoof*
141) Sayyid bin Tawoos
142) Intisharaat Jahan
143) *Mathnawi Manawi*
144) Maulana Jalaluddin Rumi Balkhi
145) Intisharaat Maula
146) *Miratul Uqool Fee Sharh Akhbar Aale Rasool*
147) Allamah Muhammad Baqir Majlisi
148) Darul Kutub al-Islamiyah
149) *Muruj az-Zahab*
150) Husain bin Ali Masudi
151) Maktabe Tijaratiya Kubra, Misr
152) *Masaib al-Masoomeen*
153) Wathiq bin Abdur Rahman Yazdi
154) Mulla Abbas Ali Printing Press
155) *Maalimul Madrasatain*
156) Allamah Sayyid Murtada Askari
157) Mausisa Baasa
158) *Maani al-Akhbaar*
159) Shaykh Sadooq

160) Intisharaat Jame Madrasain
161) Mojam Rijal al-Hadith
162) Ayatullah Uzma Sayyid Abul Qasim Khoei
163) Manshooraat Madinatul Ilm, Qum
164) Mafaateehul Jinaan
165) Muhaddith Qummi
166) Sazman Chaap O Intisharaat Muhammad Ali Ilmi
167) Maqatilut Talibiyyin
168) Abil Faraj Isfahani
169) Dar Ahya Uloomiddeen, Beirut
170) Maqtal Husain
171) Abul Moayyad al-Maufaq bin Ahmad al-Makki Akhtab Khwarzmi
172) Maktab Mufeed, Qum
173) Maqtal Husain
174) Abdur Razzaq Muqarram
175) Mausisa Baasa
176) Al-Muntazim Fee Tarikh al-Umam wal-Mulook
177) Abi Faraj Abdur Rahman bin Ali bin Muhammad Ibne Jauzi
178) Darul Kutub Ilmiyah, Beirut, Lebanon
179) Muntahaiul Amaal Fee Tawarikh an-Nabi wal Aal, (Muarrab)
180) Shaykh Abbas Qummi
181) Intishaaraat Jame Madrasain
182) Manaqib Aale Abi Talib
183) Ibne Shahr Aashob
184) Intishaaraat Allamah
185) Manaqib Murtazviyah
186) Muhammad Salih al-Husaini at-Tirmidhi al-Mutakhallis Bakshafi
187) Chaap Bambai, Muhammadi Printing Press
188) Minhajul Bara-a Fee Sharh Nahjul Balagha
189) Mirza Habibullah Hashmi Khoei
190) Bunyad Farhangi Imam al-Mahdi (a.t.f.s.)
191) Mausuat-e-Kalimat al-Imam al-Husain
192) Muahad Tahqeeqaat Baqirul Uloom
193) Darul Maroof Lit Taba-a Wan Nashr
194) Al-Mizan Fee Tafseeril Quran
195) Allamah Sayyid Muhammad Husain Tabatabai
196) Manshooraat Mausisa al-Ilmi Lil Matbooaat, Beirut
197) Mizanul Hikma
198) Muhammdi Rishahri
199) Markaz Nashr Maktabul Allam al-Islamiyah
200) Nuzhatul Majalis wa Muntakhabul Nafais
201) Abdur Rahman Safoori Shafei
202) Matba Amira Sharafiya, Misr
203) Nafthatul Masdur Fee Tajdeed Yaum Ashoor
204) Shaykh Abbas Qummi
205) Intisharaat Nuwaidul Islam
206) Nafasul Mahmoom
207) Shaykh Abbas Qummi
208) Intisharaat Islamiyah
209) Nahjul Balagha

210) Subhi Salih
211) Nashr Markaz Bahooth al-Islamiyah
212) *Nahjul Balagha*
213) Faizul Islam
214) Chaap Aftab Tehran
215) *Wasaelush Shia*
216) Al-Hurr Amili
217) Maktabe Islamiyyah
218) *Yanabiul Mawaddah*
219) Al-Hafiz Sulaiman Qunduzi Hanafi
220) Manshooraat Razi

www.ingramcontent.com/pod-product-compliance
Lightning Source LLC
Chambersburg PA
CBHW022044020426
42335CB00012B/530